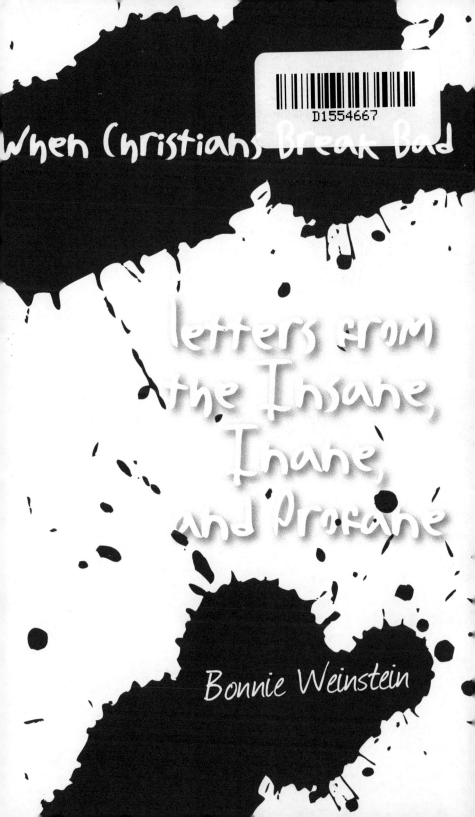

When Christians Break Bad

letters from the Insane, Inane, and Profane

Bonnie Weinstein

When Christians Break Bad

letters from the Insane, Inane, and Profane

Bonnie Weinstein

This is a Genuine Rare Bird Book

Rare Bird Books
453 South Spring Street, Suite 302
Los Angeles, CA 90013
rarebirdbooks.com

Copyright © 2019 by Bonnie Weinstein

FIRST TRADE PAPERBACK ORIGINAL EDITION

All rights reserved, including the right to reproduce this book or portions
thereof in any form whatsoever, including but not limited to
print, audio, and electronic.

For more information, address:
A Vireo Book | Rare Bird Books Subsidiary Rights Department
453 South Spring Street, Suite 302
Los Angeles, CA 90013

Set in Minion

Printed in the United States

10 9 8 7 6 5 4 3 2 1

Publisher's Cataloging-in-Publication Data
available on request

Introduction by Bonnie Weinstein

EVERY DAY, MANY TIMES a day, our inboxes at the Military Religious Freedom Foundation (MRFF) are flooded with email. We get emails from people who hate us personally and attack the foundation. We get vile and filthy emails from fake email addresses. In contrast are the emails from people who have questions, and emails from those who want to show their support. *When Christians Break Bad* contains emails sent in to the foundation and our responses to those emails. We respond to every single email, nice or nasty. People who send emails from real email addresses with real names are most interesting. The opportunity to engage, inform, then sit back and wait for a response leads to occasionally people...responding. The letters with fake email addresses get a reply and then, both the letters and the replies are posted to our site for all who may wish to peruse the mail section of our website, Militaryreligiousfreedom.org.

Since my first book, *To the Far-Right Christian Hater, You Can be a Good Speller or Hater, But You Can't Be Both* was published, I have lived and breathed every new letter and have been careful to file these letters along with their specific responses. Sadly, those files are bursting at the seams, and I have enough material to fill three books. Trust me when I tell you that just one book is more than enough for even the most jaded among us. I decided early on that if I ever wrote another book, it would contain the responses from our team of writers. I have an intriguing sense of humor, some say, in that I find some of the responses to these emails funny. I love an intelligent reply, however wasted on stupidity it may be. MRFF's greatest assets, besides Mikey Weinstein—the foundation's founder and president (my hubby), and our superstar staff—are the volunteers that do yeomen's work when it comes to responding to these haters. Their tireless efforts and energies are an incredible boost to the foundation and without whom the foundation would be a mere shadow of itself.

I feel it is of some import to give a bit of background information here so that you can understand fully our position. As defenders of the Constitution, we fight for the separation of church and state. It is the legal stance, both constitutionally and militarily, upon which the foundation and all of its actions are based.

First a bit of history; please bear with me as this is vital information and there are some details here that, when I read them, I said to myself, "I did not know that." You may find yourself thinking the same thing.

The number of times people have written to the foundation to tell us, most, not nicely, that the 'separation of Church and State' does not exist in the Constitution is staggering. While the words may not specifically exist, the idea certainty does. Those words and sentiments can be found in the writings and letters from many of the founding fathers. Their specific thoughts on the matter of the 'separation of church and state' can be found both before and after the passing of the Constitution. I offer the following examples:

"God has appointed two kinds of government in the world, which are distinct in their nature, and ought never to be confounded together; one of which is called civil, the other ecclesiastical government."

—Isaac Backus, *An Appeal to the Public for Religious Liberty*, 1773

"During almost fifteen centuries the legal establishment of Christianity has been on trial. What have been its fruits? More or less in all places, pride and indolence in the Clergy, ignorance and servility in the laity; in both, superstition, bigotry and persecution. What influence, in fact, have ecclesiastical establishments had on society? In some instances, they have been seen to erect a spiritual tyranny on the ruins of the civil authority; on many instances they have been seen upholding the thrones of political tyranny; in no instance have they been the guardians of the liberties of the people. Rulers who wish to subvert the public liberty may have found an established clergy convenient auxiliaries. A just government, instituted to secure and perpetuate it, needs them not."

—James Madison, *Memorial and Remonstrance
against Religious Assessments*, 1785

John Adams wrote in *A Defense of the Constitutions of Government of the United States of America* 1787–1788 that, "Although the detail of the formation of the American governments is at present little known or regarded either in Europe or in America, it may hereafter become an object of curiosity. It will never be pretended that any persons employed in that service had interviews with the gods or were in any degree under the influence of Heaven, more than those at work upon ships or houses, or laboring in merchandise or agriculture; it will forever be acknowledged that these governments were contrived merely by the use of reason and the senses."

The Constitution was adopted on September 17, 1787, ratified June 21, 1788, and went into effect on March 4, 1789. A favorite quote of mine, directly from the Constitution:

> "...but no religious Test shall ever be required as a Qualification to any Office or public Trust under the United States." (Article I, III)

Our Constitution was written explicitly to base America on secular rule free from religious tyranny. So, keep reading, with an open mind toward understanding /remembering history and its construing case law.

The Treaty of Tripoli is one of our go-to documents for refuting the belief that America was founded as a Christian nation. The treaty was signed at Tripoli on November 4, 1796. It was submitted to the Senate by President John Adams, receiving ratification unanimously from the US Senate on June 7, 1797, and signed by Adams, taking effect as the law of the land on June 10, 1797—a mere eight years after our Constitution went into effect.

Treaty of Tripoli states:

"As the Government of the United States of America is not, in any sense, founded on the Christian religion—as it has in itself no character of enmity against the laws, religion, or tranquility, of Mussulmen [Muslims],—and as the said States never entered into any war or act of hostility against any Mahometan [Mohammedan] nation, it is declared by the parties that no pretext arising from religious opinions shall ever produce an interruption of the harmony existing between the two countries."

Thomas Jefferson, in a letter to Dr. Thomas Cooper, February 1814, stated that, "Christianity neither is, nor ever was, a part of the common law."

In 1819, James Madison wrote in a letter to Robert Walsh, Jr. that the separation of church and state was not just good for government but also for religion: "[T]he number, the industry, and the morality of the Priesthood, & the devotion of the people have been manifestly increased by the total separation of the Church from the State."

Thomas Jefferson, in a letter to Alexander von Humboldt, dated December 6, 1813, stated that "History, I believe furnishes no example of a priest-ridden people maintaining a free civil government. This marks the lowest grade of ignorance, of which their civil as well as religious leaders will always avail themselves for their own purposes."

On May 1789, George Washington wrote in a letter to the United Baptist Churches of Virginia, and in it contained his following thoughts: "[I]f I could now conceive that the general Government might ever be so administered as to render the liberty of conscience insecure, I beg you will be persuaded that no one would be more zealous than myself to establish effectual barriers against the horrors of spiritual tyranny, and every species of religious persecution."

As Thomas Jefferson wrote in his autobiography, in reference to the Virginia Act for Religious Freedom: "Where the preamble declares that coercion is a departure from the plan of the holy author of our religion, an amendment was proposed, by inserting the word 'Jesus Christ,' so that it should read 'departure from the plan of Jesus Christ, the holy author of our religion.' The insertion was rejected by a great majority, in proof that they meant to comprehend, within the mantle of its protection, the Jew and the Gentile, the Christian and Mahometan, the Hindoo, and infidel of every denomination."

Jefferson's concept of "separation of Church and State" first became a part of Establishment Clause jurisprudence in *Reynolds v. US*, 98 US 145 (1878). In that case, the court examined the history of religious liberty in the US, determining that while the constitution guarantees religious freedom, the word "religion" is not defined in the Constitution. We must ascertain its meaning from other sources and appropriately, we look to the history of the times in which the provision was adopted. The court found that the leaders in advocating and formulating the constitutional guarantee of religious liberty were James Madison and Thomas Jefferson. Quoting the "separation" paragraph from Jefferson's letter to the Danbury Baptists, the court concluded that, "coming as this does from an acknowledged leader of the advocates of the measure, it may be accepted almost as an authoritative declaration of the scope and effect of the amendment thus secured." The first court case against the Establishment Clause and the court upholds the concept of separation of church and state. Why, oh why, are we still debating this point today?

I know I am using a lot of quotes here, but stay with me as this is a small refresher of history that gives a great perspective from which to read the contents of this book. Reading very carefully from the letters of the founding fathers, especially Jefferson and Madison, explains in black and white the thought processes behind the Constitution. While this is taught in public schools, it is not necessarily taught in the homeschooling of today, especially homeschooling with a religious bent. The dominionistic, evangelical preachers of today do no better with the matter claiming that this is a Christian Nation and use scripture, not the constitution and its construing case law to back up their claim which is why we get so many letters claiming that this is a Christian nation. With this in the back of your mind as you go through the book it will be very helpful to understand the foundation on which we stand, and that of course is the Constitution.

In 1878, the Constitutional legal concept for the "separation of church and state" became part of the Establishment Clause by law. And now, I flash forward in history to more current times with a few facts and Supreme Court case law: "One nation under God" was added to the Pledge of Allegiance in 1954. This is something that we find very few people realize. If you would like to read the original pledge it can be found at ushistory.org/documents/pledge.

Louis Albert Bowman, an attorney from Illinois, was the first to suggest the addition of "under God" to the pledge. He spent his adult life in the Chicago area and was chaplain of the Illinois Society of the Sons of the American Revolution. At a meeting on February 12, 1948, he led the society in reciting the pledge with the two words "under God" added. He said that the words came from Lincoln's Gettysburg Address. Although not all manuscript versions of the Gettysburg Address contain the words "under God," all the reporters' transcripts of the speech as delivered do, as perhaps Lincoln may have deviated from his prepared text and inserted the phrase when he said "that the nation shall, under God, have a new birth of freedom." On August 21, 1952, the Supreme Council of the Knights of Columbus adopted a resolution urging that the change be made universal, and copies of this resolution landed on the desks of the President, the Vice President and the Speaker of the House of Representatives. This led to several official attempts to prompt Congress to adopt the Knights of Columbus policy for the entire nation. These attempts were eventually a success.

The Great Seal of the United States was created and adopted in 1782, as was the unofficial motto, "E Pluribus Unum" (out of many, one). "In God We Trust" was subsequently adopted as the official motto in 1956. Then, in 1957, "In God We Trust" was first put on our paper currency, the year I was born. A law passed in a Joint Resolution by the 84th Congress and approved by President Dwight Eisenhower on July 30, 1956, declared "In God We Trust" must appear on American currency. The 84th Congress later passed legislation signed by President Eisenhower on July 30, 1956, declaring the phrase to be the national motto.

Some groups and people have expressed objections to its use, citing its religious reference that violates the Establishment Clause of the First Amendment. These groups believe the phrase should be removed from currency and public property. In lawsuits, this argument has so far not overcome the interpretational doctrine of accommodationism, which allows government to endorse religious establishments as long as they are all treated equally.

In 1971, the Supreme Court heard the groundbreaking case of *Lemon v. Kurtzman*. The case began because the state of Pennsylvania passed a law that allowed the local government to use money to fund educational programs that taught religious-based lessons, activities, and studies. This law was passed through the Non-public Elementary and Secondary Education Act of 1968.

The court ruled in an 8–1 decision that Pennsylvania's Nonpublic Elementary and Secondary Education Act (represented through David *Kurtzman*) from 1968 was unconstitutional, violating the Establishment Clause of the First Amendment, ruling in favor of the Establishment Clause. Subsequent to this decision, the Supreme Court has applied a three-pronged test to determine whether government action comports with the Establishment Clause, known as the Lemon Test, which is:

Government action violates the Establishment Clause unless it:

1. Has a significant secular (i.e., non-religious) purpose

2. Does not have the primary effect of advancing or inhibiting religion

3. Does not foster excessive entanglement between government and religion

In touching on the military aspect of the laws, in 1974 the case of *Parker v. Levy* came before the Supreme Court. "This Court has long recognized that the military is, by necessity, a specialized society separate from civilian society… While the members of the military are not excluded from the protection granted by the First Amendment, the different character of the military community and of the military mission requires a different application of those protections … The fundamental necessity for obedience, and the consequent necessity for imposition of discipline, may render permissible within the military that which would be constitutionally impermissible outside it… Speech [to include religious speech] that is protected in the civil population may nonetheless undermine the effectiveness of response to command. If it does, it is constitutionally unprotected." *Parker v. Levy*, 1974

On September 1, 2011, then-Chief of Staff Gen. Norton A. Schwartz issued a memorandum for all USAF commanders that stated plainly: "Although commanders are responsible for these programs, they must refrain from appearing to officially endorse religion generally or any particular religion. Therefore, I expect chaplains, not commanders, to notify Airmen of Chaplain Corps programs."

And, finally, the Air Force has strict rules on religious neutrality. This is binding on everyone in the Air Force:

BY ORDER OF THE SECRETARY OF THE AIR FORCE
Air Force Instruction 1-1
7 August 2012

2.11. Government Neutrality Regarding Religion. Leaders at all levels must balance constitutional protections for an individual's free exercise of religion or other personal beliefs and the constitutional prohibition against governmental establishment of religion. For example, they must avoid the actual or apparent use of their position to promote their personal religious beliefs to their subordinates or to extend preferential treatment for any religion. Commanders or supervisors who engage in such behavior may cause members to doubt their impartiality and objectivity. The potential result is a degradation of the unit's morale, good order, and discipline. Airmen, especially commanders and supervisors, must ensure that in exercising their right of religious free expression, they do not degrade morale, good order, and discipline in the Air Force or degrade the trust and confidence that the public has in the United States Air Force.

2.12. Balance of Free Exercise of Religion and Establishment Clause. Leaders at all levels must balance constitutional protections for their own free exercise of religion, including individual expressions of religious beliefs, and the constitutional prohibition against governmental establishment of religion. They must ensure their words and actions cannot reasonably be construed to be officially endorsing or disapproving of, or extending preferential treatment for any faith, belief, or absence of belief.

Okay, the history lesson is over, but please remember these very relevant facts about our history as you read these idiotic letters from people. I think all of you who read this book will realize that very little of it reflects what is normal for most of the population, far from it. Yet, it represents what is normal for myself, my husband and those involved in the foundation. This book highlights and showcases the intelligence, humor, wit, patience, anger, and frustrations of a small group of our volunteers who reply to our hate mail and I hope you enjoy the responses as much as I have. Some are caustic in tone and others seek to inform. No matter what you may think of the correspondence, it is a rough and tough job responding to these letters. I think they reflect the human side of a superb and varied team of volunteers. They do this on their own time to support and defend the Constitution of the United States and the foundation which my husband and I started in 2005. They seek to enlighten and correct the misconceptions floating out there about the foundation and the mission behind it. Sometimes to do so is an exercise in futility, still they plug away.

To understand how the book is structured, it is important to know that **my comments placed throughout the letters are in bold**, the detractors' emails are in regular font and *the responses from our fabulous MRFF team are in italics*. "Conversation" threads between Detractors, *MRFF Responders*, and **Myself** are separated by 3-Diamonds (♦♦♦).

The majority of these letters will shock you. So, sit back, fasten your seat belt and read!

Contents

Attacking the Foundation

My husband and I would lie in bed and talk about what to name the foundation. It was a back and forth, round and round, discussion with both of us offering up different ideas. We had differing opinions on what we wanted and what words we felt we needed in the title. Since so many years have passed, I am at a loss to tell you any of the specifics of those night time discussions, but I do know that we had help from an outside consulting firm and they settled on the name.

Throughout the entirety of this chapter, you will find that people are very concerned about the name of the foundation and do not particularly care for it. I personally think it has a nice ring to it. Still, the detractors are most concerned about the words, "religion," and to a lesser extent "military," and tend to offer many other options for us to use. I wonder if the foundation would receive such venomous attacks if that prickly little word "religion" were not in the title and instead the word "rights" (The Military Rights and Freedom Foundation). It is the misperception here that we are intolerant to religion, and specifically the Christian religion, that is causing the bulk of the venom that is tossed our way.

On the other hand, the letters people write indicate that they do not understand what we do. The detractors jump to conclusions upon hearing the name of the foundation that we are all about Christianity and that we are a Christian organization. They make assumptions without reading any information about us or doing any research. They then proceed to get upset and attack the foundation, my husband and I personally, when their assumptions do not pan out.

Come to find out, venturing into religious territory can be very tricky. People can become extremely defensive when they feel their religious faith beliefs are being attacked. The defenses thrown up can be downright ugly and gone are the coherent or cohesive thought processes one usually needs to write a letter to a foundation, or to anyone for that matter. You will have to trust me on this one, because, unfortunately, I know this from experience. And, as usual...*they can't spell for shit!*

♦♦♦

Subject: Your organization stinks

(Name withheld)

.

Dear Mr. Stinky

I am writing in response to your email to the Military Religious Freedom Foundation ("MRFF"). Unfortunately, I am at a loss as to how to respond to such a juvenile taunt as "Your organization stinks." After all, despite the long hours necessary to fight for the religious freedom of all our brave men and women in uniform, all of us at MRFF still shower regularly and are generally minty fresh.

To the extent you intend to claim that our mission to protect religious freedom throughout the military stinks, I am confident that our thousands of clients would disagree. I am saddened that you believe fighting for the rights of those brave enough to sacrifice so much to fight for our rights "stinks."

Blessed be,

Tobanna Barker
MRFF Legal Affairs Coordinator

.

I love this response from Tobanna and thought it the perfect letter to start off with as she is just so on point.

♦♦♦

Subject: Patriotism at its worst

You guys are a bunch of homosexuals and lesbians are you not? True only to your sexual perversions? Not a patriotic bone in your body? Rampant with Hiv and disease, eager for others to be like you? Filth in NM.

(Name withheld)

No, no we are not.

Dear Mr. (Name withheld):

I am writing in response to your email to the Military Religious Freedom Foundation ("MRFF"). I have had the privilege of responding to many emails received by MRFF and I usually explain MRFF's purpose, which is to protect the religious freedom of all soldiers, sailors, Marines, cadets, and veterans. Yet, your email does not mention anything about religious freedom, but only claims that its board members and volunteers are "homosexuals and lesbians" who you assume to be "rampant with [HIV] and disease." This statement is childish, hateful, and ignorant on a number of levels.

I am tempted to explain how sexual orientation has no connection with patriotism, that most sexually transmitted diseases are actually more prevalent among heterosexuals, etc. However, you clearly gave up on learning long ago. I somehow doubt that someone who cannot even form a complete sentence would understand complex ideas, such as religious freedom or sexual politics.

Instead, I simply suggest that you retreat back into your own lonely world and perhaps entertain yourself with that nine-piece jigsaw puzzle that has had you stumped for weeks. MRFF is busy defending the Constitutional rights of the men and women in uniform who so bravely fight for our rights.

Blessed be,

Tobanna Barker
MRFF Volunteer

Subject: You people have to much time and money.

Realize and meditate on what an absolute waste to mankind you are.

(Name withheld)

.

Hi (Name withheld),

Your terse message arrived. The subject line is incorrect. The substance of the message was childish. Given the avalanche of stupid messages we've received lately, I'll assume you are part of the mindless herd that chooses to lash out in ignorance without any interest in understanding the facts of the situation. If, unlike so many of your fellow true-believers, you're interested in knowing the actual facts of what happened and why, please feel free to write back and I'll clear things up for you.

Best,

Mike Farrell
(MRFF Board of Advisors)

.

Mike,

got way better programs to spend my time on than you

(Name withheld)

.

Name withheld,

I'm sure you do, (name withheld). Sesame Street comes to mind.

Mike Farrell

.

Ha! I love this response!

Throughout the book, I will occasionally present some of the news articles and background information which will give context to some of the emails that we receive. Here is an article that came out after we "went into action," and the email we received because of it is below the article:

A prayer breakfast at Fort Riley set for Monday as part of 1st Infantry Division's "Victory Week" celebration has been rescheduled, and the retired three-star general who'd been invited to speak—and whose invitation to a similar event at West Point in 2012 met with fierce opposition—won't be asked back.

Retired Lt. Gen. William "Jerry" Boykin, a 36-year Army veteran and longtime member of the special operations community, was to address the morning gathering at the Kansas base, but "due to a number of scheduling conflicts ... the breakfast will be rescheduled for a later date," 1st ID spokesman Master Sgt. Mike Lavigne said in a Wednesday email.

The day before, Military Religious Freedom Foundation founder Mikey Weinstein sent multiple emails to 1st ID commander Maj. Gen. Wayne Grigsby on behalf of his advocacy group, demanding the leader "immediately withdraw" Boykin's invitation. Weinstein's email included a report from another MRFF staffer on Boykin that brought up, among other issues:

- The general's statements while in uniform comparing the global war on terrorism to a holy war against Satan.

- Widely reported remarks, also during his time in service, that he had confidence in an engagement with enemy forces led by a Somali warlord because "I knew my God was bigger than his."

- Statements made after his retirement claiming Islam is "not just a religion, it's a totalitarian way of life" and should not receive protection under the First Amendment.

Boykin, now an executive vice president with the conservative Family Research Council, could not immediately be reached for comment.

◆◆◆

Subject: Your foundation

Hey just wanted to send you atheist supremacists a congratulatory note on your minor victory over decent people in Kansas due to one weak willed leader. Yes, I even heard how you laughed mockingly at him for his poor excuse. Maybe he deserved that for not having the courage to stand up to you in the first place and then not being able to admit he buckled to a pathetic group like yours. Well, enjoy your little victory for now. No matter how many decent people you harm today your actions will ultimately be dealt with on the Day of Judgement. Unless you repent of course but the hate in your hearts may be so deep that you would rather cast you lot with the beast of the pit of darkness than ever accept God's merciful grace and stop persecuting Christians for simply living out their faith. It is all too obvious that your atheist group is not about fair mindedness. Since your attacks seem to be primarily limited to Christians though I suspect anyone who truly believes in Yahwey would be fair game. Your group is definitely about driving believing Christians out of this nation by all means you can find eventually devolving, as such deep seated hate always does, into physical violence when the opportunity presents itself. First you stop Christians from simply being able to speak, then drive them out of work to starve out them and their families and then move in for the physical kill. You have heard it before I am sure, Either accept the Mark of the Beast or you shall not buy or sell. I have to admit it is somewhat fascinating to see Bible prophecy being fulfilled even if only a small part at your hands in my time. Rest assured you along with the army of darkness you have aligned yourself with will get it's day in court so to speak. Just so you know, you already lost over 2000 years ago. But for now, congrats on your minor victory in expanding your immorality and darkness over America just a little bit more.

(Name withheld)

.

We at MRFF currently represent thousands of armed forces and vets... about 96% are Christians...I am not all that religious but still pray thrice a day in Hebrew...I'm Jewish and damn proud of it too!...nearly 300 folks comprise MRFF paid and volunteer staff and well over 80% are Christians.... tell me again how we're all atheists?!....and tell me why that would even matter?....don't atheists enjoy the VERY same civil rights that YOU do as a "Christian"?....all we at MRFF care about is ensuring that the time, place and manner in which ANYONE in the military feels that they must deploy their faith complies with Constitutional and DoD laws and regulatory standards... it's always the Great Commission vs. the Great Constitution...get it?...is THAT so hard to understand??...seriously??

Mikey Weinstein

◆ ◆ ◆

Subject: Despicable org.

You guys belong to the KKK ??

.

Hi Despicable,

No, we don't. Do you? As you may be aware, the KKK is a racist, radical Christian cult not unlike some of the other religious extremist groups whose efforts to infiltrate the military threaten our treasured freedom of religious belief or non-belief. These are the groups we oppose and work to expose.

I hope that answers your question.

Mike Farrell

.

Let's hear it for Mike Farrell....and yes, for those of you who are asking if he is the Mike Farrell from *MASH*, he sure is.

A posting on YouTube shows Maj. Gen. Craig Olson speaking at a National Day of Prayer Task Force event. In the speech, Olson refers to himself as a "redeemed believer in Christ," who credits God for his accomplishments in the Air Force.

During his 23-minute address, Olson spoke of "flying complex aircraft; doing complex nuclear missions — I have no ability to do that. God enabled me to do that."

"He put me in charge of failing programs worth billions of dollars. I have no ability to do that, no training to do that. God did that. He sent me to Iraq to negotiate foreign military sales deals through an Arabic interpreter. I have no ability to do that. I was not trained to do that. God did all of that."

At the end of his speech, Olson asks the audience to pray for Defense Department leaders, who "need to humbly depend on Christ." He also asks them to pray for troops preparing to deploy again so they can "bear through that by depending on Christ."

Mikey Weinstein, CEO of the Military Religious Freedom Foundation, has sent a blistering letter to Chief of Staff Gen, Mark Welsh, arguing that Olson's comments violate an Air Force instruction, which prohibits airmen from endorsing a particular faith or belief.

◆◆◆

The following emails were sent to us after we objected to the completely sectarian nature of Olson's speech.

.

Subject: Free America

How dare you call yourselves the military religious freedom foundation! That's right, I purposely used lower case characters! You people disgust me! You have nothing to do with freedom or religion. As far as I'm concerned you're one step away from Hitler's Nazism. Isn't it special how a pop-up comes across the screen asking for donations as soon as your website is accessed. I wouldn't dream of donating ten cents to your vile and disgusting organization. Ever heard of the First Amendment? Thousands and thousands of American fighting men and women have fought for Major General Craig Olson to say the wonderful kind words he spoke in honoring The National Day of Prayer and you have a problem with it? I say, take your problem and every whinny scumbag that agrees with you and get out of my FREE AMERICA!

(Name withheld)

♦♦♦

Subject: You people are Scum! I hope you all Rot in Hell with all your RagHead buddies! You are a Disgrace, and the fact you even call yourselves military is a joke!

.

Dear (Name withheld)–

I am writing in response to your email to the Military Religious Freedom Foundation ("MRFF"). The entirety of your email appears to be contained in the subject line, as the body of the email is blank. Your apparent inability to correctly send a simple email is fitting – your message is just as empty as your head.

I cannot respond to your accusation that we at MRFF are scum and should rot in hell because you have not included any facts or arguments supporting these claims. Consequently, you have wasted my time. You are nothing more than an oxygen thief.

If you would like to assert an argument supported by facts, I will be happy to respond. Until then, just try to watch your step – I have the feeling you fall down a lot.

Blessed be,

Tobanna Barker

◆◆◆

Subject: Re: sign on HAWAII MILITARY BASE

JUST WHEN IN THE HELL ARE GROUPS LIKE YOU GOING TO PROTEST SOMETHING WORTHWHILE. FOR INSTANCE THE CORRUPT POLITICIANS IN WASHINGTON AND PLANNED PARENTHOOD. IN STEAD YOU STICK UP FOR THE ASS HOL-S THAT DID THE DIRTY DEED IN NEW YORK. YOU FOLKS SHOULD HAVE BEEN IN THE TWIN TOWERS ON THAT DAY, IF YOU SURVIVED , PERHAPS YOU MIGHT SEE THINGS DIFFERENTLY. JUST WHO IN THE HELL DO YOU THINK YOU ARE. DO SOMETHING RIGHT FOR YOUR COUNTRY AND PRAY FOR YOUR OWN SALVATION, LORD KNOWS YOU NEED IT. ON SECOND THOUGHT, THAT WOULD NOT WORK ASY YOU MUST BE DEVIL'S IN THE FLESH.

(Name withheld)

.

(Name withheld),

DO YOU SEE ANYTHING IN OUR NAME REGARDING POLITICS? NO! WE DEAL WITH RELIGION IN THE MILITARY. PERIOD.

WHO IN THE HELL DO YOU THINK YOU ARE FIRING OFF THIS EMAIL WHEN WHAT YOU SAY DOES NOT PERTAIN TO US. TAKE YOUR RANT TO SOME OTHER RIGHTS ORGANIZATION.

YOU HAVE TO BE THE MOST IGNORANT PERSON THAT EVER EMAILED US OUT OF THE THOUSANDS WE HAVE RECEIVED.

LET ME EDUCATE YOU ON WHO WE ARE AND WHAT WE DO. WE ARE NEITHER AN ATHEIST NOR AN ANTI-CHRISTIAN ORGANIZATION. SEVENTY-FIVE PERCENT OF THE BOARD, ADVISORY BOARD, VOLUNTEERS AND SUPPORTERS ARE CHRISTIANS AND 96% OF OUR ACTIVE AND RETIRED MILITARY CLIENTS ARE CHRISTIANS.

WE DO NOT ACT ON OUR OWN BUT ON THE COMPLAINTS OF OUR SOLDIERS WHO SEE THE BLATANT TRAMPLING OF THE

CONSTITUTION AND SUPREME COURT RULINGS.

WE ARE NOT DEVIL'S IN THE FLESH BUT UPHOLDING OUR LAWS.

YOU, ON THE OTHER HAND, DON'T CARE ABOUT OUR LAWS.

IT SICKENS ME THAT CHRISTIANS COME ON THIS SITE AND SPEW NONSENSE.

I'M GIVING YOU RIGHT BACK THE ANIMOUS YOU SHOWED US.

NOW, TAKE YOUR SORRY DUMBASS TO SOME OTHER WEBSITE THAT WOULD ACTUALLY CARE WHAT YOU SAY.

Pastor Joan
MRFF Advisory Board Member

·

In her reply, I think Joan thought the only way she could possibly be understood was to respond in kind, therefore ALL CAPS was the way to go! Who would write a letter to a foundation entirely in CAPS? Is this the only way they feel that they can get their point across? Well, let me answer my own question, probably so. Of all of the letters we receive at the MRFF, less than 1% are well written.

♦♦♦

Subject: Hello

Mr. Weinstein
You may claim that The Military Religious Freedom Foundation is the sole nonprofit civil rights organization dedicated to ensuring that all members of the United States Armed Forces fully receive the Constitutional guarantee of both freedom of religion and freedom from religion, to which they and all Americans are entitled. However, the American Center For Law and Justice would disagree with that. According to them, your organization is a threat to religious freedom both within the military and outside it. You obviously don't know anything about the origin of the United States at all.

(Name withheld)

Hi (name withheld),

I think you are sadly suffering from tortured, poisonous and totally wrong information about MRFF...the disreputable and disgusting ACLJ ("American Control should be under the Laws of Jesus") is a particularly putrescent and pathetic source for that...as to the history attendant to the origins of the United States, may I kindly refer you to the books from our esteemed MRFF Sr. Research Dir., Ms. Chris Rodda, "Liars For Jesus Volume 1" and "Liars For Jesus Volume 2", check them out, bro...and perhaps do your homework a tad better before you come out throwing stones, little sport...the shit you wrote to me is part of Free Speech...but the reply is part of the Free Consequences you must face for writing that opening crap...poor manners there...you can make your point without being an asshole, eh?........

Mikey Weinstein

♦♦♦

Subject: False Military Religious Freedom Foundation-Mikey Weinstein":

" ******* REPENT TO JESUS ONLY-GET RIGHT WITH THE BIBLE ONLY-STOP ASSAULTING THE TRUTH/CHRISTIANS-I HIGHLY RECOMMEND WORLDWIDE SONLIFETV.COM OF JIMMY SWAGGART MINISTRIES TO YOU!!!!!!!

The First Amendment to the U.S. Constitution guarantees an airman's right to express his faith, and the National Defense Authorization Act specifically states religious beliefs must be accommodated by the Armed Forces!!!!!!!

I am outraged that "False Military Religious Freedom Foundation-Mikey Weinstein" spearheaded-supports the removal of a life's personal testimony article written by Col. (name withheld) from "The Stinger!!!!!!!"

To deny Col.(name withheld) his right to write a story about his personal faith, while allowing others to post non-religious material clearly demonstrates a distinct case of religious assault-discrimination!!!!!!!

I demand that you immediately justly respect and honor the religious liberties airmen are entitled to, and to clear up and right this wrong matter quickly!!!!!!!

******* OUTRAGED-MAY ONLY THE TRUTH WHICH IS GOD'S
TRUTH THE BIBLE GO MARCHING ON!!!!!!!

(Name withheld)

.

Dear (name withheld)

*Jimmy Swaggart? You want Mikey to follow Jimmy Swaggart? The minister
that was caught with prostitutes twice is the one you follow? The one who
cheated on his wife and cried for forgiveness and then cheated on her again
and said to his congregation "The Lord told me it's flat none of your business."*

*As an ordained minister in the Assemblies of God I DEMAND that you run…
run as fast as you can from this man who should have never been able to
enter the pulpit again. It IS the congregations business to call out a supposed
man of God for his whoremongering.*

*"For this ye know, that no whoremonger, nor unclean person, nor covetous
man, who is an idolater, hath any inheritance in the kingdom of Christ and
of God." Ephesians 5:5*

*Clean up your own act before you point fingers at other people. You're
following a whoremonger. Apparently Jimmy taught you to judge others when
he didn't want the congregation to judge him. That makes him a hypocrite
and he should have no place in the ministry – ever!*

*You need to repent for following a man who had to start his own radio and
TV station because no one else wanted him. He's only in it for the money.*

*I suggest you watch the old movie Elmer Gantry. You will find similarities
between Swaggart and Elmer. Maybe your eyes will be opened then.*

*Pastor Joan
MRFF Advisory Board Member*

.

Dear (name withheld),

Since you did not sign your letter, I will address this to (name withheld),

I felt compelled to respond to you in light of your uninformed claims. First off I am an evangelical Christian who has been in the ministry - both militarily and civilian - for over 37 years. I just retired as a command Chaplain; There was a time that I felt Mikey and his efforts were misguided; however, I took the time to research and even went to the recusant position of meeting with him. And now I consider him a friend.

Let's set the foundation, Mikey is a practicing follower of Judaism. Secondly he feels everyone has a right to follow their religious beliefs or no beliefs, as they see fit. I know you will not believe this but he has stood up against groups that seek to stop Christian beliefs. So; with this said, just basic understanding of Judaism would preclude your tenant that he espouses the heinous acts meted upon the innocent people of France. Please research before you accuse as Mikey, like myself, have an enormous love and respect for human life - aim the evil where it belongs; in the actions of the individual or groups involved.

Thank You For Your Time,

CH (COL-R) Quentin Collins

♦♦♦

Subject: Your a disgrace

Mikey,

You need to remove the word "military" from your groups name. I am a veteran and ashamed of your letter in regards to the General and his speaking about his Christian values. Why don't you show the American Veteran's who really donate to your group?

Let us be clear Mikey, DO NOT group us veteran's into your shameful anti-Christian tactics.

(Name withheld)

.

Veteran (Name withheld),

I'm a veteran (just like almost every involved with MRFF) and I love what MRFF does to protect service members from religious persecution and extremists. I'm happy to be represented by such a great group. So no, we won't be removing anything.

Dustin Chalker
Veteran

◆◆◆

Subject: Which of you served in the military

You are a very sick bunch of people. Which of you served in the military?

(Name withheld)
Captain, US Army airborne infantry

.

Almost all of us, actually. Personally, I was an Army combat medic for nine years with deployments, a Combat Medic Badge, Purple Heart, etc.

And thanks for noticing that I'm sick. I have a horrific incurable disease called Constitutionalitis. The symptoms are pretty mild and manageable until I see someone in uniform violating the Constitution, then I get all inflamed and have angry mood swings. The best treatment is a good court ruling.

Regards,

Dustin Chalker
MRFF Athiest Affairs Advisor

◆◆◆

Subject: Watching you suffer

What is the difference between your piece of shit- Un American organization and those ISIS extremists whom you mirror as an organization. Meaning you both want Christians to be openly silenced and persecuted for their beliefs. Fuck you and you Left wing Liberal Beliefs in which you keep pushing on Real Americans!!! Your organization is no different than those enemies of America. Why don't you move to those countries and join their Jihad! Your a disgrace to Americans who have died for your freedom....May Jesus Christ have mercy on you....Cause I know conservative American Christians would love to watch you suffer

(Name withheld)

·

(Name withheld)

What you said here is very telling: "Christians would love to watch you suffer". That sums up pretty well why we do what we do. Because sick people like you want to cause harm to others in the name of a pacifist. Strange, isn't it?

One of many differences between us and ISIS is that we are supportive of a secular government while ISIS (and apparently you as well) support theocratic government. Next, we are non violent. We don't participate in our advocate the use of violent force to accomplish our goals (as you have in your message).

I hope this clarifies things for you.

Cheers,

Blake A. Page
Military Religious Freedom Foundation
Special Assistant to the President
Director of US Army Affairs

♦♦♦

Subject: Stupidity

Wow. I really don't know what to say to stupidity. Read the name of your" foundation." It's not religious freedom for "some". It's either all or nothing. God rained down hail-free and brimstone on Sodom and Gamorrah. He'll not keep His hand from a country that was FOUNDED on religious freedom but that now has done a copmlete 180.

·

Hi (Name withheld),

I understand that you find it hard to know what to say, but if you're interested in making a point it would be helpful if what you ended up saying made sense. Both the name of our foundation and the meaning of the name is clear to us. We defend the freedom of belief for those in the military. And we point out that the military, being part of the government, must be dutiful in separating Church and State, just as Thomas Jefferson and others said.

So when the law of the land, as indicated by and supported by the Constitution, says you can no longer discriminate against gay people's participation in the military, a religious believer who does not share that belief must either change his position, hold his tongue or leave the military. And now, when the law of the land recognizes the right of gays and lesbians to marry, the same applies. I hope you will choose to understand that.

I don't know how old you are, but when President Truman, over 50 years ago, declared that the military was to be fully racially integrated, many who considered themselves Christians, some of them clergy, declared it profane and sacrilegious. Like you, they thundered on with carefully chosen Biblical references. Happily, they have since either seen the light or been assigned to the dustbin of history. I wish you enlightenment.

Best,

Mike Farrell
(MRFF Board of Advisors)

◆◆◆

Subject: Mitary Chaplains

Your so called "group" is so ridiculous that I thought you were a JOKE when I first heard about you!

You spew vile HATE for Christians, and anyone else who had any sort of religious beliefs, while foolishly claiming it is "intolerant" and "hate speech" to not be just like YOU! How intolerant can you be?!

You are MASSIVELY outnumbered by Christians! We are so tired of your antics and are NOT going to tolerate much more of your pushing your Godless, "do what I say" agenda!

Leave Christians, and all non-atheists ALONE! Keep pushing you agenda on us and we will stand up against you! Our sheer numbers will be no match for your whining ways and you know it!

If you were really concerned about "tolerance" you would mind your own business and leave others alone to think, believe, and worship how they please!

BACK OFF! We are done with this and the push back is beginning!

.

To Whom It May Concern,

I normally do not engage in responses to criticisms of the Military Religious Freedom Foundation (MRFF); but, felt compelled to here. I am a Military Chaplain and have been for a very long time. There have been numerous occasions where I have been approached about things that MRFF has done or are accused of doing, and as such, I have developed a friendly relationship with the director/founder (due to my desire to see for myself). First off I must assure you that he is not trying to crush Christians. He and his organization have sought to assure all religious and non-religious practices be maintained and enforced. He is a strong supporter of the First Amendment so accusing him of spitting vile hate is ludicrous. I can assure you that he has never spit on me and he has a great deal of respect for me and my position as I have of him. The idiom that I recommend is: research the positions before you lash out as not doing so will leave you in a precarious position. Criticism is good when provided in a non-threatening way. Your position is easier to consider when not filled with anger.

Respectfully,

A MRFF Supporter and Military Chaplain

♦♦♦

Subject: what a twisted bunch of people

Your entire foundation is severely sick and twisted.

You people are talking about supporting the u.s. constitution yet want to separate religion/beliefs from military/gov?

I am not a believer in any one faith but believe in one supreme creator. I don't care what you people believe.. When a sign reads may god bless, I take that to mean whatever god is yours.. Even your satanic one..

Why aren't you going after the Federal Reserve to remove in god we trust from the one dollar bill? You afraid that might expose the fact the federal reserve is not a part of the government? Ya I though so.. you people are weak and pathetic.

And finally, I find it somewhat hilarious you guys are claiming to be constitutionalist, yet you have zero understanding of the premise behind it. It was written with natural law in mind.

Do you understand that? Natural law, gods law, natures law...Your dads a lawyer, he should know better.. I am literally in a state of shock and awe over your hypocrisy latent throughout your organization and understandings of anything.

But Americans are just dumb sheep, off to the slaughter.

People see who you are.. and your one world government won't happen.

·

Dear Twisted,

I see you bought into the lies concerning Mikey and the Military Religious Freedom Foundation. You make a lot of assumptions that have no merit concerning us. The person behind the development email address is not Mikey's daughter. "You people are talking about supporting the u.s constitution yet want to separate religion/beliefs from military/gov?" The Constitution— not us—makes it very clear about the separation between religion and government entities.

Our military is secular—which includes those of other faiths or no belief system—and it must not advance one religion over another according to the Constitution, Supreme Court rulings and the Unified Code of Military Justice. Religious activities must be in the hands of the Chaplains on Chapel grounds, not in the hands of the Commander on base-wide grounds.

If the sign in question is not moved or taken down, then under the Free Exercise Clause other faiths must be allowed to put up signs next to it.

Pastor Joan
MRFF Advisory Board Member

♦♦♦

Subject: Someone is pouting!

MLFF, You people really need to find a worthwhile issue to direct all that anger towards. I am nonreligious, but fine Christians to be much more honest and trustworthy than all other people! Let them pray and stop this compulsive pouting!!!! I would never support your stupid cause!

.

Hi point missed,

You miss the point, which is no surprise since you are apparently unable to recognize the problem at hand. The issue at hand has nothing to do with Christians being good people, it has to do with the inappropriateness of a military organization appearing to promote one religious belief system over others.

In the case at hand, that inappropriateness is not only demonstrated by the act of a military unit publicly praying, which violates the separation of church and state, but also intrudes on the rights of those members of that unit who do not share that particular faith but are required to take part for fear of negative consequences that may befall them as a result of non-participation.

What you think of as anger on our part is a combination of frustration and disgust at the continuing attempt by a certain Christian sect to impose itself on our military in violation of the law and the regulations of that same military.

Perhaps if you were more discerning you'd recognize the fact that the Christians you find "to be much more honest and trustworthy than all other people" are actually deeply divided in the way they perceive and practice their Christianity. The sect in question here holds itself out as the one true faith and condemns all others, including other Christians, who don't accept its view.

I wish you discernment.

Mike Farrell
(MRFF Board of Advisors)

♦♦♦

Subject: Fuck off Mikey

MRFF (Mikey's Retarded Faggot Federation)
Entire group of PUNKS!!!!
Mikey is the king bitch and the organization is filled with a bunch of anal butt monkeys who swallow each other's loads while wearing camo fatigues and high heels!
Fuck off!!!

This kind of "interesting" imagination blows my mind. I would just never put my imaginative process to coming up with such horrific screed. Even if I were being forced to write stuff like this, I'm not sure I could! I think it takes a special kind of mind...

♦♦♦

Subject: Serious Joke

You people are a serious joke and will be judged by your beliefs and actions in the end. There will be no heaven for you and your supporters,the good lord above will see to this. Your whole movement is a sad excuse to draw attention to yourselves and your hopeless cause. This country was built on the belief of Christianity. If you don agree with it that's fine keep it to yourself. Don't think you can change the rest of the world to believe in the sterile environment you would like us all to live in. Just crawl back in your caves and stay out of everyone's businesses. God bless the u.s. And God bless those that believe in and aren't afraid to practice religion publicly

Dear St. Peter,

I want you to see this message because (Name withheld), here, seems to think he can take your job. I always looked forward to seeing you at the gate when my turn came, but here is this guy who thinks he's the one who decides who gets in and who doesn't. He apparently doesn't remember what "pride goeth" before.

If he shows up there looking to push you off base, do me a favor before you smite him, will you? Tell him he forgot about the prohibition on judging others. Tell him he doesn't know the history of his own country. Tell him true Christianity is not under attack and doesn't need to be defended by arrogant blowhards. Stun him with the knowledge that the MRFF, while made up of people of many different belief systems, is over 95% Christian, just not the thin-skinned pretend-Christian who lashes out ignorantly because of a lack of faith. You might add, if you will, how frustrating it is to look down from your perch and see the hash so many self-important schmucks have made of the simple faith your boss put together when he was here. In the meantime, we'll keep doing what we can to make this country safe from the religious bigotry you hate by protecting everyone's right to believe as they choose. Take care. I'll check in with you again from time to time just to say hi.

A MRFF ally

♦♦♦

Subject: Military and Religion

First of all thank you for your service.

Second I really don't understand people like you that want to remove religion from America. You say that you support the Constitution but you like others think it reads, "Freedom FROM Religion" not "Freedom OF Religion". It is to protect us from a STATE run religion not from all religion. As long as all religions are treated equally I see no problem with a soldier praying or writing about their belief in their God.

(Name withheld)

·

This letter was respectfully written, something I greatly appreciate.

Dear (name withheld),

I think you misunderstand and have been fed lies by some other media source about what it is we do. We do not inhibit anyone's right to pray or worship how they please in the military.

We do, however, conduct two primary missions: we ensure the military as an institution remains religiously neutral and we protect the rights of service members to not have any religion forced on them by others.

Many people rail MRFF as an atheist organization and nothing could be farther from the truth. 96% of our over 39,000 clients are practicing Christians who come to us for help because they are afraid their careers will be put in jeopardy should they seek help through official channels. There is a very pervasive movement in the military that breeds fear for speaking up in defense of your religious rights. The vast majority of the time our clients are being religiously discriminated against by extremist Christians for not being the "right kind of Christian." That is something we do not tolerate, the Constitution does not tolerate, and that commanders SHOULD not tolerate but often do because it is the status quo.

We are working very hard to stop that. We do not tell people not to worship. In fact we highly encourage everyone in uniform of any creed or religion to worship however they see fit so long as they do not trample upon the Constitutional rights of others.

I hope this clears up questions you had but should you wish to inquire further I will be glad to answer any questions you do have.

Very Respectfully,

Paul Loebe
Special Projects Manager
Military Religious Freedom Foundation
Chicago, IL

*Disclaimer: Although I am a Marine Staff Sergeant I do not speak on behalf of the Department of Defense, United States Marine Corps, or any affiliated branches.

♦♦♦

Subject: Gen Boykin

To Whom:

Read a story that contained comments by your organization on: a speech: "In a speech at a National Day of Prayer Task Force event, Maj. Gen. Boykin

The only thing out of line is you and your organization. Free speech not only applies to you, it is a right to all! Considering that he spent a good part of his life defending free speech, this attack on him is pointless and just displays mindless hatred.

Grow up!

(Name withheld)

·

Dear (name withheld),

Here at MRFF we fully support the General's rights to free speech. What we don't support is the use of military rank to advance religious principles. Now, you might say, "all he did was talk about how great it is to be Christian." Sure, but he did so in the wrong time, place, and manner. He did so while wearing in uniform at a public venue operated in part by the government. There is actually precedent for generals being dismissed for using their rank and uniform to further religious principles. Do a quick search for Jerry Boykin if you're not already familiar with the story.

Cheers,

Blake

·

Blake

Wrong again! He was relaying a personal story i.e. life journey. He was not promoting or endorsing Christianity. Again, tolerance goes both ways! You are waking the "sleeping giant". Keep it up!

(Name withheld)

Dear (name withheld),

I'm sure you're suggesting that you and your ilk would like to overthrow the government and impose a Christian theocracy over the United States with your sleeping giant remark. Either that or you're suggesting that you and yours would like to take up and and hunt down and kill people like myself. I've heard it all before. I would very much like for you to take a moment and sit down with those close to you, perhaps your children if you have any, and tell them in detail how you feel about violence, murder, and the like. If you can't do that with confidence your threats are hollow. On the other hand, if you can do that with confidence, if you do believe in a waking giant and support a wave of theocracy overpowering the United States, I recommend you study history. Theocracy will always be a destructive force. No matter what the religion, marrying it with governmental authority breeds bloodshed and human suffering unlike anything else humanity has ever devised. Which Christian military organization was it that fought under the motto (translated to English) "God With Us?"

Cheers,

Blake A. Page
Military Religious Freedom Foundation
Special Assistant to the President,
Director of US Army Affairs

♦♦♦

The following is a very nice letter of thanks that was sent in to us after we were able to achieve a positive outcome.

Subject: I Am Evangelical Christian and MRF Foundation Helped Us

My rank is (withheld). And I am a U.S. soldier stationed at Fort (name withheld) in (state withheld).

I am evangelical Christian and a member of The Foursquare Church. And have been since I first accepted Jesus Christ as my personal Lord and Savior. And was born again as a 7th grader living in California. I have eternal life in Christ.

Recently I asked my supervisor to help me approach my commander and ask him to stop taking the Lord's name in vain all of the time. I understand that this is the Army and soldiers will cuss. But our commander says "Jesus F—ing Christ" all the time and I and other soldiers find it offensive to our faith in Christ. Our commander says this all of the time and not just a few times a day or night. It is his go to phrase.

My supervisor declined to help us talk to the commander and did not say why? But he told us about the Military Religious Freedom Foundation. He gave me a phone number to call Mr. M. Weinstein.

Mr. Weinstein answered my call his self and took down all of the facts to the problem. He was nice like my supervisor said. He talks fast and acted even faster.

Mr. Weinstein spoke to some people above my commander in our chain. And we have seen that the cussing has suddenly just plain stopped.

My supervisor says that the commander was very angry at first when he got called in to see his superior unit commander due to Mr. Weinstein's phone call. But now he has cooled off and is not that angry. Even though (name and rank of commander withheld) said that since he's Christian too and because of that he could not be accused of offending other Christians because of his cussing. But that is not true!

I and my other battle buddies are very thankful for this help from the MRF Foundation. Even though we know that Mr. Weinstein and the

MRF Foundation is not yet a follower of Jesus Christ. He and the MRF Foundation helped us all the same.

I do not want to offend Mr. Weinstein or the MRF Foundation but we will pray that they all come to know the love and peace of walking with Jesus Christ. Thank you all at the MRF Foundation for helping us when we needed you to help. Because our supervisor wouldn't. And he's Christian too. Like our commander is.

May God Bless the MRF Foundation with the love of His only Begotten Son.

(Name withheld)

◆◆◆

The following letter came in very recently, and I thought a love letter that validates precisely what we do was the perfect end to a chapter filled with, well, what it is filled with!

.

Subject: Critical

I was aware of Mikey Weinstein's work and the work of MRFF before I joined the Chaplain Corps, but I was surprised first and then impressed by how aware many military chaplains were. Unlike me, who thinks the work of MRFF is critically important to the integrity of military chaplaincy, many of my colleagues were afraid. They felt threatened by the power and success of MRFF's work. Ultimately, these chaplains are afraid because they think a win for MRFF and the tens of thousands of service members represented by them, is a loss for them. "Mikey" was a four-letter word to them.

For those of us who care about the men and women serving our nation, and believe they deserve to be treated with dignity and justice, we are facing a deeply entrenched system of fundamentalist Christianity that funds the interlocking cruelties homophobia, trans-phobia, misogyny, Islamophobia, antisemitism, and Christian-supremacy. These forms of bigotry betray unit cohesion, compromise mission readiness, and preclude chaplains fulfilling their job description. This is not about political positions or theological commitments; it's about good order and discipline. MRFF's work is crucial to the strength and well-being of our military service members and the operations our nation's military at-large.

(A MRFF supporter)

Again with the Jews

THE BACKBONE OF THE foundation is the people who support it through generous monetary donations, monthly recurring donations, as well as donating themselves (of their personal time, effort, and energies). It takes all of our paid staff, volunteers, and supporters to make this foundation work.

Our clients who come to us for help are never charged and are never asked to donate to this charitable foundation. This is actually a bone of contention between me and my husband. I have picked this bone from time to time especially when a tremendous amount of effort and energy (more than the usual) is being put into action for one situation. Of course he works hard for everyone, but when the occasional exceedingly time-consuming case comes along, I might suggest mentioning that we are a charitable foundation and need financial support to keep the foundation up and running.

While gone are the days when we survive month to month, we operate on a very lean budget and survive year to year, December being a critical fundraising time for us. I sometimes would like people to get a glimpse of the time, efforts, and energies it takes to work on these various cases. I think most people would be shocked at the amount of time just one case can take. However, my husband flatly refuses to mention donations when taking on or finishing up cases. Thus, I find chapter two, "Again with the Jews," to be repulsively ironic.

These less than intelligent thinking people (you won't find much political correctness or any type of kind verbiage in this chapter so I thought I would throw that in) think of my husband as a Jew first, not Jewish, but not just any Jew, rather a money-grubbing Jew. And yet, Mikey is one of the most generous people I know. He is generous (perhaps overly so) of his knowledge, his access, his time, and his money. Here, I present one of the thickest chapters, one with by far and away the most material to go through, all because of the fact that my husband and I are Jewish.

By the time you reach the end of the chapter, you may find yourself somewhat desensitized to it all. I hope that does not happen as I hope you find each letter as bad (or worse) than the one before it. These days we must stay vigilant to what is going on around us and not allow the hateful and racist context of these letters become the norm. Right now, you may be thinking that you have never read or seen anything of the like, but I have. Unfortunately, this is normal for me. What I do not want is for it to become normal for you.

Subject: Finally, the Air Force grounds Mikey Weinstein

Get your Jewish money out of your pocket and see what it says. Then read the Bible.

(Name withheld)

.

Dear (name withheld),

"Jewish money"???

I strongly doubt that Mikey has a shekel on him or even in his home!! He almost certainly uses U.S. currency when shopping or when doing the other things Americans do.

As for what I suspect is your presumption that U.S. currency has anything to with Dog or Jesus (who by the way was an orthodox Jew and never heard of Christians). You appear to be just another bigoted Christian nationalist who lives under the misapprehension that there actually is a Dog and that he wags his tail when you bark.

What actually gives you the impression that anyone gives a crap about what you think or that your narcissistic emesis will act to change anyone's thoughts or actions?

Marshalldoc.

.

Dear (name withheld),

This does confuse me, I have to say. People like you, who apparently believe in a Jew and feel they were saved by a Jew yet delight in indulging in such crass antisemitism, cause me to wonder if they understand the meaning of hypocrisy.

That ever trouble you?

Mike Farrell
MRFF Board of Advisors)

◆◆◆

Subject: stiff necked jews at Fort Campbell

Micheal Weinstein your little plan to cause trouble for the spirit filled followers of Christ Jesus at Fort Campbell will fail.

Christ Jesus in Acts branded jews a stiff necks people and your neck 'Mr. jewgooder" is the stiffest of all hellbound jews.

The jews at Fort Campbell don't need new leader.

They already have a new leader. It is Christ Jesus! Halleluyah and Huzzah! His Army is America's army.

They jews don't need no leader other than the only True Son of Man. (John 14:6)

Stiff neck jews like you and that Mize lady deserve our pity but that is all.

(Name withheld)

.

You poor, pathetic fake Christian. It's not spirit that fills you and your fellow followers, it's dread. You are clearly too ignorant to recognize the difference between devotion and revulsion, which is what any genuine Christian feels when exposed to the moronic drivel being spewed by fear-filled bigots like you. Those of you who have the audacity to claim to follow Jesus and use the pretense of faith in order to justify the hatred and panic that fills your perverted hearts are beneath contempt. If you had the brains to comprehend the hypocrisy of your words you'd be on your knees begging forgiveness instead of wasting your breath and our time.

Mike Farrell
(MRFF Board of Advisors)

Subject: Jew coward

leave Gen (name miss spelled) alone you treasonous little jew coward of ZOG. The Gen. loves Jesus and is loving bringing that to the World as the Bible tell us too. Did some checking up on you mickey and you slime children at the air force academy. Weak cry baby all. not surprised to find the Truth. that you all tortured good Christians there.

Now you cry when We of Christ fight back? haHa payback is bitch especially for jew cry babys like you little jew boy. Who thinks he's a real man. and your wife deserves to be so cripple And We of The Lord pray you have brain hemorrage where your eyes pop out. and your shitjew blood streams out of ears.

(Name withheld)

·

Dear (name withheld),

It is good to see communications such as you have just sent to Mr. Weinstein. They help immeasurably to illustrate true religious bigotry and total disregard for honesty.

Your communication demonstrates why good, thinking people must be alert to the trap of religious hegemony and what dangers lurk therein.

Rick Baker
Capt. USAF (MedRet)
MRFF Volunteer

·

One of Mikey's friends wrote in to tell me that calling Mikey a coward is like calling Schwarzenegger "Peewee Herman." I must say, I do agree. My husband may be many things, but never a coward.

Subject: ICE needs to deport mikey

You uppity commie kike. You little white man wannabe.
You jew persecutor of our pure Christian soldiers.
I hope you just drop dead and get you fucking corpse eaten by starving spic
immigrants from mexico.
Then they can just shit out their little mikeymeal. After ICE throws they
wetbacks back over the border to taco land where they all belong.And
where do you belong mikey? ICE needs to throw you back to the jew camps
to burn like your grandpappy burned. And as your daddy burns even now.
STOP THE MRFF EVIL AGAINST AMERICA SOLDIERS! BRING THE
SWORD AS JESUS DID! Matthew 10:34)

(Name withheld)

.

Dear Coward,

*You turd. You unspeakable excuse for a failed human being. The ignorance in
this vomit-filled attack on Mikey and the MRFF says more about your poor
withered soul than any response can describe.*

*The level of self-disgust your wretched, putrid, love-starved words betray makes
me want to weep for you and anyone infected by your presence. Your message
provides evidence that Neanderthals have survived. Scientists will be intrigued.
That you arrogate to yourself the right to speak for "pure Christian soldiers"
brings shame to Christianity.*

Mike Farrell
(MRFF Board of Advisors)

Subject: Flag Folds for Christ and Familys

You fucking jewfuck mickey WHINEstein. You don't even know that our flag is folden then given to the familys of dead soldiers to help them know there sons are now with Jesus. Yes the very same Jesus who you mffr jewfucks crucified for few pieces of silver. How that work out for the jewish race? You are cruel to be the jewfucks you all are. The Air Force is right to have these flags foldings to be about Jesus The Christ. Cause Jesus is for the familys. Oh do you have it coming mickey. You been asking for it and Jesus will answer. We pray to Him you croak in pain and fear and you're family gets no flag at all ever at your funeral.
When you get to hell with your jewskin on fire you can kiss the flag of satan your daddy. Hes a jewfuck just like you and the mffr.

(Name withheld)

.

Dear (name withheld),

Thank you for reaching out to the Military Religious Freedom Foundation. Unfortunately, Mr. Weinstein is unable to directly address every email he gets and has thus forwarded me your email. Reading your very interesting–if somewhat nonsensical email, I get the sense that you have failed to grasp a few important details related to the issue you have written in about.

Here are the salient facts that you appear to have missed:

The Military Religious Freedom Foundation is an organization whose sole purpose is to protect soldiers from the abuse of their right to practice the religion of their choice.

The Air force is currently infringing on the rights of soldiers by including a Christian-specific flag-folding ceremony, but failing to offer the same support for soldiers of other faiths.

A flag-folding ceremony is an event meant to honor the sacrifice of the dead for the nation whose flag is being folded. The flag is presented to the next of kin as a symbol of gratitude and respect to them for the sacrifice made by a loved-one. Attempting to blanket this ceremony in religious rhetoric cheapens the sacrifice of a human life first by refusing to acknowledge that it is a sacrifice by replacing it with the idea that the dead's actions were some sort of reward-seeking behavior and second, by excluding individuals who don't subscribe to whatever religious rhetoric is being used. Do you know what people actively seek to gain celestial rewards through their own deaths? Suicide bombers.

Cordially,
Reverend CD

♦♦♦

Subject: fuck you jew

Army Rangers will always have Jesus and visa virsa you jew asshole.

(Name withheld)

.

Dear (name withheld),

…And they're welcome to him, idiot. Just don't push him on everybody else. Your anti-Semitic imbecility is noted, by the way. Did it ever occur to you that Jesus was a Jew?

Mike Farrell
(MRFF Board of Advisors)

♦♦♦

Subject: Missed a few jews?

Seems Hitler flubbed eliminating your family seed when he had the chance mickey?
Win some lose some.

See ya around.

(Name withheld)

.

Oh, this one is sick.

.

Dear (withheld)

I am writing in response to your email to Mikey Weinstein, which includes as the subject, "Missed a few jews?" As an initial matter, I must point out that his name is Mikey – not "Mickey." While I find it interesting that you can apparently have so much contempt for a man without bothering to even learn his name, it also says a lot about your character (or, rather, lack of character).

To answer your vile question – Yes, Hitler did fail in his attempt to brutally murder the entire Jewish population of Europe (though not for lack of trying). I am not familiar with Mikey's personal ancestry, so I cannot say whether he has any direct family link to that atrocity. I also doubt you have any personal knowledge of his lineage since you can't even get his name right. Regardless, I am only one of thousands of people who are extremely thankful for Mikey and his tireless efforts to protect the constitutionally protected religious freedom of our brave men and women in uniform.

It is truly an honor to be part of Mikey's team that is the Military Religious Freedom Foundation. Yet, I am forced to read the ignorant and hateful words of such despicable people as you. "Win some, lose some," I suppose. However, I have the benefit of being on the winning side – every moronic, contemptible letter we receive only empowers us and assures us that our mission is true. I assure you – you don't want to see me around.

Blessed be,

Tobanna Barker
MRFF Legal Affairs Coordinator

♦ ♦ ♦

Subject: Mikey the Jew

Dear Mr. "Mikey" Weinstein,

Let me start by saying that I neither expect, nor will this e-mail address above allow, a reply from you or any of the other leftist bandits in your misnamed so-called "Military Religious Freedom Foundation."

As a Pastor of a large church of The True Gospel of Jesus Christ and former military chaplain, I can only say that people like you and your people are the lowest scum of the earth. You personally are the worst. Suddenly you all are attacking our Army for their "Crusader" names and logos? None of that hurts one single person. You make mountains out of molehills. You "represent" crybabies.

You all pretend to "fight" for "equality of religion in the military" but that already exists for all. You hunt without mercy good Christians in the armed services who only want to share The Good News with those who may wish to listen. Nobody is ever coerced or forced under duress. It's all quite voluntary and respectful. You and your people are liars to say otherwise.

You all just hate our Lord and Savior Jesus and want to replace Him with either Allah, Satan, Karl Marx or "none." Or maybe Buddha or witches or 2 hundred Hindu "gods".

I see that you are a jew too. How interesting? No, I am not an antisemite and have even some friends who are also jew. But it is hard not to consider what your people did in rejecting the Son of God and turning Jesus over to the Romans. It is hard not to see the "Judas" in a jew like you, Mikey Weinstein.

Remember what happened to Judas, Mr. Weinstein? Leave the Army alone, "Mikey"

Happy Unthanksgiving to you and your communist people from hell.
(Name withheld)

·

Oh, that's right. Go ahead and throw shit in an email, then block your address so you will not get any blowback. That, my friends, is a coward, a complete and total coward.

♦♦♦

Subject: you have hurt the Air Force

Mr. Mikey Weinstein of the MFFR,

I guess you and your group of followers think your helping our military but your not.

I am in the Air Force and one of my biggest missions is to bring my troops to Jesus Christ.

I am a NCO leading many and witness the Gospel and Word of Christ to my troops for who I responsible every chance I get on duty or not. In uniform or not. Whether they ask me or not. The Word is the only light and the life and truth. It is water for those who thirst and food for those who starve. My troops love hearing it. And I love preaching it.

None has ever complained to anyone even once. Until a few days ago. Your name and the MFFR came up in anger and fear against the Lords Word.

My wife and me and others looked at your website. Did some more research on you all. Very eye opening to see such devil hatred from the MFFR. Tools of of the dark one. satan dwells in your house.

You all represent the sin and evil in our nation. MFFR has damaged the military by stopping the Word from being preached. Without the Word none may be saved.

I was sorry to see that your jew but it made a lot of sense to us. Jews of your blood betrayed and murdered Christ. And His blood is forever on their hands and their children hands.

How does that feel to have slaughtered the Lamb of the Lord? Make you feel like a big man jew? You think you help in the Air Force? You killed our Savior by your jews nature.

Our Air Force rejects you. Our military and country rejects you. The MFFR is only welcome by satan.

We will pray that your days of life will be shortened by the Lord. He will come for you and your kinsmen and helpers like a theif in the night.

You all will helpless to stop your destiny.

We pray that you and the MFFR will suffer by flames for all eternity for your sins of defiance and stiff neck jew nature against the Word.

.

Mikey,

He is the reason the MRFF exists.....

He is the reason you get emails all day long...

He is the reason the Air Force is losing fine young troops, not wanting to deal with his NCO spreading" the word at work....

He, and people like him, are the reason LGBT airmen commit suicide because they don't think they can turn to him for help.....

He is the downfall of our military......

You Mikey, are the hope people have in the fight against jackasses like this one.

Thank you for what you, Bonnie, and the entire MRFF do.

He needs to leave the service... folks like him will never change... sad

MRFF Supporter and friend

♦♦♦

Subject: jew Noses

Question- why do all jews have such big noses?
Answer- because they keep stick them in places where they don't belong.
Object lesson- Mikey keep your jew nose out of the business of Christians in the armed services.

Post Script- oh and fuck you by the way!

.

Question: Why do cowards hide behind fake addresses?

Answer: Because they embarrass themselves with their own stupidity and are too ashamed to be openly associated with themselves.

Object lesson: Self-hatred manifests itself in surprising ways.

Post Script: Jesus was a Jew.

Mike Farrell
(MRFF Board of Advisors)

♦ ♦ ♦

I finally figured out what the next hate email with the subject "Just another jewboy" was about. To make it clear to you, I have included a news article that was in the *Air Force Times*, which explains the situation.

.

The Air Force Academy is once again looking at whether God has a place on the football field after an advocacy group complained about the Falcons holding hands and praying in the end zone before games.

The academy is looking into the matter, but not everyone is opposed to the football team praying in public, said academy spokesman Meade Warthen.

"The Air Force Academy Inspector General opened a third-party complaint and referred the issue to the athletic department for an informal inquiry," Warthen said in an email to Air Force Times. "Friday morning we received an opposing viewpoint requesting cadets continue to be afforded the right to pray. Thus, we are being prudent and deliberate in our review of this issue."

The Military Religious Freedom Foundation, a group that opposes proselytizing in the military, complained about the Air Force Academy football team praying after its Nov. 28 game against the University of New Mexico, but that did not stop the Falcons from praying in the end zone before their Dec. 5 game against San Diego State University.

"This end zone praying is just another territorial conquest of the religious Christian right," said MRFF founder and president Mikey Weinstein. "This stands in a long line of conservative Christian acts like this."

The advocacy group has been at odds with the Air Force and the academy before.

In June 2005, an Air Force task force report found incidents of proselytizing at the Air Force Academy. For example, then-head football coach Fisher DeBerry hung a banner in the football team's locker room that read: "I am a Christian first and last. ... I am a member of Team Jesus Christ." DeBerry announced in December 2006 that he was retiring from the academy.

Warthen said the academy is "attentive to all religious freedom concerns."

"The Air Force is dedicated to maintaining an environment in which people can realize their highest potential regardless of personal religious or other beliefs," he said.

However, the Military Religious Freedom Foundation currently represents 144 Air Force Academy cadets, faculty and staff, including five players of the academy's current football team, said Weinstein, who did not express confidence in the athletic department's inquiry.

"Allowing the Air Force Academy to investigate itself — this is simply the fox investigating the hen house," he said. "We expect that we'll get nothing positive out of this and we'll continue to take a look at whether our clients could possibly get 'John' and 'Jane Doe' protections to go into federal court to seek an injunction."

◆◆◆

Subject: Just another jewboy

Mickey WHINEsteen: just another pushy little jewboy with a law degree big mouth and a chip on his shylock shoulder against Jesus Christ helping our military. So typical of his breed. Ungrateful the whole lot of them. Ho hum-boring.

GO Air Force Falcons football team! GO Tim Tebow! Go Jesus!

And YOU GO to your place in hell jewboy mickey. We will rejoice as you roast forever aflame.

(Name withheld)

Dear (name withheld)

Last time I checked Jesus was Jewish. It's his followers who aren't. ... In more ways than one.

With best wishes,
(MRFF ally)

Dear Clueless Football Fan,

I want to use another word that started with an "f", but somehow, I was able to restrain myself. I'm sorry your brain is so small as to not understand the problem. However, being a rational being and a non-christian myself, I totally get it. I feel sorry for those kids on the football team who take a knee because they don't want to look like a schmuck by not participating. Boy, that's a real team building experience. Probably why the team couldn't beat Navy, New Mexico or San Diego State. Did any of those teams publically pray before the game? Hmm – maybe their god is more powerful than your god. Obviously, your god didn't give you much of a brain as you really have responded in such a childish way. What really ticks me off is a-holes like you and the USAFA football team leaders trying to turn my alma mater into a madrassa for your bronze age religion. Go back to your sandbox and don't come out until you grow up.

Signed, class of 77 grad and proud classmate of Mikey Weinstein

♦♦♦

Subject: Beauty and The 666 Beast

AF Academy ashamed of Mikie Wienstein and let the football team pray to their Lord and Savior Jesus Christ. America is a Christian nation duh!

Your the devil in the flesh Mr. jewish and you can just go back to he## with Carl Marxist and Lenin!!

Megyn Kelley called you out once and she can do it gain you evil demon.

(Name withheld)

"Carl Marxist." Seriously? Sometimes you just can't make this crap up and John Lenin by the way, was cool as shit!

Dear (name withheld):

If I have the name wrong, my apologies—I'm trying to deduce your name from your email since you didn't sign your brief missive. Thanks for writing to the MRFF, as it gives me an opportunity to disavow you of some serious misconceptions.

First misconception—"AF Academy ashamed of Mikie Wienstein." I think your contention is that the USAFA community is 'ashamed' of the efforts of Mikey and the MRFF? That would be a tremendous overstatement. To be sure, there are some members of the community, both stationed at USAFA and among its graduates, who oppose our efforts. That is what makes American great, that we can agree or disagree with one another openly. But I would contend, based on what I hear from many of my fellow graduates and from individuals I know who are currently stationed at USAF, that a MUCH larger percentage of the USAFA community supports our efforts. That is because the majority of people understand that protecting the rights of everyone is not a 'win-lose' proposition. In other words, respecting the rights of a non-Christian, or a non-believer, does not take any rights away from a Christian.

Second misconception—that Jesus Christ is the "Lord and Savior" of the USAFA football team. The USAFA football team is a military organization, and like every other organization in the US military, it has no 'savior'. Individual members have their own beliefs, and each of them is fully entitled to those beliefs (including non-belief). The problem comes when the organization begins to take on the hue of a particular sectarian religious belief. Doing so violates both relevant USAF regulations and the US Constitution. That is what happens when team members, in uniform and on duty, conduct a public spectacle that promotes a specific sectarian religious belief.

Third misconception—"America is a Christian nation duh!" While that is a common refrain offered by some Christians, it is not even close to true. America is a pluralistic nation, comprised of a diverse group of citizens who represent every manner of belief and non-belief. Our Constitution was written expressly to recognize, respect, and accommodate that diversity. Every citizen has the same rights and freedoms under the Constitution, a document which was expertly crafted so that it favors no particular religious belief, including Christianity.

Fourth misconception—Mikey Weinstein is "the devil in the flesh", "Mr. jewish" (whatever that means), and an "evil demon" I gather from your overall commentary that you are a Christian. As such, and as a Christian myself, I struggle with the notion that name calling does anything to give glory to God. But in any case, I know Mikey very well—he can be strident, unyielding, and undiplomatic... and he is also a man of great honor, character, and integrity. Yet while I don't think he has ever won the title of "Mr. Jewish", he is in fact Jewish—and in my view, anyone who would attempt to use that as an insulting epithet is a bigot of the worst kind.

Anyway, thanks again for writing. If nothing else, you've reminded me why it's important that I continue to support the efforts of the MRFF.

Peace,

Mike Challman
Christian, USAF veteran, MRFF supporter

♦♦♦

Subject: devil brain jew

hey bald jewboy

we hope we pray Jesus rips that kike smirk right off your fucked up jew face we see everywhere our military is sacred to Jesus and your fucking it up trying to take the only Son of God out of it praying for your devil brain to explode right threw your eyes and ears you coward wizard then you can enjoy the sulfur fumes as your are consumed in Lake of Fire for your 2nd death -Revelations 21:8

enjoy Albuquere!

.

Mikey

They are real tough from that side of the keyboard, aren't they? These emails are very interesting to me. You see, you're like a lab rat in my little experiment. I know of no one else that has more negative prayers directed at them. All these emails and hostile prayers only suggest that either G-d isn't real, or he is unwilling or unable to answer prayers. The more you get these, the larger the dataset.

Deep breath, Mikey!

.

A bit of relief here is needed in the form of some fun facts. I thought it would be a good time to include some real facts about people who happen to be Jewish or are of Jewish ancestry.

At least 194 Jews and people of half or three-quarters Jewish ancestry have been awarded the Nobel Prize, which accounts for 22% of all individuals so recognized worldwide between 1901 and 2015. In the scientific research fields of Chemistry, Economics, Physics and Physiology/Medicine, Jews make up 26% worldwide and 38% of all US recipients. Among women laureates in these same fields, the worlds Jewish percentages are 33% and 50% among the US recipients. Of organizations awarded the Nobel Peace Prize, 22% were founded principally by people of half-Jewish descent. Since the turn of the century (the year 2000), Jews received 25% of all Nobel Prizes and 28% of those in the scientific research fields. To put all of this into perspective, Jews currently make up approximately 0.2% of the world's population and 2% of the US population.

The Military Religious Freedom Foundation has been nominated eight times for the Nobel Peace Prize.

♦♦♦

Subject: JEW

you don't like the Gospel of Jesus Christ on the vet admin clinic POW table mickey? your a lying decitfull ,backstabing money loving, dirty lawyer. Christian hating traitor to America. in other words your a goddamn JEW!

we hope they make it a nation holiday when you croak and rot in hell. too bad its to late for the ovens for you and you're little storm troopers mickey. Or is it?

(Name withheld)

.

Dear (name withheld),

Thank you for naming yourself after the worst anti-Semite to ever walk the face of the earth. You saved me from calling you that name.

What you wrote is nothing new or original. In fact, your namesake said it first.

In Mein Kampf (I read the whole book) Hitler wrote-

"I believe that I am acting in accordance with the will of the Almighty Creator: by defending myself against the Jews, I am fighting for the work of the Lord."

Although Hitler did not practice religion in a churchly sense, he certainly believed in the Bible's God. Raised as Catholic he went to a monastery school and, interestingly, walked everyday past a stone arch which was carved the monastery's coat of arms which included a swastika. As a young boy, Hitler's most ardent goal was to become a priest. Much of his philosophy came from the Bible, and more influentially, from the Christian Social movement. (The German Christian Social movement, remarkably, resembles the Christian Right movement in America today.) Many have questioned Hitler's stand on Christianity. Although he fought against certain Catholic priests who opposed him for political reasons, his belief in God and country never left him. Many Christians throughout history have opposed Christian priests for various reasons; this does not necessarily make one against one's own Christian beliefs. Nor did the Vatican's Pope & bishops ever disown him; in fact they blessed him! As evidence to his claimed Christianity, he said:

"My feelings as a Christian points me to my Lord and Savior as a fighter. It points me to the man who once in loneliness, surrounded by a few followers, recognized these Jews for what they were and summoned men to fight against them and who, God's truth! was greatest not as a sufferer but *as a fighter. In boundless love as a Christian and as a man I read through the passage which tells us how the Lord at last rose in His might and seized the scourge to drive out of the Temple the brood of vipers and adders. How terrific was His fight for the world against the Jewish poison. To-day, after two thousand years, with deepest emotion I recognize more profoundly than ever before the fact that it was for this that He had to shed His blood upon the Cross. As a Christian I have no duty to allow myself to be cheated, but I have the duty to be a fighter for truth and justice... And if there is anything which could demonstrate that we are acting rightly it is the distress that daily grows. For as a Christian I have also a duty to my own people."*

Martin Luther's 1543 pamphlet On the Jews and Their Lies *was a "blueprint" for the Kristallnacht. Shortly after the Kristallnacht, Martin Sasse, Bishop of the Evangelical Lutheran Church in Thuringia, published a compendium of Martin Luther's writings ; Sasse "applauded the burning of the synagogues" and the coincidence of the day, writing in the introduction, "On November 10, 1938, on Luther's birthday, the synagogues are burning in Germany."*

Great job in pointing out that you do mirror Hitler.

Is it too late for you to take the cowardly way out of this world like Hitler did and join him? I'm sure he'd love to see you and compare notes. Or, maybe he would be angry at your for plagiarizing his words.

That would be too funny.

Pastor Joan
MRFF Advisory Board Member

.

Dear (name withheld),

I am writing in response to your email to the Military Religious Freedom Foundation ("MRFF"). However, I must admit I had to double check the date of your email to ensure it was sent during this decade since the vile you spew against people of the Jewish faith belongs in a historical fiction novel. What a sad life you must have with so much misplaced hatred.

You accuse Mikey Weinstein of being "lying" and "deceitful" (actually, you claim he is "decitfull," but that is not a word, so I assume you meant "deceitful"), yet you fail to set forth a single lie he has told. Ignorant people like you are the reason MRFF fights for the religious freedom of every soldier, sailor, airman, Marine, cadet, and veteran – and your hateful emails only give us strength to continue fighting.

I have bad news for you, "adolfii"—your apparent idol is the one rotting in hell. But don't worry—I am confident he has saved a place next to him for you to spend eternity.

Blessed be,

Tobanna Barker
MRFF Legal Affairs Coordinator

♦♦♦

Subject: Why we hate you

Hey Mikie

Its not only because your a thievery jew that we hate you.

Its' not just because your a liberal that we hate you.

Its not because your a queer lover that we hate you.

Its not just because you love musloms more than Americans that we hate you.

You know why we hate you?

Because you hate Jesus & Jesus' bible and all of His followers.

Just kill yourself mikie and make everybody happy. Especially your country and its' soldiers.

(Name withheld)

Dear detractor,

I'd like to offer up a challenge to your moral courage. If you actually have the intestinal fortitude that Mikey shows every day, I challenge you to do the following:

- *Print off the email you just sent us.*

- *Record yourself reading this out loud, with your face clearly visible, after announcing your name.*

- *Show this video to your mother and father, brothers and sisters, employer or employees, pastor or congregation.*

- *Record their responses to your pitiful lack of moral scruples and perverse deviation from everything your religion teaches.*

- *Send us that video with permission to put it out on the world stage.*

Sack up or shut up.

Sincerely,

Blake A Page
Military Religious Freedom Foundation
Special Assistant to the President
Director of US Army Affairs

.

Blake sure did make my day when I read this reply!

♦♦♦

Subject: Pat robertson is right about You

We hate you little jew trouble-maker Michael Weinstein. We hate your jew wife and we hate your jew children. We hate everyone at vomit drinking Military religious Freedom foundation. We hate everything about you. Why? Because we are commanded to serve Jesus Christ of Nazareth the Prince of Peace and our Lord.

And who are we? We are everywhere the Lord Jesus is. You will never stop us all.

And Jesus hate all of you too. You stole the oath to Christ away from our soldiers. Just like you crucified our Lord and savior. And tried to blame romans. Blood on your hands little jew Michael weinstein.

Pat robertson is right about you. To expose you but good. For all of us to see. You all frighten the air force because your in league with husiene obama and satan.

But you don't frighten us. We are military families washed in the Blood of the Lamb. The Armour of the Lord Jesus protect us from you and your wicked followers of the devil. Perish and burn followers of michael weinstein. May you children and wife rot before your eyes forevermore.

(Name withheld)

.

Dear (name withheld), (although that is not likely your real name) –

You are incredibly wrong in every aspect of your vile, disgusting diatribe:

- *Pat Robertson is not right about MRFF and Mikey Weinstein. I strongly suspect that he knows he's not right, too — yet he apparently believes that lying for Christ is an ethical thing to do.*

- *No one "stole the oath" from anyone. Every Air Force member who wishes to include "so help me God" in his/her enlistment oath can continue to do so. Your grasp on the facts of the case are even more tenuous than your grasp on proper spelling, grammar and punctuation.*

- *You claim to be following the commandments of Jesus Christ, yet you spew hate the likes of which is unrecognizable in the light of Christ's teaching and example.*

- *Your nasty, mean-spirited, ignorant attacks on Mikey and his family are inexcusable.*

- *You claim not to be frightened, yet you attack with the fervor of on terrified by something he has not taken the time to understand.*

I pity you, and I also wish that you would refrain from identifying yourself as a Christian. Those of us who love and serve Jesus Christ are worshiping a very different God than whatever god it is you appear to worship.

Mike Challman
Christian, AF veteran, MRFF supporter

.

Thank you everyone for these responses. You are marvelous, and it makes me feel safe knowing that you have our backs.

.

Dear Anti-Semitic Tommie,

Your phony name and address and your hatred is of little importance to the thinking people of the world. Yours is a life wrapped in bigotry and prejudice and if he actually exists, Satan will welcome you to the dark bowels of Hades as an equal partner in the downfall of mankind.

I'm afraid it is you who will rot in the presence of good people and although we do not and could not in good conscience wish your family harm, we hope that they will find a way to safety and immunity from your inflated ego.

You put yourself on an equal level with Jesus when you could not even hope to kiss His footprints.

I am a former Air Force Officer and Rescue Pilot, having served two combat tours in Vietnam. I can assure you that Mr. Weinstein could never have frightened me or my crew but only encourage us to keep independent thought and allegiance to the secular regulations and instructions to which we took our solemn oath.

My advice to you is not to let your imagined relationship with Jesus cause your downfall.

Rick Baker
Capt. USAF (Ret)
MRFF Volunteer

♦♦♦

Subject: Mikey is Kikey

you won't find too many kikes in the US military because it's the goyem's job to die for the chosen. If it smacks of manual labor, kikes will back away from it like a cheese filled sausage. Fucking kike bastards, I hope they are nuked if Jizz-real attacks Iran.
Kikes make better fuel than they do human beings

(Name withheld)

.

To the Nazi who wrote the email, above:

Mikey's busy. I'm responding for him. Do you have any statistics to back your claim regarding the number of Jews in the United States Military? I thought not. The rest of your rant is equally unfounded. Rest in peace — soon!

Sincerely,
A real American patriot, an American military veteran, and, of course, another Jew

♦♦♦

Subject: nigger out and jewboy in jail

Stay out of Arizona KIKE. fuck you jewboy mickey wienstein. just as soon as the arab sandnigger is out of the white house you will go to jail with that cunt hillary for stopping bibles from given to veteran hospital soldiers. Stop the word of Christ? Christ will stop you're words jewboy.

(Name withheld)

.

While I assume this is a fake address, the usual coward's hideout, let me only pass along this thought, in the unlikely hope you'll ever see it.

You are a disgusting; pathetic human being and I use the last two words advisedly.

Mike Farrell
(MRFF Board of Advisors)

♦♦♦

Not too long ago, I started seeing multiple parentheses on each side surrounding a name and I did not understand what that was all about. So, I did a little research. I now know more than I care to about the alt-right and their blatantly anti-Semitic memes. In a very sterile nutshell, the alt-right will put multiple parentheses around names to indicate Jewish names and then follow it with anti-Semitic attacks on that person. Of course, that is putting it very simply, but you get the idea.

.

Subject: It had to be a (((jew)))

The moment I read that stupid jew-friendly article today in military.com I just knew there would be a stinking jew in that wood pile
Not a nigger in the wood pile at Langley AFB. A jew. Of course. And there it was.
The name once again of one of the greatest threats to American democracy and our military power still alive.
(((Mikey Weinstein))).
What a shylock Christ-hater.
Can't you just do your country a favor and choke to death on the next bagel you eat?
Soaked in the blood of Christian children like your kike family tree did.
Time you disappeared little jew.
No more wood piles for you to infest.
Wood burns you know.
Let's just visualize the beauty of whimpering jew (((Mikey Weinstein))) on fire just like the others in WW2 Deutschland.
Eliminate the wood piles and bye-bye (((Mikey Weinstein))).

.

You, sir, are a truly sick puppy. And, since this is likely a fake address, a cowardly, cringing, probably too-often abused sick puppy.

A MRFF ally

♦♦♦

Subject: Enough with the Jews already

Mr. Mikey with the Jewish last name,

We're sick of hearing that bullshit about how the Jews don't get equal treatment by the marines and all.
Who cares if they can't put up their minhorah for Hanikkah?

The Jews owe a debt to every Christian who has fought in America's wars to allow them to even be allowed to reside in our nation. After getting kicked out everywhere else in The Lord's Green Earth for doing your typical Jew treachery America still lets you stay. Know your Jew place Mr.

.

Hey punk who hides his ignorance and bigotry behind a fake address.

I went through MCRD when you were probably in diapers. And judging from the colossal stupidity of your rant, you're probably still wearing them.
Read the Constitution if you can, punk, and think about it.

Mike Farrell
(MRFF Board of Advisors)

♦♦♦

Subject: jews have that certain smell

you know, Mikie. That jew smell of murdering the innocent Lamb. The Son of God.
The same Son of God who's resurrection we will celebrate on Sunday.
Try as you might to keep Jesus out of our military you will just even more nail yourself to the cross of satan.
And you will burn in hell forever.
Every day will be a Dachau day for you. Every night will be a Kristallnacht.
For all eternity.
Hell smells like Mikie. Hell smells like jews.

(Name withheld)

.

Hey shithead,

Why don't you climb back into your mother's asshole where you were born from. That's why you smell like a pot of dog shit. Without Jews you wouldn't even be alive—and that alone is a big mistake. I'm a living breathing Catholic retired Marine Corps Master Sgt. who had to deal with stinkin' assholes like you my whole career, and thanks to the good Lord you will do yourself in. I have dealt with and served with Mikey Weinstein and MRFF for ten years and he is a true hero among the military, one who helps save military members from the savages of some of their Christian asshole shithead commanders, much like you are you crumbling useless shit ball. If you even know how to read look up all the Jewish scientists, military leaders, and inventors, and medical geniuses who made it so you asshole could live past twenty-five. You stink like stale cat shit and dog dung especially when you breathe, which wont be too long I hope. Leather ass.

A MRFF Supporter

♦♦♦

Subject: Fuck Tray Crowder puppet of jewboy Weinstein

It figures that jewboy Mikey weinstein would eventually find a white simpleton housenigger to do his anti Christian hate bidding for him. Right kikey mikey? Your just crematoria firefuel destine for hell's flames anyway.l And now you got hat faggot fairy white trash pretender Tray crowder to step up to bat for you. How much did you pay the pretend hillbilly to do your jew dirty work weinstein? 30 pieces of silver? Supid kike. Judas crowder. Your both traitors to Christ Jesus and his promised land of America. And our soldiers who spread the love of the Son of God. Peckerwood crowder is about as southern as mikey jewboy weinstein is caucasian. It would be laughable if it wasn't so serious. Fuck you weinstein! Fuck you crowder! hope you die in front of you kids and burn in hell for the apostasy you fuckers are.

MAKE AMERICA GREAT AGAIN!
JEW TRASH AND THEY WHITE CRACKER PUPPETS WILL NOT REPLACE US!
HAIL VICTORY! HAIL TRUMP!

(Name withheld)

My blood never fails to run cold when I read this particular email. "Hail Victory, Hail Trump!" scares the shit out of me!

◆◆◆

Subject: typical of a jew"

As soon as my husband who is an U.S. Army senior NCO leader showed me who was behind this supposed "scandal' at Fort Gordon we both just said "of Course".

Only a conniving jew of the likes of the infamous mikey weinstein would try to attack a friendly barbecue by the chaplains for all the soldiers to enjoy. Hey mikey why do you hate Jesus so much and his followers?

And nobody was ordered to be there at all. If they say they were they are just liars all of them.
Probably jews arabs and atheists. Pretending too be soldiers.

Sharing the Gospel of the Son of God with our nation's young war heroes was just a innocent picnic of love for sinners to learn how to rid themselves of sin thru Christ.

It could only be jacked up by some hell bound hook nose. With a anti-christian agenda of hate towards Jesus Christ.

Hey mikey stay away from our soldiers and just go count and polish your pennies.

Christ will curse you mikey weinstein and all off your children and their children too.
We hate you. The Lord hates you.

(Name withheld)

⋅

Dear (name withheld),

Are you an adult? Where did you learn to spell? Did you learn grammar in the same place? I found myself, in reading this tract, wondering if you were home-schooled, possibly by someone who was filled with fear and chose to hide in the arms of a Bible-totin' fundamentalist who pretended to be a Christian while knowing nothing about Christianity. There are a lot of them, you know. There are a lot of so-called Christians who are actually hucksters and thieves. They prey on frightened people like you who are content to stay huddled in ignorance rather than dare to venture out of their caves and expose themselves to the world.

It's too bad, too, because the real world is a pretty nice place. But instead, frightened people like you accept themselves as ignorant fools and become lost in a sad, dark world filled with bigots and cowards who train them. It's a lonely, miserable place filled with fear and anger and spite and lies. Despite their claim to know the "truth," these 'teachers' defile what you refer to as the Gospel of the Son of God with putrid garbage like you've tried to copy down in your message here. It's truly pathetic that anyone could so debase the name of Jesus by associating it with the filth you've managed to spout here. I suspect you don't realize you've made yourself the dummy to their ventriloquist. And, sadly, you're more Mortimer Snerd than Charlie McCarthy.

If you ever treat yourself to a free thought – that's a thought unshackled from the bilge you've apparently been fed for years – I encourage you to find something clean and ponder it for a minute. It might be a rock; it might be a flower; it might be a cloud. It might, if you actually are a "mom," as you suggest, it might be a beautiful, innocent child. If you can do that, take a deep breath and drink in the pure innocence before you.

That rock or flower or cloud or child isn't filled with fear and hatred and jealousy. It has no need to lash out at Jews or Arabs or atheists or any other being. The rock and flower and cloud can't be poisoned by the hatred you've been taught to spew. But the child can.

I hope you'll give it a chance you've clearly never given yourself.

Best,

Mike Farrell
(MRFF Board of Advisors)

♦♦♦

Subject: Messy dead daddy

Hey mickey,

I just read about you the MFFFR trying to stop another national prayer lunch at a Air Force base in Alabama.

My wife and I are in the Air Force stationed in California. You have so many who hate you at our base. Like our whole Bible study.

And you are so wicked as to try to stop the love of Christ at just a simple annual prayer event?

So what if the Wing Commander made the invite? Non Christians don't have to come if they don't want to. No one has to accept the Gospel.

The Wing Commander is just trying to steal souls back from satan. Nobodys forced like you say.It's freedom OF religion not freedom FROM religion mickey. Your a lawyer and should no better.

The jews and atheists and queers in the military always come running for little mickey to fight Jesus Christ for them. Same with the muslims. And the dot indians.

And your always just so happy to fight for satan against our Lord right mickey? Makes us wonder why? What's in it for you?
But we know. Satan pays you well. jews love the $$.

30 pieces of silver mickey? (Matthew 26:15)

A lot of our friends here in Bible study think your asking for an ass kicking. Your way overdue boy.

The internet says you have kids and a wife and grandkid.
My wife and me and our Bible study just hope you die slow in pain right in front of your wife and kids.
Piss your undies and shit your trou. Bleed out thru your eyes and ears and mouth. A blessed site to see.

My eyes have seen the glory of the coming of the Lord. So Jesus is coming for you mickey.

Let your family learn the lesson of what not to be like.

Messy dead daddy is the bible lesson of the day.

You have it coming and Jesus will administer His devine justice on mickey. His devine wrath is on you.

The Son of God will take your wicked life and kick your whineystien ass all the way to the fires of hell.

You live in sin and will burn in sin. Always and forever. Fire unending and no hope left.

How's that 30 pieces of silver working out for you now mickey? You and judas too peas in a pod.

Can we have a Halleluyah!
(Airmen for Christ and His Kingdom in America)

Dear Airman,

From the ugliness enfolded in the email you sent to my friend and brother, Mikey Weinstein, a suggestion: it's time to locate a new bible study group, as the current one you are in lacks the discernment of who Jesus of Nazareth is. Or, is that even the Person you are called to be a follower of...

When was the last time your Bible study leader reflected on:
Matt 22:14: "Many are called by few are chosen." I dare say as it appears from revealing your heart to all of us, not often enough.
It is also quite apparent the soul-void such as you house, coupled the inability to grasp concepts such as respectfulness, compassionate, truthfulness, clarity of accurate information, YET foremost, the Christian walk. I can only ponder what it is that has lead you to be so negatively revealing to someone you have never met, nor personally spoken with prior to sending out such vile hatred wrapped in contempt, for so many to read. Do know we recognize you clearly, Airman, as the Trash bins are filled with the many who have come before you. The damage you have done is only to yourself, along with those you travel with. More than likely you'll never be able to comprehend any healthy distinctions, as your focus appears to be a

finely crafted presentation of conveying evil. It's ALL yours, fully, Airman, and not Mikey Weinstein!

So as one who seeks daily to walk an authentic life with the Prince of Peace, I accept His teachings by saying, peace to you and yours. . .Yet the ones of notable harm, well we leave in the hands of our law enforcement for them to deal with.

Peace, A MRFF supporter

♦♦♦

SUBJECT: ADVICE TO (((MIKEY)))

(((Mr. Weinstein))),

We all understand that you were born with a big "hate Christians" chip on your shoulder (what jew wasn't?) but don't you really think it's about time for you to leave the national stage, sir?

Afterall (((Mikey))) you've had a good run of pretending to "fight back" against the obvious good will of followers of Jesus in the armed services and made all of that nice fame and beaucoup $$ (what jew doesn't like the fame and $$? Just look at your fellow tribesmen in Hollywood).

This is now the long awaited time of serious political and religious realism. Whether you and your libtard acolytes like it or not our new President embodies the good will of the people of this country. We "Make America Great Again" by ridding ourselves of the crybabies and weak-willed who prey on those who actually built this country from nothing. Umm, that would be ridding ourselves of the faux justice fighters such as you (((Mikey))) and your deceptively named anti-Christian (((MRFF))). To say nothing our our former president, Nancy Pelosi and Chuck Schumer.

It is just a fact that the real builders of America were and are predominantly white and Christian and heterosexual males. It's not "bad" for us to simply recognize and celebrate that fact. It's just the truth, sir.

And our great country's military has also been made great by the dominant presence of white, Christian and heterosexual males. Try as you might to rewrite history you will fail (what jew doesn't love to rewrite history?).

Think it over (((Mikey))). You've outlasted your usefulness to your country and are now just a constant plague and pestilence upon it's military forces.

You had your time. Now it is our time.

Leave the scene gracefully before time catches up with you and reminds you that you're not wanted or needed anymore.

Perhaps open a nice retail sales clothing store, do comedy standup or sell some matzoh ball soup?
Maybe become a diamond merchant? It's in your genes to do it.

We don't want to hear your big mouth replying to our request so don't waste your efforts.

signed,
Defenders of American Military Mighty

.

Dear Defender,

Not really sure of what you are defending and most likely this is a bogus email address; however, I thought it would be a modicum of effort to dispel some of your diatribe. Let me begin with your "hate Christians" statement. For a person to "hate", they must reconcile their feelings with their actions. You see "Defender" MRFF has a huge number of clients and the overwhelming majority of them are Christian. Seems counter-productive, wouldn't you say, to protect the very people that Mikey so "despises"? Your ignorance really has shown through as you have only reacted with emotion and failed to engage your intellect. Finally, your stereotypical characterization of people of Hebraic descent made me laugh out loud. Please, jewelry store/retail clothing outlet? Maybe you should throw "Carpenter" into the mix, as Jesus (called the Christ) was one. As a Born-Again, Spirit-Filled, Christian Pastor who happens to be a retired Military Chaplain (Colonel) I proudly help Mikey one his journey to assure everyone has a voice. As an Advisory Board Member for the Military Religious Freedom Foundation, I see when people like you lambast Mikey, we are on the correct path.

Respectfully,

Quentin D Collins, US Army Chaplain (Colonel-Retired), Ph.D, CPC, ELIMP
MRFF National Advisory Board

♦ ♦ ♦

Subject: liar

You're a liar, you typical Jew.

.

You're a fool, you typical bigot.

Mike Farrell
(MRFF Board of Advisors)

♦ ♦ ♦

I have included a statement here from Mikey Weinstein. It is necessary to insert here so that you understand what the writer of the letter with the subject line "you suck mickey joosteen" is upset about.

.

Statement by Mikey Weinstein, MRFF Founder and President

The latest confirmed removal of an illicit sectarian Christian bible display from the Tobyhanna Army Depot POW/MIA memorial comes as simply the latest in 5 consecutive Constitutional wins initiated by the Military Religious Freedom Foundation (MRFF) for the purpose of ensuring religious (and non-religious) liberty and inclusion within our armed forces as well as the good order, morale, unit cohesion and discipline of our brave warfighters and uniformed servicemembers.

However, the fact that the latest removed Christian Bible bore the official name and motto ("Excellence in Electronics") of the Tobyhanna Army Depot, as well as imagery depicting a military radar defense system, indicates that the scourge of undue Christian fundamentalist, theocratic-militaristic fervor still remains a devastatingly serious national security issue of the highest order throughout all service branches. Illustrating the gravity of this failure to comply with Constitutional and DoD directives, at Tobyhanna alone no less than 115 servicemember clients (86 of whom are Christian) sounded the alarm to MRFF requesting that we intervene to stand up and address their grievances.

While we are somewhat encouraged by the swift moves on the part of Colonel Gregory D. Peterson, the Commander of Tobyhanna Army Depot, and the rest of the senior Tobyhanna Army Depot leadership to remedy this crisis in constitutional compliance, we are confused that it took so long on their part to notice a display so clearly and prominently violative of established rules, regulations, and norms governing the role of religion in the military. The elaborate and unconvincing apologias claiming that a third-party, private organization—the Veterans Council—was responsible for this conspicuous offense indicates, at the very least, the glaring Constitutional blind-spots of base leaders towards these exhibitionist displays of sectarian Christian supremacy which constitute violations of service members' basic civil rights. However, we also have a right to wonder if this case of purportedly Christian conceit is now, within the pressure-cooker of widespread public scrutiny, transforming into a case of Christian deceit.

We vigilantly call on the Department of Defense to immediately condemn, investigate, and root out those DoD and private entities who time and time again willfully conspire to erode and undermine the foundational, Constitutional barrier separating church and state within the U.S. military.

Now, as before, the purpose of the Military Religious Freedom Foundation is clear: to put an end to a calamitously unconstitutional environment within the United States Armed Forces whereby the legally-bankrupt "exception" evidently turns out to be the Christian fundamentalist "rule."

Michael L. "Mikey" Weinstein, Esq.
Founder and President
Military Religious Freedom Foundation
mikey@militaryreligiousfreedom.org

♦♦♦

Subject: you suck mickey joosteen

you should have the bible of Jesus shoved up you jooish asshole inch by inch by Navy SEALs
leave the POW-MIA tables alone mickey whiningsteen
no one wants your jooish nose in the Lords business anyway
(why are all your noses so big anyway? its true and hitler has the pix to prove it)
JESUS CHRIST IS KING!

Dear, (name withheld)

We get a lot of mail from people with questions about the mission of the MRFF and we get a number of expressions of concern from people who don't understand the U.S. Constitution. We try, when we get them, to reply in a way that helps people understand how important it is to support the rights we are blessed to be able to enjoy as Americans.

Unfortunately, we periodically get ugly and hateful mail from brainless, bigoted twits like you, who demean the name of Jesus by pretending to be Christians in order to somehow justify their lonely, hate-filled lives. Ignorance, Joe, is understandable and can be cured by education. Stupidity, on the other hand, when exhibited in the manner you've chosen, appears to be genetic and is probably a life-long deficit. Cowardice, while quite often the primary characteristic of bullies and bigots, is another quality you and your ilk demonstrate with regularity.

It's a shame. And I'm sure it not only embarrasses real Christians, but is likely the causative factor in a phrase my uncle used to use: "Jesus wept."

Mike Farrell
(MRFF Board of Advisors)

When nasty bigots talk, it comes out sounding disgusting and dangerous. If you have been able to get this far into the book I think you will agree that it is beginning to all sound the same. Sad and pathetic, all under the shade of the Bible. I do not mean to sound jaded here but these are Christians, or at least they believe themselves to be. Yet, I invariably hear from friends and supporters and my own mother that this is "too sad" and "I hope you know this person is not a Christian or a representative of Jesus." My first thought is that they are sincere in saying this and most likely correct. It is a knee-jerk reaction to want to defend your honestly held religious beliefs especially when you consider yourself to be a good person, but getting right down to the nitty-gritty, they too are "judging." What a conundrum! My favorite Bible verse is "Judge not lest ye be judged" and I am probably the worst at keeping this sound advice. So, I say with the best of them that these haters just hate and they do so all while knowing nothing, or not having studied anything, of the Bible they profess to know so well.

Wrong, Wrong, and Wrong Again

MORE OFTEN THAN NOT, when I am unsure of a fact I ask someone who would know more than I do. Usually, my husband does, and will give me some information to enlighten myself of the facts. Failing the availability of such a knowledgeable person, I would go to a library for a little old fashioned research. The internet is also a possibility, as Googling has become an easy source of information for me. The bottom line is, no matter my means of finding out information, what I end up with is a plethora of pertinent and accurate information which I can use to educate myself as to the fact and speak to the subject matter with accuracy.

One or more of these methods of fact-finding is readily accessible to most of the population in the United States today. So, why is this next section such a large chapter? I believe "wrong and wrong again" points to a level of society of individuals who have become entirely lazy. Very little time, if any, has been taken to fact check before pounding out angry diatribes full of misinformation on a subject matter which is very clear they know nothing about. I feel, before writing a letter into a foundation, or anywhere else for that matter, the letter writer should have an inkling of the facts. There is also the possibility that letters such as this could be written with "correct me if I'm wrong, but…" or "Am I correct in thinking," which would open up a bunch of information or dare I say, cause enlightenment. Having seen so many of these letters, I can tell you that very little thinking or any kind of fact-checking has remotely entered their brain. We often get e-mails that say almost the same thing, but by different people. I believe these individuals are simply following "orders" to write letters with a fill-in-the-blank option. The resemblance is too uncanny to be anything else but a fill-in-the-blank handout.

Subject: Atheist

There is no atheist in the fox hole. Mikey Weinstein is a liberal idiot. The phrase was well noted by ex-ww2 soldiers.

(Name withheld)

.

Dear (name withheld),

There are loads of atheists in fox holes. Burying your head in the sand does not change the reality that exists in the world around you. You are a true representation of the Grand Old Party. Willfully ignorant and proud of it. Perhaps if your head were not so well entrenched in the hole of your choosing the light of wisdom would have an opportunity to reach you.

Cheers,

Blake A. Page
Military Religious Freedom Foundation
Special Assistant to the President
Director of West Point Affairs

♦♦♦

Subject: Sincerely

I sincerely hope the next administration kicks you out of your position and title so hard you feel it for the rest of your life. Your anti Christian drivel is the afront to the nostrils of millions of Americans. Shame on you, you nasty man.

Enjoy your last 2 years in this position. I have a feeling when we are free of Obama in 2016 a lot of the dirt will be wiped off when he goes.

And thank God for it. It can't come soon enough.

Very sincerely

(Name withheld)

Dear (name withheld),

It's stunning, I must say, to read such a misbegotten message from one who can spell, use punctuation correctly and, while being decidedly critical, refuses to stoop to the level of vulgarity and obscenity that adorn most of the messages we receive from those who dislike what they perceive as our work. You do fall, unless I am misreading, into familiar political territory, but that is, of course, your right.

As regards the sum and substance of your message, you are operating from a number of false assumptions. Let me explain:

First, neither Mr. Weinstein nor the MRFF has any "position and title" in association with the Obama Administration. Given that fact, no matter the tone or the party next in the White House, our work will continue

Second, the MRFF is not a political organization and has no political role. We are made up of people of many different faiths and varying political viewpoints.

Third, there is nothing remotely "anti-Christian" associated with the work of either Mr. Weinstein or the MRFF. The work we do is to protect the right of the men and women in our military forces to their freedom of choice as regards belief. Because that protection includes warding off the efforts of a certain fundamentalist, dominionist sect of Christianity to force itself into a position of dominance in the U.S. military, many assume, as you appear to, that our opposition to the efforts of this totalitarian sect means that we oppose Christianity. Nothing could be further from the truth. In fact, over 90% of our members/supporters are Christian, some of them clergy.

Fourth, there is no need for Mr. Weinstein or anyone associated with the MRFF to feel shame for protecting the constitutional rights of our service women and men. If fact we take pride in it.

If you'd like more information, I should say correct information that comes without the hysterical slant applied by the would-be-dominant-dominionists and their ilk, I'll be happy to oblige.

For now, the only shame attached to anyone is that which associates itself with "nasty" messages based on ignorance.

My best to you,

Mike Farrell
(MRFF Board of Advisors)

.

Oh, (name withheld),

We get a good chuckle when anyone writes to us stating that Mikey has a title and position with President Obama concerning religious tolerance in our military. There is no such office (title and position) created by the White House and Mikey has never received a paycheck. You've been lied to.

The last time Mikey ever held a 'title and position' by a President was working for over three years in, and for, the West Wing of the Reagan Administration as legal counsel in the White House. In his final position there, Mikey was named the Committee Management Officer of the much-publicized Iran-Contra Investigation in his capacity as Assistant General Counsel of The White House Office of Administration, Executive Office of the President of the United States.

A proud MRFF supporter

.

When we left Washington DC, and all of the politics, I was never so happy to be out of there. I had had my fill of the political life, the traffic and congestion. I saw our environment as a small cross-section of our society and I missed the broader representation of life that I saw available to us elsewhere, say, for instance, New Mexico. The part that made me sad was that we were leaving a lot of family living in the area and one of my very best friends on the planet. As it turns out, you don't have to live in the same state to remain friends! It was, of course, a uniquely worthwhile time in our lives and now history. That being said, I cannot imagine going back.

♦♦♦

Subject: Go suck an egg!!!

Mr. Weinstein,

As a US Naval veteran, you are an affront to my senses. You have no understanding of what "Freedom of Religion" means and you are working to degrade our military. I'm sure you have already been enlightened concerning the term "wall of separation" and its source (not the Constitution).

I served for your right to speak and support your ridiculous notions. You may continue to do so but not without my undying opposition and that of my worldwide family.

(Name withheld)

.

Dear (name withheld),

As a US Army veteran, you are an affront to my senses. You have no understanding of what "Freedom of Religion" means and you are not working to defend our military. I'm sure you have been enlightened concerning the term "wall of separation" and its source (multiple US Presidents, drafters of the US Constitution, opinions of the SCOTUS, etc.).

I served for your right to speak and support your ridiculous notions that religion should be allowed to rule our country. You may continue to do so, but not without my undying opposition, that of our worldwide family, and the obnoxious repetition of the failure of theocratic campaigns over time.

Blake A. Page
Military Religious Freedom Foundation
Special Assistant to the President
Director of US Army Affairs

.

Dear Blake,

Proud of your nice little title? You may continue to go suck eggs. Glad that Jesus will one day rule the entire world and we will no longer have to suffer your hatred,
(Name withheld)

(Name withheld),

Any movement that confuses disinterest with hated is woefully deluded. Your wet dreams of a blue eyed, blonde haired, Skoal chewing, plaid wearin' sweet baby Jesus riding down from the clouds on his favorite pet dinosaur to smite me for my wicked ways makes about as much sense as me telling you too watch out for the evil Lord Sauron because little Frodo Baggins hasn't made it to Mordor with the one ring yet. To me your religion is a fantasy. I don't care if you believe it's true. That's your right. Have fun with it. In the same way I wouldn't go out of my way to find and disrupt the local dungeons and dragons gathering, I don't care what believers do while believing in the right time, place, and manner. Now, if one of those dodecahedronites decides to try to order a service member to wear their wizard robes in formation I'd take issue. Same thing when someone of your persuasion tries to order a service member to partake in that religion. It's not right. Even one of the countless authors of the errant words of your God admits that forced religion stinks in his nostrils. (Although to be candid I don't know what forcing religion smells like, but apparently Yahweh finds it offensive)

Anyways, have a great day and may his grand noodly appendage bless you with a bounty of good fortune today on your quest to suck eggs...

—Blake

♦♦♦

Subject: Hello

Hello,

I would like you all at the MRFF to know you will never find an atheist in a fire fight. Men who have never called on the name of the Lord will do so in a hurry and be saved in a instant.

Life is eternal and you choose where you live it. Accepting a free gift is all it takes. Reach out and take it today...

Now, I will willingly walk into combat tonight for you knowing I will stand in the presence of my God if I am killed. You should be fearful today to know you will stand before God one day and answer for all the lives you turned away from this free gift of salvation through His Son.

Thank you and have a good day!

(Name withheld)

.

(Name withheld)

Nearly the entire staff of MRFF is former service members, including many war veterans. I was an Army combat medic and Iraq veteran with a Purple Heart for injuries sustained in combat and a Combat Medical Badge for providing care under fire. And I'm an atheist, just like ~20% of the unit that I fought a war with, and the numbers are similar throughout the rest of the armed forces (far higher than the general population, by the way). Now that you've been corrected, I would appreciate it if you NEVER lie and insult the character, virtue, and service of atheists in the US Armed Forces EVER again.

Dustin Chalker
MRFF Atheist Affairs Advisor

♦♦♦

Subject: Mikey

When you get what you want we will inhabit a world full of people who are utterly remorseless (planned parenthood). When this comes to pass Mikey what will protect you. Our president had to liken crusaders to modern muslims to justify the present day blood bath occurring on the Middle East. I can't think of any overt acts of violence perpetrated in the name of Christ, but I can think of 10's of thousands of horrors committed in the name of muhammad. To compare the organization who appears at every natural disaster in the world, or war zone, or any atrocity to devil worship is sick. You have to trudge into the past to justify your current hate. Like it or not the constitution is full of our Christian God. There are more of us than you. You have moved to quickly and we are awake to your horrible ways. Persecute those who cherish life and embrace those who kill unborn children. I am not sure of your end game or what you expect to accomplish by your terrible nature. hope you don't get what you want Mikey because we believe and we will fight hard to defend our RIGHTS. I have never seen more frightening developments around the world and I am sure you people think you are somehow above the fray you are creating. You are not Mikey, you are known to millions and your advocacy of a world that allows a place like Iran to possess nuclear weapons will ensure the world you seek will come to pass. When chaos rules where will Mikey RUN. (Name withheld)

·

Dear (name withheld),

You wrote: "I can't think of any overt acts of violence perpetrated in the name of Christ". You could've stopped that sentence at "I can't think" and we would've gotten the point.

I am 100% certain that you've never read the Constitution, but you haven't let that stop you from having a strong opinion about what you think it says, have you? Like it or not, the US Constitution is a completely godless document. That's a fact.

I don't know what you think Planned Parenthood has to do with MRFF. I guess I shouldn't assume that you're thinking at all since we've already established your deficiencies in that arena.

Find something different to do with your time, (name withheld). Get a hobby. Read a book. I'm sure there is something better that you could be doing, rather than vomiting your ignorance all over the internet.

Dustin Chalker
MRFF Atheist Affairs Advisor

·

Dear (name withheld)—

I am writing in response to your email to the Military Religious Freedom Foundation ("MRFF"). As upset as you appear to be with MRFF, I assure you it is nothing to how upset I am about the time I lost attempting to decipher your rambling, ignorant, stream-of-consciousness email.

You attempt to express some vague political opinions about Planned Parenthood and nuclear weapons, yet you fail to mention a single act by MRFF with which you disagree. The closest you come to even almost referencing the work of MRFF is the statement, "Like it or not the [C]onstitution is full of our Christian God." This is simply not a fact—there is absolutely no mention of God anywhere in the Constitution.

To the contrary, the Founders very specifically decided to create a government based on democratic principles, rather than religious principles. The First Amendment protects the freedom to practice any religion (or no religion) – not just Christianity. It further prohibits the establishment of any particular religion. Additionally, Article 6 provides, "No religious test shall ever be required as a qualification to any office or public trust."

These are the constitutional protections we fight to ensure for all brave men and women in uniform. You say you will fight to defend your rights, yet we are the ones fighting to defend rights. From what I can tell, you don't do anything other than steal valuable oxygen from those around you.

Blessed be,

Tobanna Barker
MRFF Legal Affairs Coordinator

◆◆◆

My husband loves to say that information is better than no information. With that in mind, I have included an article on Operation Christmas Child.

.

The commander of a support squadron at Dover Air Force Base, Delaware, told the unit's airmen and civilian employs Tuesday that an evangelical group's email soliciting them to help with a Christmas charity was "not sent at my direction and is not endorsed in any way by me or any level of command."

Lt. Col. Donald Tasker, commander of the 436th Force Support Squadron, issued his statement in a squadron-wide email following a review of the charity group's solicitation for volunteers by the 436th Airlift Wing Commander Col. Michael W. Grismer Jr.

The charity group's email was forwarded to everyone in the squadron on Oct. 14 by Tasker's secretary, Valencia Branch. The email sought volunteers to help pack more than 5,000 gift boxes that would be sent to "children in desperate situations [to show] that God loves and values them."

"Many have never heard of God's incredible Gift of Salvation though His Son," the email stated.

Weinstein said his group got involved after 14 squadron members complained of the solicitation for the Operation Christmas Child campaign.

Weinstein told Military.com that the problem with the solicitation is that it was sent to everyone through the official email of the 436th Force Support Squadron commander's secretary. For all intents and purposes that is perceived as having the commander's approval, he said, which lends itself to charges of undue command influence to promote religion.

Retired Army Chaplain (Col.) Ron Crews, executive director of the Chaplain Alliance for Religious Liberty, on Tuesday issued a statement defending Branch's email to squadron members.

"We should be commending members of the Air Force, not condemning them for wanting to serve orphans," Crews said. "The e-mail announcing a volunteer opportunity in no way violates any Air Force policy or regulations, especially since the program involved is a federally approved charity."

Crews said his group hopes that Tasker "will stand behind those under his command who simply make others aware of how they may serve others if they so choose."

The Chaplains Alliance is made up of chaplain endorses—those who provide chaplains for the military. Crews said the group speaks for more than 2,600 military chaplains.

Weinstein said there was a right way for Dover airmen and civilians to support the campaign, but Branch's email was not it.

"There's no problem with this [campaign] if it's done through the chaplain's office," Weinstein said.

The same campaign, sponsored by Samaritan's Purse, an evangelical Christian charity and relief organization headed by Rev. Franklin Graham, was held at Hurlburt Field, Florida, in 2013. But the event was organized there by the base chapel's Protestant parish coordinator and held at the chapel, according to an official Air Force feature on the event at the time.

A member of the 436th Force Support Squadron at Dover told Military. com on Monday that the solicitation sent by Branch was not the first religious-oriented email mass distributed to the squadron.

Bryant Jordan can be reached at bryant.jordan@military.com. Follow him on Twitter at @bryantjordan.

.

Subject: Operation Christmas child

You people have alot of balls trying to shut down a Christmas toy drop for children in need or low income family's and even miltary family's... Christmas is a Christian holiday and for you people to want punishment for the 436th FSS commander's secretary is absolutely ridiculous. Tell your so call leader of a husband to back off...who cares if the miltary wants to give toys away to children...hope you have a nice day

(Name withheld)

.

Dear (name withheld),

Thanks for writing to the MRFF, because it gives me an opportunity to correct a terrible misconception on your part. The MRFF has not tried to "shut down a Christmas toy drop for children." Not even close to the truth, although I realize that is the way the situation is being misrepresented by conservative media outlets.

The ONLY thing to which we've objected is the manner in which Operation Christmas Child was communicated. Specifically, the communication was done via the "official" command structure, and that is contrary to governing law and regulation. As a 'current military member', you should know as well as I do that the military is very hierarchical, and that military leaders wield a tremendous amount of authority over subordinates. As such, military leaders at all levels are enjoined from using their official position or the color of their authority to promote any sort of sectarian religious belief, be it Christianity, Judaism, Islam, Atheism, or any other conceivable belief.

Make no mistake, Operation Christmas Child exists for the primary purpose of Christian evangelization, it's not a non-sectarian effort. With regard to military involvement in such an event, and as I'd hope you well know as a 'current military member', the military has other appropriate means of promoting this sort of charity, notably the chaplaincy. That is the avenue that should have been taken in this case.

Lastly, I give great credit to the commander at Dover for responding quickly and appropriately to this issue. It's a crying shame that so many conservatives are calling for his head, accusing him of lacking leadership skills, or lacking a spine, or both. The truth is that he recognized that the manner in which this particular event had been communicated was not appropriate, and he took decisive action to set things straight.

From my perspective, those who are screaming about the objection raised by the MRFF, and the response by the commander, may be ignorant of the rules that govern this sort of thing in the military. Or perhaps more likely, they may suffer from the malady of Christian Exceptionalism—that is to say, a belief that Christian proselytizing is immune from the rules that govern such activity and is not bound by the limits of the US Constitution. Such people are wrong, of course.

Thanks again for writing, and thanks for your service.

Peace,

Mike Challman
Christian, USAF veteran, MRFF supporter

♦♦♦

Subject: OCC Orphan Scandal

Dear Weinstein and all you that work under him:

How incredibly sad that you went after a guy trying to help orphans have a nice Christmas. I feel sorry for you, as it is only the Christian values of a free nation that allow us all to have the liberty, prosperity, and compassion even to do such a thing as care for orphans. Why pursue such a bitter course as you've taken?

May you come to know Him who've you pierced. And may you know His great love for you.

(Name withheld)

.

(Name withheld),

I think you have us all wrong... We did not stop that program at all, good ma'am... We simply required that the program be administered by the military chaplains and not the commanders... For the sake of your lord, would you please do your homework before you cast stones at us?! Also, I didn't "Pierce" anyone... Thanks for reaching out and take care,

Mikey Weinstein, Founder and president,
Military Religious Freedom Foundation

◆◆◆

The following article appeared in *The Stars and Stripes* after we intervened in the matter of improper placement of a Bible on a POW missing man table.

.

Advocacy group pushes Navy to remove Bible from Okinawa POW/MIA display

The Military Religious Freedom Foundation has filed a complaint with the Navy over a Bible being included into a POW/MIA display at U.S. Naval Hospital Okinawa.

The complaint—addressed to Navy Medicine West commander Rear Adm. Paul Pearigen—demands the immediate removal of the Bible from the hospital galley display, the immediate removal of accompanying written materials that describe the United States as being "founded as one nation under God," a Japanese translation of these materials and an independent investigation into who put up the display, as well as "appropriate disciplinary measures" for those responsible.

.

We received the following hate mail after this report was published.

.

Subject: POW/MIA table

What an appalling take on religion!! As per status quo of liberals, you go on the attack to whomever disagrees with you. (ie: God in the Constitution)

May I gently remind you this nation was founded on Christian faith. If someone who was a POW or family member of a POW would request their book of faith be included, there would be no negative reaction when the request was explained. We Christians do not hold the market in believing in a supreme being.

My father was not a religious man but deeply believed in God. He spent 3 1/2 years as a POW of the Japanese in the jungles of Burma Thailand as a POW/MIA. His family had presumed he had died until he came home from the war.

I ask that you research the hellish conditions of starvation & torture of these POW's so you can better comprehend & have more empathy for anyone who has lived like an animal to survive—and some didn't make it.

I feel sadness for the Jewish & Muslim men who felt offended. Surely, there was a better compromise than the knee jerk reaction of removing the Bible. Each and every man who has endured the unimaginable deserves the same respect & honor as the next man.

(Name withheld)

We also received the following love letter in response to the same issue.

·

Subject: Thank you

Mikey,

I would like to express my deepest gratitude to you and the entire staff of the Military Religious Freedom Foundation.

I am a patient at a local Akron, Ohio VA medical facility, and they had a missing man table display which prominently displayed a Christian New Testament bible. This had deeply disturbed me, as I strongly felt that the religious demographic of the MIA/POW's was not exclusively Christian; and that by having the bible representative of faith for all in fact divided and segregated all.

Within 15 minutes of contacting your Foundation, my phone was ringing with your call.

You displayed great compassion and understanding to my beliefs.

You did not come across as an Anti-Christian attack dog like so many wrongly make you out to be; you were genuinely interested in bringing equality to all Soldiers, all veterans, of ALL faiths, or even none.

Realistically the only way to do that is to remain truly neutral, and not show preference towards one religion, or give the appearance of preference of one religion over another.

I did my homework prior- I knew you advocated for Atheists, Christians, Muslims, Hindus, and many other faiths in the past. Your attitude, logic and passion for equality displayed in our phone call gave me 100% confidence that I had the right advocate.

Within 24 hours, your foundation had contacted the VA. Once again, rather than be a brutish bully many would like to portray you to be, you worked with he VA administration to come to a beneficial understanding that gave equality to the veterans serviced by the outpatient clinic.

Within 72 hours, the bible was removed, and the table was set as it should be.

Many Christians felt they were persecuted or attacked, and started to cite the National Alliance of MIA/POW Families Website as the authoritative directive on how the table is set, which includes a bible. We know, and the VA administration agreed that the NAOMPF is a private organization. ANYONE can register an organization as non-profit, then create a website and post an "authoritative" list. Unless its a .gov website, it isn't authoritative.

Next came Chaplain Ron Crews, a fierce Christian agenda propagandist. To understand Chaplains, you must know that they are ordained in their secular religion, and their first priority is the conversion of Soldiers. As an afterthought, they attempt to "counsel" all Soldiers. They are also governed by AR 165-1 which forbids many of the opinions Chaplain Crews spouts, yet he is the go to guy for Christian media citation. His credibility is shot.

Every media outlet with a Christian agenda, and some politicians, took your media piece, twisted it, added their own NON-credible sources, and pushed it out as if next you were going to go into their homes, steal their bibles, and physically restrain them from going to their private place of worship.

None of the Christian media outlets dared show your whole article, or have a hyperlink to it, as that would reveal their twists, misquotes, ommitances and they would fall from their false moral high ground.

Lastly, as the Christian attack pieces flooded the media, and thousands of comments were posted online spewing the hate calling us honorable war wounded veterans cowards, and death threats started to be posted, you continuously called on a daily basis to check up on me and see how I was handling things.

I have a Purple Heart and a Bronze Star with "V" Device. That means I intentionally and continuously put myself in harms way. I was prepared to take a bullet for my fellow Soldier. ANY fellow Soldier on the battlefield. My sacrifice was for ALL Soldiers, of ALL faiths and beliefs.

I truly believe what you do, fighting religious oppression in its many forms, and getting into the hate, the bitterness, and the threats to bodily harm and life is its own battlefield; and I believe that you are prepared to "take that bullet" for ALL Soldiers of ALL faiths.

After 15 years and 5 deployments, my war is done. I hope that one day we'll find that equality and yours will be too.

(Name withheld)
A Republic, if you can keep it - Benjamin Franklin.

♦♦♦

Subject: I think you are missing the point

At first I thought you were doing a good thing, then I started reading on and on about your cause. Look everyone who comes to this country has a right to worship as they see fit but to say that the United States needs to keep God out is very, very wrong. This nation was based on *Christian principles,* if it wasn't for God our nation would never have survived. As this nation pulls further and further away from God the greater is the danger that we as a nation & we as a people will no longer exist. I spent over 10 years in The Marine Corps and we have always said for God, Corps, & Country, notice how God is first then the Corps and then the Country last. That is how it should always be, God has to be first in everything we do because without God's good grace we would have never existed. This other crap saying that we are offending other people is a load of shit, everybody says we have to accept people as they are but yet you will not accept us praying or even mentioning God. This political correctness crap is for the birds, we have more important things to worry about.

Right now is a very critical time in our history, we have Muslims living in this country and at the same time we are at War with Islam. I have no problem with Muslims as long as they are peaceful and arewilling to live among us as honest, good hard working Americans. But as we have seen and what we have seen now Radical Islam and what they are capable of doing. It scares the Hell out of all of us, and they do not know how to coexist among others, even amongst their own. Trump was correct in saying we need to close the borders to anyone that is of Muslim faith until we can find a way to be able to distinguish between radical Islam and non-radical Islam. To be honest I believe there needs to be unannounced inspections of all Mosque until they are determined that they are not teaching radical Islam in their churches. That should also go to any church who's congregation starts blowing buildings up or conducting mass murder for the sake of their religion.

(Name withheld)

·

Dear (name withheld),

Let me see if I understand you correctly. You believe that the United States government is at war with Islam. Specifically, with Islamic practitioners who wish to take power over others and co-opt government authority. You also believe that the United States government exists to bolster your religion, and that your religion ought to have state sponsored authority.

Do you notice anything, dare I say it, hypocritical? I'm an American. A veteran. A taxpayer. A small business owner and newly minted job creator. I'm not Christian. In your view does that last label compromise my ability to carry the first I listed? In your view is my identity contradictory?

To be very clear, I believe that any religion that makes a person happy, without taking from or imposing on others, should be freely and vibrantly celebrated. Pray to whomever you like. But don't dare try to steal my country from me. Don't contribute to the erasure of our country's original

motto. E Pluribus Unum. If you must forget it, recognize that I will not, and that the Military Religious Freedom Foundation will not.

Cheers,

Blake A. Page
Military Religious Freedom Foundation
Special Assistant to the President
Director of US Army Affairs

◆◆◆

Subject: Waterboard Whinigstein

Michael Weinstein we hate you!

All red blooded Americans hate you. God hates you.Get out of America NOW!How dare you support the ousting of that brave airman at the retirement ceremony from simply reaffirming that America and its flag are God-given and that America is God-blessed. You atheists and jews can't get it through your stiff-necked heads that we are a Christian nation intentionally by birth and history. And we always will be. Why do you think the pilgrims said prayers at Plymouth Rock. God His Son and the Holy Spirit are what America brings to the fallen world.Our Muslim president may support you but his term is over thank God in January.You need to be locked up and waterboarded until you accept the Lord Jesus Christ as the full sinner you are.

(Name withheld)

•

Hi (name withheld),

You're just flat wrong about so many things it's hard to know where to start. I'm a red-blooded American and Mikey is a friend of mine. You don't know him and choose to hate him out of ignorance, which is sad.

As your use of the word "support" suggests, the "ousting of that brave airman," as you choose to think of him, wasn't Mikey's idea, nor was it his doing. That was the action of the commander in charge who, if you'd bother to read and understand the reports, specifically barred the man from speaking as it was an official event and there are official, actually authorized, words to be said at that moment. "(T)hat brave man" had evidently been specifically told he was not to participate and chose to push his way forward anyway. At a private, not-military-endorsed event, people can say what they choose, but that's not the case at an official event.

You're welcome to your opinion about the formation of this country, but you have the history and the facts wrong.

It is interesting, may I add, that you appear to believe what you suggest about the president of the United States and also are apparently a fan of waterboarding. Sad, but interesting.

Mike Farrell
(MRFF Board of Advisors)

◆ ◆ ◆

Subject: West Point

Dear Mr. Weinstein—let me join in the chorus of outrage about your actions against the Army Football team—my response is simple- it is none of your damn business what goes on in the Army football locker room. Butt out-

But since the issue of religion has been engaged, as it now happens, you have now forced your religion-which I gather is NONE atheism- on the Corps and the football team- so tell me why you, and those like you, have not violated the 'church-state' clause? The absence of .religion. is a religion. And now no 'religion' is the prescribed and accepted religion.

But I am sorry you were offended- but you are a big boy now so get over it and mind your own damn business.

(Name withheld)
Class of 19xx
USMA

•

Dear Mr. (Name withheld),

Thank you for writing us with your concerns. Don't worry, we're certainly not offended and have heard them all before.

The first point of contention that you've brought up is the tired line that we should just "butt out" and ignore our clients' requests for assistance. As it is our sole mission to respond to requests for advocacy by members of military organizations, we can't do that. If you'd like to oppose what we do, you might find collusive ideas with an organization like ISIS, which aspires to have religiously inspired governments fight holy wars with one another and oppress their citizenry.

To your second point, secularism is not a religion by any definition. Secularism means specifically not having anything to do with religion. The loss of special privileges, while painful to many Christian Nationalists or theocrats, is not subordination. It is equalization. These three statements should clear things up for you:

We won because of a god! = Establishment of religion (unacceptable if made by a representative of any government organization in the execution of their duties thanks to the first amendment)
We won as a team! = Secular (religiously neutral and acceptable under our laws, does not establish or infringe on religion)
We won because there is no god! = Impedes religion (unacceptable if made by a representative of any government organization in the execution of their duties thanks to the first amendment)

The absence of religion is not a religion in the same way a bowling league is not a non-stamp collecting, non-horse riding, non-cycling, non-political, non-whatever else you'd like, organization. Not participating in something is not a positive affirmation of any belief. If I haven't made the point clear enough yet, I recommend that you research Lemon v. Kurtzman and read about the SCOTUS' ruling.

There is very real danger in the iniquitous form of government that is theocracy. Our country fights such governments, and factions, regularly. If you want holy war, the first step is to build a holy regime. That lesson has been learned over thousands of years of senseless death. Our country was founded as a secular republic, E Pluribus Unum, for good cause.

I truly don't mind that you are offended by the first amendment of our Constitution. Get over it, or steep in anger. It's entirely up to you.

Cheers,

Blake A Page
Military Religious Freedom Foundation
Special Assistant to the President
Director of US Army Affairs

.

Blake, I am sorry that you are lost and choose like all liberals to believe that evolution is your answer which has already been proven wrong by the second law of thermodynamics and that liberals to date have no answer of where humans come from other than some bowl of soup and evolved from monkeys. The God of the bible has been proven by bible prophecy where things proven have come to pass and more are coming to pass. Just like liberals to believe in global warming which can also be proven wrong. They say that the polar caps are melting and that humans cause this but, I say that the polar caps are also melting on Mars and there are no humans there. In fact, they are melting but, it is due to changes on the Sun. You see, I have a masters in astrophysics and know what I am talking about. The purpose of liberalism is for government to control people through economic and religious means but, I and conservatives do not fall for such bull crap.

(Name withheld)

·

Dear (name withheld),

Attempting to impose the second law of thermodynamics on a segment of an open system falls flat. If you truly had a masters in astrophysics you would know this. Conflating liberalism with atheism is another huge misstep for someone claiming to have an education. Atheists can be from any political party. Liberals can be from any religion. If you doubt that human efforts are causing global warming, great. You're a member of the .01% of the scientific community that holds that position (assuming you have a degree at all). We do have an answer for where humans came from, but you lack the mental faculties to comprehend natural selection, so I needn't waste any efforts sharing the basis of all biology with you. If the good of the bible were true, Jesus would have returned within the lifetime of his disciples as promised. He's 2000 years late to the prophecy.

Blake Page

♦♦♦

Subject: Separation Clause

MRFF,

The term "separation clause" refers to nothing found in the U. S. constitution. The idea that honoring God is separate from our governance is a false concept proposed by those who seek to undermine the corner stone upon which the founders built the structure of government - ". . . endowed by their Creator . . ".

I will pray for your spirits that you will know the true peace and love that can come only from God.

Blessings,
(Name withheld)

.

...sorry, (name withheld), the word "God" appears NOWHERE in the Constitution for a reason..we do however have GENERATIONS of bedrock caselaw which incontrovertibly carves a deep chasm between church and state in America...just as The Founders fully intended...please spare me your disingenuous prayers...pray perhaps instead for your OWN enlightenment about how our wonderful country works...

all best,

Mikey Weinstein

.

Dear (name withheld),

Please name ten modern countries that have governments that are explicitly based on a religion. Shouldn't take long, just start in the Levant and work your way out. Feel free to include rebel factions like ISIS, to make your research go by a little quicker.

Now, what exactly is it about those countries that you admire so much? Is it the "strong leadership" they demonstrate by siphoning the fruits of their population to prop up the gods of the state? Or is it their viciousness in dealing with other countries that have slightly different state-gods?

A separate assignment: on a scale from academically negligent to maliciously stupid, how would you describe the decision made by the founders of this great country to exclude mention of it being a Christian state in our Constitution?

If you don't blame the founders, which of the three branches of government across all of our country's history do you think was misreading our laws as they continued to uphold (for whatever crazy reason) that the United States is not founded on the Christian religion, but rather is a secular state that does not advance or impede any faith?

Sincerely,

Blake A Page
Military Religious Freedom Foundation
Special Assistant to the President
Director of US Army Affairs

◆◆◆

Subject: Freedom from religion?????

No such thing as freedom from religion in the Constitution. You can cling to your atheism and falsehoods. I'll stick to God and guns.

(Name withheld)

.

Dear (name withheld),

Please be advised that the MRFF does not "cling to atheism and false hoods." We represent thousands of lloyal & patriotic military members, veterans & civilians who have requested that their US Constitutional freedom from religion be respected & protected. 96% are Christians who do not want someone else's version of Christianity imposed upon them. We proudly serve them to insure they are not denied this historic American individual liberty.

Your statement "No such thing as freedom from religion in the Constitution" is incredibly ignorant for a 21st Century American adult & contrary to facts, history & law. Attached is a rational explanation in plain language of the factual, historical & lawful relationship between our Constitution, the military & any religion. Hopefully, you will find it enlightening.

Most Sincerely,

John Compere
MRFF Advisory Board Member & Texas rancher

.

Again no such thing as freedom from religion in America. You have the right not to participate or purchase something you don't believe in.

You can't be free to practice your religion and free from all others to practice their's. Very basic logic

(Name withheld)

.

...in the US we are all free to practice our faith or lack thereof as long as it is in a time, place and manner which complies with the United States Constitution, it's construing Federal an State caselaw and, in the military, all DOD directives, instructions and regulations...if "following your faith" violates those precepts, you're an outlaw and, if you do it in the military, you will be a target of MRFF! "Very basic logic ..."

Mikey Weinstein

♦♦♦

Subject: Relationship

You guys have it all wrong. Why not spread the Gospel? Are you afraid of something ? A military that truly has Faith in the Father, Son ,Holy Spirit. Will do their job very proficiently. They will listen to their leaders and follow through with the task they are given. If one chooses not to attend or want to not listen that's their option. This nation was formed and founded with lots of prayer read your history . So in other words I Totally disagree with what you are attempting to do. Look at our nation , God was kicked out of schools years ago , we, our nation is behind in every thing. Third world nation's can beat us in academics now days, Patriotism is no longer accepted in schools, no pledge of allegiance, no love of country and what we once stood for. Our nation is so worse off than it has ever been, no morals. No grounding. Parents is where it starts then schools that have upright teachers with proper morals not this left wing garbage that's being instilled in young very impressionable minds. Look around you or you have blinders on. I totally disagree with liberal mission.

(Name withheld)

.

Hi (name withheld),

Nope, not afraid of anything. No one here is opposing your right to "spread the Gospel." In your case, were you in the military, that would be a right we'd be sure to protect. But you see, in the military, which is part of the government, one is only free to "spread the Gospel" on her or his own private time. Because of the First Amendment's protection of free choice of belief or non-belief, one cannot try to push one belief system over others because it violates the separation of church and state.

Your belief system holds that "a military that truly has Faith in the Father, Son, Holy Spirit… will do their job very proficiently." That may be so in some part of the world or in your imagination, but in America everyone doesn't believe in the Father, Son and Holy Spirit, so it can't work here.

You see, much as it pains some people, in America one is free to believe as you do or not, and each person's choice of belief or non-belief is just as important as yours. And the same is true of any other aspect of that person's citizenship.

You have lumped a lot of what you perceive as social problems together under the assumption that they're all the result of one thing: not believing as you do. Hard as it may be for you to understand, it is exactly that kind of narrow mindedness that causes the problems you list, not the the fact that some lack your perception of God or godliness.

It's a shame that you can't understand that people who are not your kind of Christian, people who may well be believers but just not the kind that needs to shove it in everyone's face or demand that everyone bow down in their chosen way, can be just as decent and loving and compassionate and Christlike as you seem to think you are. And, like it or not, those who believe in Allah or Yahweh or Krishna or The Great Spirit and those who believe there is no god or there are many gods are also just as good and decent and thoughtful as are you. Maybe even more so.

Your idea about taking the blinders off might a good self-prescription. Think about it.

A proud MRFF supporter

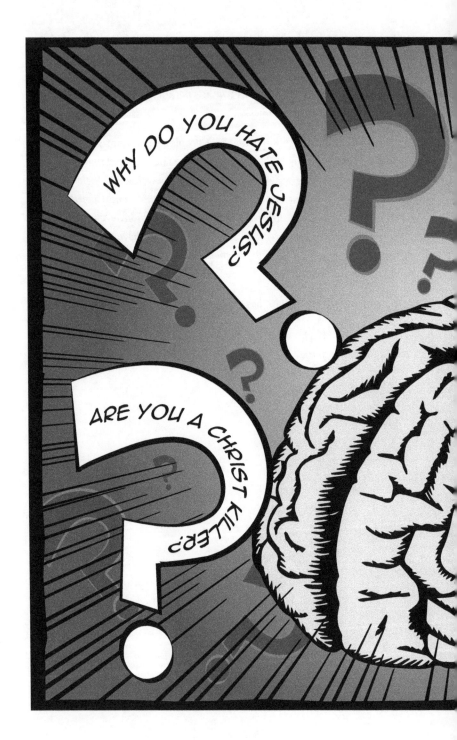

You Have Questions

WHILE LEARNING PUNCTUATION IN grade school, I found the principles of when to use a question mark very straight forward; commas, not so much, but when and how to use question marks came pretty easy to me. I liked the question mark. For some reason, this part of grammar and spelling has proven difficult for a lot of those who write to us. I follow a pretty simple rule, I ask questions when I want answers. Simple enough. Further, but not to complicate matters, when I ask a question, I end the question with a question mark.

With this in mind, I would like to think that people who write in with questions want answers. One would reasonably assume that to be the case, but for the most part in this chapter it's not. If you just want to state your opinion about a subject, do so, but to couch it as a question when you do not want an answer or are not going to listen to the answer is disingenuous at best.

This leads me to mention two other issues. These letters are perfect examples of a lot of things, for sure, but mainly I find that this chapter clearly shows it is not what a person says but how they say it. That is one of the reasons why I like the responses from our team so much. They give like they get but also when approached in even a small degree of civility, that is what is returned.

My second issue on the matter of emails is content without intent. Unfortunately, we understand all too well the intent of most of these emails, however, I have an issue with a generation of society that would email rather than pick up a phone. It is in listening that you get intent, something that is not available as well when the word is written. I can write "oh, for sure" and even in context it may not be clear what I mean. However, if you heard my voice you would know immediately if I was speaking sarcastically or emphatically. I am not for one moment suggesting that these kinds of detractors call us, I am speaking more to a general point. One of my pet peeves is with the advent of the internet we are developing a culture of paper tigers and communication that is lacking in personal, face to face communication.

♦ ♦ ♦

Subject: Re: Do Christian Fanatics in the Military Endanger National Security? Like the Christian Fanatics that stormed Normandy and now have THE CROSS over their graves?

(Name withheld)

.

Mr. (Name withheld),

Is there a point you're trying to make here? I get a sense of hostility in your message, but I'm unclear just what it's about.

Are you objecting to people having crosses over their graves? Are you concerned that some who were not Christian have nonetheless had their graves marked with a cross? Or is your point that you object to the term 'fanatic' being attached to the word Christian?

If the latter, is it your intention to suggest that Mikey has somehow besmirched the memory of those who took part in the D-Day invasion? If so, I assure you that's not only an inappropriate but a foolish thought.

If I'm getting warm, though, let me only say it's surprising to me how thin-skinned some Christians seem to be. Some who claim to be followers of Jesus seem quite ready to take umbrage at any expression of concern about inappropriate behavior on the part of self-professed Christians, seeing such an expression as an attack on the entire faith and all who are part of it.

I find that hard to understand. Certainly we know there are many self-professed Christians who have taken advantage of others, who have seduced or robbed or manipulated innocents for their own advantage. We can know about such things and still understand that the behavior of such a person doesn't taint the entire faith. That would be silly.

But it's important to be able to speak the truth about such behavior, wouldn't you agree? And when doing so results in angry outbursts calling on the memory of those who perished while taking part in a battle to save civilization, for example, isn't that a bit over the top?

Perhaps you have an issue with the idea that the term fanatic can ever apply to the behavior of one who has chosen to follow Christ. But what about the Christian who murdered Dr. Tiller because he performed a medical service for women who needed to terminate a pregnancy? Or what of the poor, apparently demented man who killed three people in a clinic in Colorado Springs because he had been misled into believing they were selling "baby parts." In a less dramatic but just as subversive way, what of Christians who damn and demean people whose faith does not meet the standards they believe necessary to qualify as Christian enough. What of Christians who condemn, sometimes quite loudly and vigorously, people who have the audacity to be Hindu or Muslim or Jew? Zealotry and fervent belief can become problematic, I trust you understand, and predatory behavior gives evidence of fanaticism.

So please understand that Mikey's concern with those Christian fundamentalists trying to infiltrate themselves into the military leadership, those who intend to turn our country into a theocracy and make our military into "Jesus's Army," are among us, and they are rightly thought of by those who believe in the freedom of religious or non-religious choice, as fanatics.

Best,

Mike Farrell
(MRFF Board of Advisors)

♦♦♦

Subject: questions

Dear MRFF

I understand that you have joined in the fight to remove Bibles, Bible Verses, Speech about the Bible, and references of or from a Christian stand point from the military. Is this correct? Are you putting money, time and or effort to remove Christian beliefs from the military? WOULD YOU DO THIS IF ISLAM WAS THE ONE IN QUESTION?

I expect an answer to EVERY question.

Thank you for your time.

(Name withheld)

Dear (name withheld),

The answer to EVERY question you've asked is as follows: No. No. And stupid question, but sure.

We don't have the authority to ban anything anywhere. We are a nonprofit advocacy group which serves the singular purpose of giving a voice to those in our military who cannot safely speak for themselves. On the matter of bibles in POW/MIA displays, we notified leaders at several installations that existing US law and military regulation was being violated. Fortunately, those leaders had the good sense to recognize that this is a country of laws, and regardless of how much consternation it causes Dominionists, separatists, Christian nationalists, or subversives of any other variety, we don't have free reign to pick and choose which laws to follow without consequence. If that limited public forum were opened to the inclusion of other holy texts, the bible could have stayed. It was ultimately the decision of the leaders at those installations.

Our organization spends its time, money, and effort fighting theocracy, and defending our clients. We do not have any ability to remove individual's beliefs. We do fight against state sponsored religion in the way our Constitution demands any patriot ought.

If the United States government made a real effort to promote Islam as the state sanctioned religion in the same way it so often treats Christianity, we'd be first in line to smack that nonsense down. Our secular government's design doesn't get to pick winners or losers when it comes to personal faith.

You're welcome,

Blake A. Page
Military Religious Freedom Foundation
Special Assistant to the President
Director of US Army Affairs

◆ ◆ ◆

Subject: Concerned

Hello. To whom it may concern.

I am a bit confused. This organization is so busy trying to erase anything Christian for all military functions, so far the latest not getting a speaker to speak for the prayer breakfast, which I was going to attend up until found out its no longer going to be one for Victory Week....what about out civil rights as a Christian? Do we not count for anything? Just looking for clarity and understanding

(Name withheld)

.

(Name withheld),

You certainly still have your rights to expression. There is a succinct analogy that might help here: Your right to swing your fists stops at the bridge of my nose. In the case of Jerry Boykin, he's used his position to infect his subordinates and others with the virus of Islamophobia. He's made patently un-American claims publicly and on record which make him unfit to be a mentor in any way to any active duty service members. He was forced to retire after violating countless regulations and was such a stain on the uniform he wore that he earned direct condemnation from the President himself. As we learned in Parker v Levy, not all speech is protected in the military. Not if it detracts from the mission. Boykin is an ideological defector from the United States and flouts his belief that this country should be over thrown and a theocracy built in its place. He's spread conspiracy theories about our current president. His message is not religious, is political. He is a lobbyist, not a pastor. As such, he has no business having access to the impressionable minds of our young service members. I hope this clears things up, but if you have any more questions feel free to ask.

Thank you,

Blake A Page
Military Religious Freedom Foundation
Special Assistant to the President, Director of US Army Affairs

.

Mr. Page,

Thank you sir. I appreciate it.

V/r,

(Name withheld)

◆◆◆

Ok Let me just get this right. You all MRFF think the black negroes girls at west Point are heroes for making a black fist in the air?

(Oh but we can't call them niggers right?)

And that raghead ay-rabs and fagots in the army are heroes too?

But that Jesus Christ (who is GOD) is the enemy who you must crucify and shit on?

You can just go live with the girl niggers and sand niggers and queers mikey wiensteen.

Get sick and choke to death on your own kike vomit jewboy.

.

Let's jump back to the dark ages. After all, life was so much better, right?

◆◆◆

Subject: God in the Constitution

In Article 7 of the US Constitution it states "in the Year of our Lord"

Who are the Founders referring to?

(Name withheld)

.

Dear Mr. Name withheld...

Clearly, you been listening to David Barton and believe his ridiculous claim that the date on the Constitution is part of what he laughably calls "the attestation clause of Article 7," and that you haven't actually looked at a copy of the Constitution yourself. If you did actually look at the Constitution for yourself, you would see that Article 7 consists of only one short sentence, and all that this one short sentence says is how many states needed to ratify the Constitution in order for it to go into effect, and that the words "in the Year of our Lord" are not part of Article 7. The date follows Article 7 for no other reason than that Article 7 happens to be the last article of the Constitution. It is not part of the body of the Constitution, as Mr. Barton would have his followers believe with his ridiculous claim of its being the "the attestation clause of Article 7."

I suppose you also believe the other part of Mr. Barton's claim — where he claims that the inclusion of the words "the Independance of the United States America the twelfth" in the Constitution's date make the Declaration of Independence a part of the Constitution, thereby also making the Declaration's references to a creator, nature's god, etc., part of the Constitution and coming up with his grand total of there being seven references to God and/or religion in the Constitution.

This "attestation clause of Article 7" claim of Mr. Barton's is so utterly ridiculous that I actually devoted an entire chapter of my new book to explaining the utter ridiculousness of it. I am attaching a copy of that chapter to this email, and sincerely hope that you will take the time to read it, or at least look at the pictures.

Chris Rodda
Senior Research Director, Military Religious Freedom Foundation

·

Dear Chris

Thank you for responding to my email. Let me re-phrase my question. Before the signers of the Constitution signed their names to the Constitution, they dated their work being the Seventeenth Day of September in the Year of our Lord one thousand seven hundred and eighty seven.

Who was the "Lord" they referred to?

(Name withheld)

·

(Name withheld),

Well, obviously, since the western world's dating system is based on the alleged birth date of the Christian lord, it's the Christian lord.

Now, let me ask you a question. If dating documents "in the Year of our Lord" held such an important religious significance to the founders, why didn't they also date the Declaration of Independence "in the Year of our Lord"?

Chris

◆◆◆

Subject: Opinion about the bible removing

Really ashamed a veteran of the U.S. has the bible removed out of the lobby. I saw it on Fox News. I mean REALLY! What if it was a porn magazine would he have had it removed also? I get offended every day by something just tell the guy to put his big girl panties on and just get over it and move on....that Bible was probably placed there to help someone who needed it. Shame on your group and I would not support you for sure. I Love America and our Vets who served but this is just ridiculous and that is why I thank our veterans for serving and giving me MY Freedom to express this opinion also.

God Bless!
(Name withheld)

.

(Name withheld),

Ours is a nation of laws. Your hurt feelings don't negate the US Constitution and sixty+ years of judicial precedent. Shame on you for sleeping through civics and sympathizing with theocrats.

Cheers,

Blake A Page
Military Religious Freedom Foundation
Special Assistant to the President
Director of US Army Affairs

Subject: Mr. Weinstein Why?

Mr. Weinstein, it seems to me and my fellow Air Force Academy grad classmates that you are pro-gay, pro-abortion, pro-Islam, pro-atheist, anti-Christian, anti-Jesus. anti-Bible, pro-females (over males), anti-Christmas, anti-military, anti-USAFA, anti-guns, anti-Israel and pro-Palestinian? Why are you so wrong on every issue that makes America the greatest country in the world, sir? How did you ever even manage to graduate from our esteemed Academy? Shame, shame on you and your Academy graduate children too.

V/R

xxxxxxx x. xxxxxxx, USAFA Class of xxxx

.

Mr X,

You are approximately one-third right. Indeed, Mr Weinstein is pro-gay, pro-Islam, pro-atheist, pro-female. (As for abortion—I won't speak for him, but there are many loyal and patriotic Americans serving in our Armed Forces that disagree on this hot topic). But, you have the latter two-thirds wrong. He is also profoundly pro-male (i.e, pro-gender equality),pro-Christian, pro-Jesus (at least concerning his teaching and ideas of acceptance and forgiveness), pro-Bible (i.e., pro free speech, free practice, free press), distinctly and demonstrably pro-military (virtually ALL of his family is or has served), pro-USAFA (defending hundreds of cadets from bullying and discrimination), pro-guns (since he needs to defend himself and his family against an astonishing number of whacko death threats on an almost daily basis), pro-Israel (duh!), and pro-Palestinian in that he support universal human rights of self-determination, respect, etc.

Please give specifics on where he is wrong. Is he wrong for supporting and defending the most perfect government document ever written by man (The Constitution)—to which I've affirmed my intent to support and defend for over THIRTY-(number withheld) years of active duty—and its guarantees of free practice and anti-establishment? Is he wrong to support subordinate military members from being forced to practice religious beliefs (or eschew their beliefs) in order to placate a superior or protect their opportunity for retention and promotion? Let's remember, well over 90% of his clients are practicing, devout Christians who have come to him as their only recourse against bullying superiors who think that they are 'not Christian enough' or not of the right flavor for advancement in that superior's "Air Force." Should he and the MRFF NOT defend the Jewish or Muslim or Hindu cadet or airman against blatant bias—as we all would defend those subjected to racial or gender bias? In other words, what problem do you have, how is he wrong is insisting that our Department of Defense and all its members: treat others with respect; treat others as valuable individuals able to contribute to our defense; expect that in the work place superiors and all members maintain the kind of religious and political neutrality that makes our military the envy of the world and a model of (simultaneously) effectiveness AND diversity that reflects our population. Please, do tell me where he is wrong with cases and specific actions that I can address.

Until then, my friend and fellow member of the Long Blue Line, you can SIERRA-TANGO-FOXTROT-UNIFORM.

Sincerely,

An Active Duty Senior Air Force Officer and USAFA Grad

♦♦♦

Subject: US Constitution

Hey Mikey,

If you would ever take the time to read our US Constitution you will find that there is nothing in that document that says anything about separation of Church & State.

Therefore, are you just trying to be a bully because you are an atheist and have no respect for anything to do with the Christian religion?

Your day will come when you meet your Maker to tell him why you are doing what you are doing.

(Name withheld)

Dear (name withheld),

As Mikey is busy defending the religious rights of our military members, I have been asked to respond to your email.

First, I'd like to know where you got your law degree or other formal, accredited university or college training in understanding our Constitution. Mikey is not only a lawyer, he was an Air Force lawyer ("JAG") for ten years. If you have comparable credentials, bring them on.

Second, the Constitution and Bill of Rights both offer protection from government imposition of religion on anyone. That is what Mikey is fighting against. When anyone "witnesses" in uniform, on duty, to his or her underlings, the military environment translates that as use of governmental authority to favor those who, regardless of their own upbringing and personal beliefs, suddenly start attending his church, his bible study, and etc., while showing less than fair consideration of those who don't — even if they, too, are Christian! It is taken to mean that the latter are not true Christians or not Christian enough! The others are non- Christians who also find themselves treated unfairly, often dangerously so, and that includes on the battlefield.

Such leadership behavior is extremely detrimental to unit cohesion, good order, and discipline, all of which are needed for our military to do its job. Such leadership is also unconstitutional, so the leaders doing it are breaking their military enlistment oath to "protect and defend the Constitution." One cannot both protect the Constitution and defy it at the same time.

You are free to argue semantics, i.e., the representative phrase "separation of church and state" all you want. Mikey and the rest of MRFF will do what is truly American and patriotic, keeping our oath, defending our Constitution, and, most of all in this regard, protecting the religious freedoms of all our military members, regardless of their personal beliefs.

Sincerely,

A true patriot, an American veteran, and a staunch MRFF supporter

♦♦♦

Subject: How Many Jews?

Hey there Mikey. Quick question for you in honor of the Holiday Season.

(Q) How many jews does it take to crucify the Son of God?

(A) All of them. All the time. Everywhere. (jews have a nose for deicide)

Happy Easter Christ Killer.

·

Hey there,

Quick question for you in reference to the holiday season.

(Q) How would Jesus feel if he saw that a true Christian sent a stupid, ugly, bigoted, anti-Semitic comment to someone he didn't know, a comment condemning an entire people, of which he happened to be a member?

(A) Not too bad. He'd weep for the stupidity of the poor lost, demented soul who sent it, but he'd be comforted in the thought that a true Christian would never stoop to doing such a thing.

Sleep well.
A proud MRFF supporter

♦♦♦

Subject: Fort Carson

Read about you below. How long have you hated Christians and loved muslims? You do know they want to annihilate Jews as well as Christians.

"The enemy that Army and Air Force personnel at Fort Carson are trained to fight has now formed a battle with them on their own turf in Colorado Springs, Colorado. All it took was a couple of complaints from irate Muslims and those who support them, and officials at the base bowed down to Islam."

(Name withheld)

·

Hi (name withheld),

I know where bigotry comes from, but I've never been clear about willful ignorance. Now, thanks to you, I have a bit more clarity about the latter. I suppose if a person treats himself to a steady diet of stupidity, arrogance and fear, it can become kind of hypnotizing.

If you're at all open to things like facts, I'd be happy to help you. I fear, however, that you may have chosen to lose yourself in the hypnotizing trio mentioned above. However, since I tend to be an optimist, I like to say true things because sometimes they pierce the veil of willful ignorance. Here are some: No one here hates Christians. We believe Christians have the right to practice their faith. Everyone here believes Muslims also have the right to practice their faith just as believers in other faiths have. And, in addition, everyone here believes people who subscribe to no faith at all have the same right.

BUT—and this is important—people in the military who want to practice their faith or belief system must do so in the proper time, place and manner. We also know that Muslims do not want to annihilate Jews, Christians or anyone else. You are confusing, apparently, radical extremists who do not represent Islam, for all Muslims. That is as wrong as it would be to assume all Christians are represented by the man who murdered Dr. Tiller, or Robert Dear, the man who killed people in Colorado Springs, or Timothy McVeigh.

You see, (name withheld), there are facts and there is ignorant bigotry. You've taken your pick, but it's not too late to do a little clear thinking.

Best,

Mike Farrell
(MRFF Board of Advisors)

.

Mike,

I take offense at you idea of "stupidity, arrogance and fear". As far a stupidity, have you read the Koran and the references of "killing" all unbelievers? Over 100 times it says this. Maybe the stupidity is on your part unless you can explain those references. This is the guide all these people believe and live by. Why haven't they condemned the killings by "extremists" the way

Christians condemned Tiller, Dear and McVeigh? I believe the "ignorant bigotry" is on your part, not mine. Arrogance? I am a retired teacher who wants to live a long life in the country I love. My arrogance left me a long time ago and I wonder if the arrogance might be on the part of MRFF in "dictating" how someone should or should not believe. Fear? Are you afraid you might lose your job if you found the truth and it didn't agree with your colleagues?

"It's not too late to do a little clear thinking."

·

Oh (name withheld), please. You're happy to spout nonsense, but when called on it the result is you "take offense"?

Actually I have not only read the book but I know many Muslims, none of whom hate you or me. Nor are any of them about to dedicate themselves to annihilating Jews, Christians or others who don't share their faith.

Have you bothered to read the Bible? Does stoning children at the city gates appeal to you? Has it occurred to you that things change as people grow? Do yourself a favor. Visit a mosque and ask people there about their need to murder nonbelievers. If you're open to trying something daring like that it might wake you up.

The fact that you choose to believe that Muslims haven't condemned the behavior of the extremists who defile their religion demonstrates your unwillingness to actually reach out and find the truth of what's happening. And frankly, it makes me tired. The idea that one who was once a teacher, presumably of children, is so full of fear and hatred that he's willing to spew this kind of garbage is terrifying. Xenophobes and demagogues should be barred from teaching. It's a relief to think you're retired, but it's horrifying to think about the damage you may have done before you left.

No one at the MRFF is dictating how someone should or should not believe. You may cling to your sad and sick convictions as long as you'd like, but fortunately people in authority in the military are not always as blind as you choose to be.

Mike Farrell

♦♦♦

Subject: Why Your wife has Multiple Sclerosis

Mr. Michael Weinstein our church has a single question for your to consider.

Has it ever occurred to you that the reason your wife Bonnie suffers with MS is as punishment to you from the Lord Jesus Christ?

Because of the MRRF vicious attacks constant against loving Christians in the armed services. Like you taking the Bible away from Air Force Major.

Just sayin'.

.

How kind.

.

Dear Coward who hides behind what is probably a fake address,

Your church, if it exists, is a haven of hate, a pox-filled slime pit that reeks of rotting, pus-filled, vermin infested cretins so weak in their pretense at faith that they stoop to satanic levels of stupidity and cruelty.

You, of course, betray your ignorance by your pre-kindergarten-level grammar. In pretending to speak for this poorly fabricated congregation of ghouls, you are a prime example of what made Jesus weep.

Has it ever occurred to you, " Just sayin'" why you waste precious time on this Pale Blue Dot? You appear and manifest on some cognitive level, to be irrational, void of a clear and functioning mind.

Healthy individuals would never consider attacking another's wife. They seek through examination, discussion, self reflection, grounded with/& in a wholly intact consciousness.

I offer you the below explanation on brain function, Just sayin' :

"The frontal lobe is the same part of the brain that is responsible for executive functions such as planning for the future, judgment, decision-making skills,

attention span, and inhibition. These functions can decrease drastically in someone whose frontal lobe is damaged."

Peace,
Jude

.

Dear ???—

I am writing in response to your email to Mikey Weinstein and the Military Religious Freedom Foundation ("MRFF"). I would have addressed you by name, but you apparently did not have the courage to include it in your ridiculous email.

I am tempted to explain all the ways that MRFF protects the constitutional rights of the brave men and women who sacrifice so much to protect ours. However, I must assume that, if you believe a medical diagnosis is a consequence of not practicing your particular religious belief, you are not interested in facts.

Has it ever occurred to YOU that the Lord you claim to honor would not appreciate you daring to make such declarations in his name? Perhaps anything unfortunate you or a loved one may experience should be considered punishment for such arrogance—a reminder that YOU have no authority to judge who should be punished or rewarded.

To the contrary, nobody cares about your disgusting presumptions concerning the lives of others. I sincerely suggest that if you insist on keeping your mind closed, you keep your mouth closed as well.

Blessed be,
Tobanna Barker
MRFF Legal Affairs C

♦♦♦

Besides posting our email on the web site, the emails from detractors are routinely sent out to a wide array of supporters and family and friends who are able to see firsthand what it is that we deal with on a daily basis. I love it when these people write back with personal comments of support and sympathy.

·

Mikey, Wow...there is just no end to it, is there? But, it's understandable here in middle America because Christianity has always stood for "goodness" and there has simply been no other religion except Christianity...so you are, in essence, representing everything that is against goodness. People here just don't have a frame of reference that includes other ways of thought and belief.

I roll my eyes because my frame of reference is somewhat broader, but honestly, Mikey, are looking (and judging) the elephant through the knothole in the fence. Others, of course, use whatever part of the Christian religion to justify their own aberrant behavior.

Sigh...B

·

Attacking your family reveals a level of inhumanity that causes great concern. I know my words are so little compared to what you have to deal with.... You and your family are courageous. Keep on fighting, we stand with you.

·

Hi Mikey, and Bonnie,

Please accept my deepest apologies for this thoughtless and mean spirited email as it is by far worst of all the horrible emails you and Bonnie have received. I am sending you both my love and total acceptance of who you are and what you stand for.

I hear what you say and do, I accept what you say and do and I wrap that in my love and respect for your both.

Huge hugs

·

I can't believe this kind of cruelty:

I wish there were a way that I could sufficiently apologize for "Christian" bigotry and crass stupidity. Bonnie doesn't deserve this bullshit. You don't deserve this bullshit. I won't even comment that the writer must've flunked fourth grade grammar and can't read the acronym for the Foundation's name correctly. The love of my life lives every day with the ups and downs and uncertainties of relapsing-remitting MS. What this jackass doesn't know about living with chronic illness (or about being an inclusive and loving Christian) could fill all the scrolls of all the holy books ever written.

Again, I'm sooo sorry. If Bonnie has seen this, please tell her that one of her biggest fans apologizes to her, too.

Peace & Goodness

We the People
in Order to form
perfect Union,
Justice, insure
Tranquility,
common defence,
general
the Blessings of
do

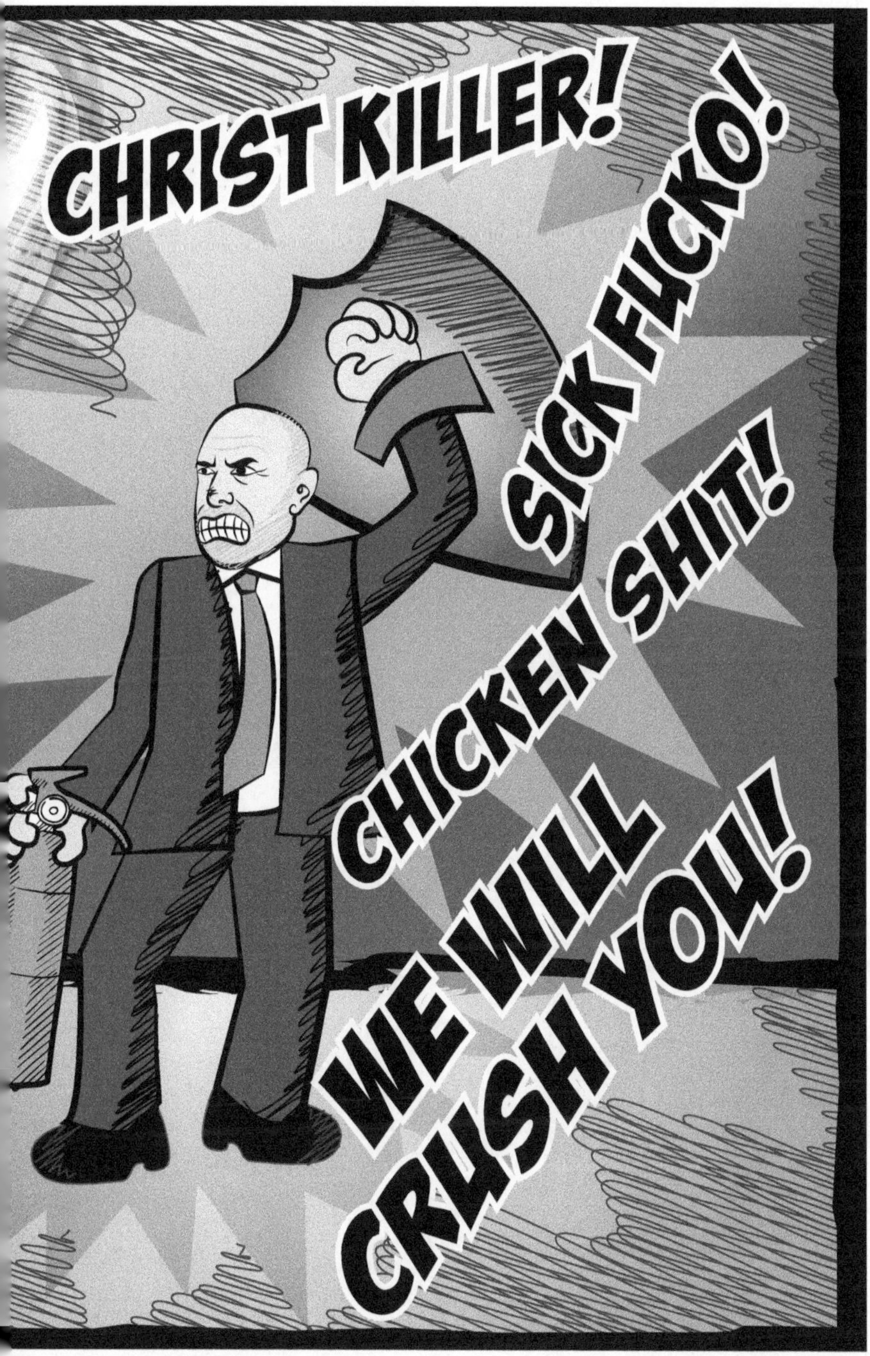
CHRIST KILLER!
SICK FUCKO!
CHICKEN SHIT!
WE WILL CRUSH YOU!

Attacking Mikey

THERE ARE LETTERS WHICH come in that attack my husband, and I am just stupefied at their hutzpah, Jewish speak for gall or gumption. I understand that people have differing views of the law, of the Constitution and its construing case law. That is their right, of course, to believe however they want to, but to personally attack someone with whom they disagree, is something else entirely. They are not attacking his actions on behalf of the foundation; they are attacking him, individually, and quite viciously so.

I thought I would take a moment here to give you a little insight into the Mikey I know.

My husband grew up in a military family, just like I did. He will tell you that he had a wonderful and idyllic childhood; a major portion of which was spent in Albuquerque, New Mexico. His family lived on-base, went to base schools, and Mike and his brothers had a safe and nurturing environment in which to grow up. Mike was in the sixth grade when his father got an assignment to the Pentagon in Washington DC. Alice and Gerry had not been back to the DC area since they left fourteen years before. Mike's mother, Alice, grew up in DC and still had lots of family there. There was not then and is still not today, military housing available when assigned to the Pentagon. Mike's parents purchased their very first home in Temple Hills, Maryland. Before the moving truck had left the driveway, a neighbor came over to introduce himself to Gerry. The very first thing this neighbor said was "Hi," followed by the question, "What religion are you?" The neighbor did not like the answer.

It was not a good neighborhood by any means but Gerry and Alice did not know that at the time they purchased the home. It was the only home they could afford in, what was even then, an expensive locale to live. Mike got into fights pretty much every day at school. He was always being attacked for being Jewish. If not for that, the local boys saw him as an intruder into their school and neighborhood. Mike never started the fights but always stood his ground. He knew that if he backed down the bullies would go after his brothers, and that was not acceptable to Mike.

The nation was rife with strife and it was particularly noticeable when Martin Luther King Jr. was shot. Rioting was happening in the schools and the streets. It was at that time in his life that Mike grew into one who would fight for others, and against the social inequities that he and others faced on a daily basis.

When my husband and I met years later, he had moved with his family to Lompoc, California, where his father was a missile launch officer at Vandenburg Air Force Base. Mike would go to high school there and get arrested for inciting a riot when he was one of the first to throw a rotten tomato at a neo-Nazi during a rally. He bought the tomato for five bucks and thought it was a very worthwhile purchase. It was at Lompoc High School that he faced continuing religious discrimination from those professing to be Christian. He and his brothers were the only Jews in the school. Mike was senior class president, his brother was junior class president, and his youngest brother was president of the freshman class. The kids tried their hardest to convert Mike. While in high school, he excelled in academics and tennis and was offered presidential nominations to all three military academies. We met during his fourth class year, freshman year, at the U.S. Air Force Academy, when as a sophomore in high school I took a girlfriend with me and drove up to the Academy to meet real men.

My husband has been from the very beginning of our relationship a great conversationalist. I was sixteen when we started dating, and I was altogether attracted to a man who could hold a conversation and had worldly opinions and views. His convictions were strong, and I loved that. He was the kind of person who would stand up for what was right and what he believed in. I thought that was very attractive. After a date, if he didn't have to get back to the Academy right away, we would talk about all kinds of things, and my world opened to others' views and opinions. The very first time I ever heard him speak publicly, I was blown away. He had graduated from McGeorge Law School and was invited back to be honored guest speaker at a dinner. He was, at the time, a White House lawyer for Ronald Reagan, and we were living in Burke, Virginia. It was also the first time we were treated as VIPs.

Before the dinner, I asked him if he had written his speech and he said no, that he did not know what he was going to talk about. I was just a little stunned at this but as they called him up to speak, he whispered to me, "I just realized what I am going to talk about." I thought that it was about time, but didn't have a chance to tell him as he was already up and on his way to the podium. His entire talk centered around not being able to sneeze while at the law school and he had everyone, including me, rolling on the floor with laughter. He received a standing ovation. I have never worried about him having to speak in public after that, which is really good as he has plenty of opportunities to do so. He never writes anything down, speaks totally extemporaneously, and always has the crowd in the palm of his hand. If ever given the opportunity to hear him speak, I would highly recommend that you do so.

Subject: Mickey sentenced to public execution

Dear Mr. Mickey Jewstein,

We have it on good authority that President Trump's national security team will soon have the MFRF dismantled and torn to the ground. In the first 100 days. You're days of Christ bashing in the armies are over jewboy.

You Mickey and your staff of jew commies and atheist and followers will be round up and tried fair for treason and sedition. There will be joy in the land! Mickey will be justly sentenced by President Trump for public execution to be televised international and all over the web. Trump himself will pull the hangman switch. Praise the Lord!

The MFRF supporters will be give life sentences at hard labor except your race traitor whore wife and diseased jew children.
They will be maid part of the servents staff at White house to clean and cook for the Trump family and wait on them. Hand and foot. Day and night year round.

We can't wait for the devine justice to come. Satan can't wait to welcome you home to the flames for the Second Death. Love the smell of jew flesh burning in the morning!

Sincerely,
American Leaders For Christ and Justice

✦✦✦

Subject: Mikey

"Reviled by the radical fundamentalist Christian far-right, Mikey has been given many names by his enemies including "Satan," "Satan's lawyer," "the Antichrist," "That Godless, Secular Leftist," "Antagonizer of All Christians," "Most Dangerous Man in America," and "Field General of the Godless Armies of Satan."

I prefer......Dip Shit.

(Name withheld)

Dear Dipshit,

You've got an odd taste in nick names. I would probably stick to (name withheld) if I were you. If you really need help coming up with something better, I'm sure we can help. There's really no need to out yourself as a dipshit when introducing yourself.

Blake A. Page
Military Religious Freedom Foundation
Special Assistant to the President
Director of US Army Affairs

·

I thought this was so funny; wit and humor are sometimes the best and only way to deal with this trash. The following letter is right out of our current reality, where politicians and certain members of society call anything they do not agree with "fake news."

·

Subject: Your whole Life is fake News

Mickey

you fight against Christians @ Fort Cambell who are trying to help the US military to bring peace to the world thru Christ.

everything you do is fake because our US Christians soldiers are peaceful and only want to share the glory of Christ.

when you die in shame your grave will say 'Here lies Mickey whose whole life was just fake news'.

we will throw a party to celebrate your dead and sending you to your place to burn in hell. It will hurt and you will scream til blood comes out of your mouth eyes and ears.

(Hell is not fake news as you will find out as soon as you die Mickey)

·

Dude,

- *Learn how to spell. Learning how to think is beyond you at the moment so start with spelling. Then try reading. I recommend the Bible. The Sermon on the Mount has its positive moments;*

- *After the rapture, may I have your car?*

- *Jesus is coming so look busy.*

- *Stop hating.*

Ambassador Joseph Wilson (USFS, ret.)

·

Mr. Wagoner,

The United States Constitution is not fake news. It prohibits our government or its representatives (which includes the military) from endorsing or promoting a religion (i.e., one of the countless versions of Christianity or any of the numerous other religions of the world). It is recommended that you read this original American establishment document and its Bill of Rights (especially the 1st Amendment) or consult a public school government teacher regarding the lawful significance.

Your diabolical diatribe reflects only on yourself indicating a shortage of self-esteem, radical religious indoctrination, and primitive tribalism. It has been my experience that any man who resorts to spewing hatred at fellow Americans does so because he cannot communicate with intelligence or integrity. Willful ignorance is difficult to dissuade when infected with apathy, acrimony & arrogance. However, we at the Military Religious Freedom Foundation endeavor to educate & enlighten.

Most Sincerely,

Brigadier General John Compere, US Army (Retired)
Disabled American Veteran (Vietnam)
Military Religious Freedom Foundation Advisory Board Member
Texas rancher
(Former member, 101st Airborne Division "Screaming Eagles,"
Fort Campbell, Kentucky)

Subject: Help make the world a better place

Consider shooting yourself in the face.

(Name withheld)

.

Dear (name withheld)—I'll need a tutorial. Maybe you could take point and show me how it's done yourself?

Blake A Page
Military Religious Freedom Foundation
Special Assistant to the President
Director of US Army Affairs

♦♦♦

Subject: Today os Hitlers Birthday

Happy Birthday to Hitler Mickey!

He did to the kikes who killed The Lamb what you do to the children of The Christ.

Don't get all self rightious and think your any better than Hitler.

Your not. Your worst than Hitler.

(Name withheld)

.

How many grammatical laws can a single bigot break in a 4-line email?

- *Spelling – a bigot's worst nightmare! Multiple instances*

- *The evil "your, you're" conundrum*

- *A new conundrum based on mispronunciation "worse vs. worst"*

- *Honorable Mentions: Reverse a surname and a first name when speaking to a person of American Nationality.*

Way to go Mr. Bigot! That computer screen may hide your face, but it doesn't hide that red neck!

A MRFF supporter

◆◆◆

Subject: One Religion?

Would you please tell Mikey to stop making shit up.

Thank you,

(Name withheld)

.

NO.

Blake A Page
Military Religious Freedom Foundation
Special Assistant to the President
Director of US Army Affairs

.

Hi (name withheld)—

Mikey has read your brief, curious email and shared it with me...and I feel compelled to ask, just what is it that Mikey or MRFF is doing that you consider "making shit up"? I'm happy to address any specifics you want to discuss... but your odd note is leaving me puzzled. To be sure, there are things that Mikey says that rile people up—he would agree that he is often very direct and undiplomatic. But the mere fact that some people don't like what he has to say, or what MRFF represents, doesn't mean that our position is not valid.

So please, let me know what you'd like to discuss and we'll have at it.

A MRFF ally

◆◆◆

Subject: Mikey

mikey WHINEstein IS AN ASSHOLE. GO FUCK YOURSELF WHINEstein

(Name withheld)

·

Hello, (name withheld)—

Thanks for your insightful and thought-provoking observations. The time that you took to articulate your position was well-spent, as it makes clear the depth of your intellect and the effort that you've extended to understand the complex issues in which the MRFF engages. However, I feel compelled to point out that the activity in which you've asked Mikey to engage is physically impossible; therefore, he will not be complying with your request. But feel free, as you deem appropriate, to continue with your own experimentation.

Peace,

Mike Challman
Christian, USAF veteran, MRFF supporter

·

Dear (name withheld),

I am writing in response to your email to the Military Religious Freedom Foundation ("MRFF"). As a volunteer for MRFF, I have had the privilege of responding to many emails received by MRFF. I usually explain the mission of MRFF; how it has assisted thousands of service members suffering from religious discrimination or persecution at the hands of their superiors; the legal requirements of the Establishment Clause, Article VI of the Constitution, military regulations, etc. I sometimes even mention that MRFF has received seven nominations for the Nobel Peace Prize.

Yet, I must admit I am at a loss as to how to respond to a scholar of such high caliber, as yourself. "WHINEstein"—pure genius! In all the years MRFF has been fighting to protect the Constitutional rights of the brave men and women in uniform who sacrifice so much to protect our rights, nobody has ever before come up that particular pun. It's funny because the word "whine" sounds like the beginning of his last name!

I also really enjoy your claim, "mikey WHINEstein IS AN ASSHOLE." It has a childlike, back-of-the-school-bus-taunt ring to it—something like, "I know you are, but what am I?" or "I'm rubber, you're glue." What a refreshing way to express a point!

These words are dripping with sarcasm, which I hope you are picking up because I'm laying it on pretty thick. Your email is nothing more than a juvenile tantrum. If you have an actual concern and would like to express it like an adult, I will be happy to address it. If you simply want to spout profanity or are looking for somebody's lunch money to steal, I suggest you look elsewhere.

Blessed be,

Tobanna Barker
MRFF Volunteer

♦♦♦

Subject: Ass Wipe weinsteins

Whenever we run short of toilet paper in the house my wife and I just print off some pictures of you and your little clan of weinstein Christ haters from the computer. Works great. Feel bad for the paper though.

Wishing you the damnation you all have coming Little Mikey Boy. Sleep well and wake up in hell.

V/R
Active Duty US Army and Proud of our Flag and our Savior

.

When I read this, my first thought was I hope they get a paper cut!

♦♦♦

Subject: WE HOPE YOU DIE

Mikey We Hope You Die

And that all your organs go into the bodies of American airmen who have been saved by our Lord Jesus Christ.

Your earthly form will then all be of Christ.

Your immortal sin-soaked soul will then be on fire with lucifer in hell forever.

And everyone will be happy.

Halleluyah! Stop attacking the faithful followers of The Only Son of Your God. Fall to your knees and beg the forgiveness MGEN Olson.

-with hatred and pity for weinstein the evil persecutor of Jesus The Christ;

Air Force Academy Graduates Who Live and Walk The Word of Christ

.

Every time the reunion comes up for the class of 1977 the foundation gets a rush of emails and phone calls harassing Mikey and myself. I have always told Mikey from very early on, that this was the work of a very few grads. In the beginning, Mikey did not believe me, but grads, they unfortunately are. So, I am not surprised when I see this low blow of an email. This is coming from a very small group of disturbed individuals who simply do not understand the rules and regulations and the constitution that they have sworn to protect and defend. Some just have a short circuit that they cannot and do not want to rewire. What is nice, and I point this out to my husband continuously, is the numbers of supporters he has that are grads, from all graduating class years. These grads and supporters value the cause and efforts, and for that and their complete show of support, I am grateful.

♦♦♦

Subject: I feel sorry for you!

I feel sorry for you! Why are you working so hard to keep people from talking about god and Jesus?
The only reason I see is that you are trying to push people away from praying and away from us talking about god.

People who worship satin try to push people away from god.

You should not have any say in how people worship. Everyone will judged by god for what they have done, and even the demons from hell know that.

(Name withheld)

.

Hi (name withheld),

Sorry, but you're a little confused. No one here is trying to keep people from talking about their beliefs. All we're doing is protecting the Constitution and the freedom of people in the military to believe as they choose. I'm sure you agree with that.

We're happy to support people in whatever they choose to believe and we support their right to pray as they choose, it just has to be done appropriately. I'm sure you wouldn't want someone requiring you to listen to an officer preaching about atheism or about Muhammad. In the same way some people don't want to have to be subjected to proselytizing in any form. That's why the Constitution establishes the separation of church and state, so everyone can believe and practice his or her belief in his own way.

I'm not sure what the "demons from hell know," but the Constitution says we can't force our own religious beliefs on other people. So that's all we say. Let everyone believe as they wish and don't try to push your belief on others. In the military, that's the rule. I hope that explains thing a little better for you.

By the way, we don't know anyone who worships "satin;" fabric is not a major concern of ours.

Best,

Mike Farrell
(MRFF Board of Advisors)

♦♦♦

Subject: Your cause

Dear Mickey:

Saw a photo of you recently. Apparently you haven't missed many meals. You seriously need to get into the gym bubba. And as an Academy grad (72) I gotta say you and your undoubtedly miserable ilk are an embarrassment to us all of us who graduated from the zoo.

Get a real life.

(Name withheld)

.

Hello, (name withheld)-

I just saw your email to Mikey (not Mickey) Weinstein. I also saw his very appropriate reply to your idiotic personal attack. Like you, I'm a USAFA grad ('85). As such, I feel compelled to say that the efforts of Mikey and the MRFF are not an "embarrassment to us all of us [sic] who graduated from the zoo." In fact, I know many grads who support the efforts of MRFF. At times, I wish more of them would be more public in their support, but then I see cretinous missives such as yours, replete with its poor punctuation, grammar, and syntax, and I understand why some of our fellow grads may be reticent to expose themselves to the sort of vitriol that you so ignorantly spew. That's not me, though.

I'm proud to stand very publicly with Mikey Weinstein and the other good people who support the MRFF. I won't deny that Mikey can be strident, undiplomatic, and unapologetically demanding at times. But I also find him to be an honorable and courageous man who has willingly devoted himself to an important fight, even though it often brings fools like you out of the woodwork to attack him. I'm also quite happy to suggest that, in my view, your immature note reveals you to be a bit of a douche.

Peace,

Mike Challman
Christian, USAFA graduate, MRFF supporter

Frankly I really do NOT care what you think. And to say you are a Christian and that you support this fat, anger filled clown is illogical and an oxymoron. The emphasis should be on moron; and clearly the moron is you.

Go about your miserable conflicted life with the contempt of most of your fellow grads. Do you seriously think most of us support your sad cause? Get real.

We had jerks in every class and clearly the two of you fit that description. Glad I didn't have to serve with fools such as you. And I suspect that you had less than an illustrious career.

(Name withheld)

·

Dear (name withhled),

Wow, you are one angry, angry man and I pity you for that… although I do appreciate the verification that you are, indeed, a douche.

Peace,

Mike

·

Your note to my dad

Dear (name withheld),

I won't waste much time on you. It must be so frustrating for you to have so little power and influence that you have to hide behind your little email and send off trollish notes to people who are making an actual difference and impact in the world. It brings me so much joy to know we're pissing you and your ilk off so much—you made my day!

Casey Weinstein
Class of 2004

·

Dear Stein:

Actually I could not care less about you and your vile Dad- a person who spends his life trying to trash others. What a role model he is for you.

And actually you are not pissing me. I would have to care what you think to be pissed off.

You must be a great officer. Probably always on the lookout to try and hurt someone who espouses religious faith. I pity the poor folks who have to work with you.

In the final analysis know this-most grads loathe your Dad. Whatever you think nothing can change that.

(Name withheld)

.

Dear (name withheld),

Well how about this (name withheld)? I'm Mikey's other son and an active duty Captain. I'll be at USAFA tomorrow all-day walking around the cadet area while proudly wearing my A-jacket with my last name on it. Why don't you or anyone of your classmates come say this stupid shit to my face and prove you're more than just a scared, sad little man who hides behind his keyboard. I stand up for my family and friends and my beliefs…. I got that from my role model AKA my dad. See you tomorrow.

Curtis Weinstein
Class of 2007

.

I am so proud of my sons. They have grown up to be beautiful and caring individuals.

.

Dear (name withheld),

I have seen the email traffic concerning you and your statements concerning Mikey (not Mickey) and the MRFF. What bothers me enough to write to you is the fact that you are a fellow graduate. I would expect a higher standard from you than I see from the ignorant, uneducated, so called Christians that normally slander and debase a truly good and caring man. If you saw one hundredth of the hateful anti-Semitic filth that Mikey gets sent every day you might have chosen your words more carefully. It sometimes causes this incredibly intelligent man to react and say something without thinking it through, which is what I expect was the case here. So I too will have to throw in my two cents worth.

So you know where I'm coming from, I am a member of the class of 1977, a History Major (you will see why I mention that later), and admittedly a good friend of Mikey (actually he is my brother). I served 21 years on active duty, most of it flying MC-130's. I retired to continue flying airplanes instead of a desk.

I think my good friend and brother (name withheld) said it all but I'll try as he did to correct the misunderstanding you and so many others have concerning the efforts the MRFF makes on behalf of all men and women in uniform.

A person's religious belief should be and is protected in this great country of ours. However, when an officer or NCO of higher rank uses their rank or command position to force ANY kind of personal religious beliefs or attitudes on a subordinate or uses it to judge a subordinate's performance and consider it for advancement, it is against regulations, but more to the point, it is just plain wrong. That in a nutshell is what the MRFF is trying to stop. You should be a whole-hearted supporter not a detractor.

Our Founding Fathers whom you invoked in one of your emails recognized the danger of state sponsored (or "correct") religion and ensured we were protected from it. They were of many different denominations, and Benjamin Franklin was actually a Deist. The MRFF is fully in support of this protection and is trying to keep a growing, frightening brand of Evangelical (?), Dominionist (?) Christianity from eroding the strength of the US Military. History has shown how truly dangerous a force like this can be. Current events are confirming it.

I truly hope you will re-examine your heart, your faith, and your thoughts on this. Reconciliation and forgiveness are most certainly Judeo-Christian beliefs. Maybe you and Mikey could exchange a new set of emails.

Sincerely

USAFA Graduate and MRFF supporter

PS. I have always thought personal attacks are childish, but to set the record straight, Bart Simpson is taller than Mikey and has a LOT more hair.........

♦♦♦

Subject: your wife and daughter

Yo, Mikey.

Your wife was really good in bed last night.

But not as good as your daughter 2 nights ago.

When they say that all Weinsteins are fucking sluts they're wrong.

They're ROCK STAR fucking sluts.

Keep up the great work keeping Jesus out of the armed services.

I'm so proud of you, your family and the MRFF.

See you all real soon.

love,

The Devil

.

Dear "Devil"—

I've had the privilege of answering many hate-filled letters received by Mikey Weinstein and the Military Religious Freedom Foundation. I must admit, I have to give you points for creativity (and grammar). Unfortunately, a bit of artistic license and a basic grasp of the English language do not make you any less ignorant or your life any less sad.

Trust me when I say that if you ever actually encountered Mikey's wife or daughters, the only thing you would be doing would be taking notes as they blew your mind with their incredible intelligence, bravery, and integrity.

I usually respond to the emails received by MRFF by explaining our mission and the mandates of the Constitution, but I won't bother. I somehow doubt you would understand. After all, I can't help but notice that you don't express any actual thoughts or discernible arguments. While you took the time to write something fairly creative, you may as well have simply written "Shut up" or some other common line from any pre-teen tantrum.

Just note that if you want to play games, you should find a different outlet— the Weinsteins are way out of your league.

Blessed be,

Tobanna Barker
MRFF Legal Affairs Coordinator

◆◆◆

Subject: Today

Mikey your a moron. You are a tabloid whore. No ones forcing anyone to pray you idiot. Reaching yet again .

(Name withheld)

.

Dear (name withheld),

When calling someone an idiot, it's generally best to make an attempt at spellchecking. When composing an argument, it's best to support your thesis with evidence.

Cheers,

Blake A. Page
Military Religious Freedom Foundation
Special Assistant to the President
Director of US Army Affairs

♦♦♦

Subject: Dispicable Mikey

Dispicable Mikey

(Name withheld)

·

Name withheld-

After going to all the trouble of sending a 2-word, 'subject' only e-mail to Mikey (akin to spitting at someone as you drive by at 60 mph)...Is that your concept of "substantive discussions"?

Not only are MRFF's points valid, the American legal system has upheld them repeatedly through the decades because those 'points' whether made by Mikey & MRFF or others in the past are all based on our only primary founding document; the US Constitution.

Now, if you want a 'substantive discussion' (which you might have had the courage & courtesy of addressing to Mikey in your initial e-mail) that can be had. Before you reply though, kindly read this essay by a former USAF chaplain, M.S.I. Morton—"End Run" which addresses the 'Tebow' exhibitionist behavior at AFA football games and why it's not just wrong but unconstitutional as well—I'm presuming that, due to the timing of your initial e-mail, that's what's bugging you.

If you have substantive remarks after reading it, or have substantive other issues, I'll do my best to address them.

Oh, and kindly,

Marshalldoc

♦♦♦

Subject: Mikey Winstein

He's an embarrassment to our nation and disgraces our military.

(Name withheld)

(name withheld), are you referring to the honors graduate of the Air Force Academy, two-time author, multi-year Nobel Prize nominee and recipient of dozens of honors and awards from various organizations? If an accomplished civil rights activist is an "embarrassment" and "disgrace", exactly what the hell are you?

Dustin Chalker
MRFF Advisor

I already apologized to Mikey for my brash words. I may disagree with many of his stances but I had no right to attack him. That was not a Response that I'm proud of. Thank you for your reply and I deserve to be reprimanded for my rudeness. God bless and have a pleasant weekend.

(Name withheld)

♦♦♦

Subject: Jesus is a Marine

I am the wife of a U.S. marine. Leave the marines alone to pray with Jesus as we all see fit. You are awful terrible man. I hope you just drop dead and nobody comes to your funeal. I hope your wife and children cries their eyes out until they shake and faint. Read about them all. Because no marine ever will mourn for you mikey. 'Semper Fi" means loyalty to the flag and to our Lord and Savior.

Not to a atheist. And no to a hateful liberal. And a pretend jew. Go back to israel and be a commie Christ hater there.

Wow, this is scary crap. A marine, really? Oh, my lord.

Good Afternoon, (Name withheld) -
Before getting to anything else, I want to thank you and your husband for your military service. As a veteran, husband, and father myself, I know very

well that when the husband serves, the whole family serves and that everyone must make sacrifices. I want you to know that I appreciate all that your entire family does to help keep American safe and secure.

Thanks, too, for taking the time to write to the MRFF and express your concerns... although I do wish the tone of your note had not been so nasty and hateful. Like you, I am a Christian and I don't believe that we represent our faith well when we say the types of things that you conveyed in your email. But I would like to chalk that up to human frailty on your part and would hope that in retrospect you can agree that such barbs are decidedly un-Christian. I realize that some in the conservative media misrepresent both the MRFF generally and Mikey Weinstein specifically as being anti-Christian atheists. That is not the truth. In fact, the vast majority (more than 9 in 10) of MRFF supporters and clients are people of faith, mostly Christians.

So why is it, you may ask, that the MRFF raised a concern about the manner in which the "Prayerful Leadership" talk at Quantico has been publicized? Simply put, the manner in which it was done gave the invitation a clear imprimatur and endorsement from the Commanding General, and that is inappropriate. Now, it may be that the effort was well-intended, but good intentions don't always mean appropriate Constitutional behavior. This sort of communication should have come from the Chaplaincy and not from the office of the CG. That is the entire basis for the MRFF objection—we are not speaking out against Christianity and we are not challenging the individual beliefs of any Marine. We are only challenging what I think is an obvious Constitutional misstep on the part of the CG; allowing her position to be used as a 'seal of approval' for a sectarian religious event.

Lastly, regarding the subject line of your email—No ma'am, Jesus is not a Marine, nor are all Marines Christian. The Marine Corps ranks include many good, honorable, brave men and women of all manner of belief (including non-belief). To suggest that the beliefs of Christians are entitled to preferential treatment over all other beliefs and non-belief is a slap in the face of every non-Christian Marine, both active duty and veteran.

The position of the MRFF is that all members of the military, both Christian and non-Christian, believer and non-believer, is equally entitled to live and work in an environment that does not give preference to any particular *sectarian religious belief... not even my own beloved Christianity. That is the basis of one of the most fundamental rights of all Americans.*

Respecting the rights of those who don't share our beliefs doesn't make us worse Christians—it makes us better Americans and better military members. I wish you, your husband, and your entire family a long and healthy life.

Peace,

Mike Challman
Christian, USAF veteran, MRFF supporter

◆◆◆

Subject: Fot Mickey Weinstein an opinion of your opinion

I won't belabor you with my beliefs or attack yours. I just want you to know that in my opinion you are a disgrace to the thousands of military officers that have gone before you and millions of enlisted people who have loyally served this nation. Many of these people perished so that you could spout your garbage. You should be ashamed and pay back the education that you received free from this country. You have used your education to bring harm to good upstanding people who happen to wear the uniform of this nation.

Mickey as far as my research has shown and in my biased opinion you have demonstrated that you are total jerk and unworthy of the gifts this nation has given you. Shame on you!

(Name withheld)

Dear (Name withheld), thanks for the reasonably civil, albeit non-specific, letter to the MRFF. I occasionally answer letters for the MRFF in addition to helping defend your right to write and express your opinion. I've been doing the former for about twelve years and the latter for over thirty. I think that would probably put me into the group of "thousands of military officers...who have loyally served this nation" you mention below.

While I'm certain there are long-serving, loyal officers and enlisted that may disagree with Mr. Weinstein and the MRFF, I'm not one of them. I met Mikey about a dozen years ago when the US Air Force Academy, through its own internal survey, discovered a problem with wide-spread, unwelcome religious proselytizing within the Cadet Wing, faculty, and staff. Both Mr. Weinstein's offspring and mine experienced that bigotry first hand, greatly affecting their cadet experience and their desire to serve after graduation—in a negative fashion. Mr. Weinstein formed the MRFF to combat these egregious efforts by THOUSANDS of self-proclaimed loyal officers and enlisted personnel to turn the US military into their own religious baptismal pond of like-minded believers. These same airmen (as well as soldiers, sailors, Marines, and coasties in the other services) thought that one simply could not serve the nation patriotically without being their kind of Christian (and you'd have to ask them what that entails—but it's not Catholic, LDS, or Eastern/Russian Orthodox, I know that) and they made that clear to their subordinates. Promotions, choice assignments, and advanced schooling were contingent on 'getting along' with the right kind of Christians. Evaluations favored those of similar religious belief even though private religious or political belief should have no bearing on job performance or evaluation.

Through the MRFF's tireless efforts, policies have slowing been shifting. The Air Force published it's instruction 1-1 clearly delineating what commanders could and couldn't do with respect to religion in the workplace. It set definitive boundaries on proselytization within the Air Force while affirming the rights of all airmen to practice their religion in their free/private time—so long as it did not infringe on the rights of all other airmen to maintain their own beliefs—or lack thereof.

Since that time, the MRFF has steadfastly urged, cajoled, and filed suit in order to force the Dept of Defense to OBSERVE ITS OWN RULES. That would seem easy, but it's not—precisely because there are so many out there that think that Evangelical, Fundamentalist Christianity is a necessary and sufficient condition for honorable service in the US military. You and I, however, both know that that is completely counter to the US Constitution which states that there should be no religious test for holding a position within the government—nor can the government establish or promote a specific religious perspective.

That's Mikey's battle and the MRFF's as well. It's my battle. Some people think I'm a jerk. Some people think Mikey's a jerk. I can live with that, and so can he. But the fact remains that he's also a very courageous jerk, completely committed to defending the rights of those that defend yours. I'm glad he's a jerk about that and THOUSANDS of officers and enlisted in our military, currently serving to defend you, feel the same way. That's why they're clients of the MRFF and active supporters of the MRFF cause. They've lived the threat first-hand and need the MRFF's help to make our military stronger, more inclusive, and more effective for our nation.

Pay back the nation for his education and the 'gifts' that he's received? He's doing that every day in ways, and at costs, you can't imagine, by defending my rights and those of my fellow airmen. I'd like to think you would support him for that as you would support an active duty officer like myself. But then I'm probably wrong because I'm a jerk who all too often expects the best of people, not the worst.

A Senior Air Force Officer and Service Academy Graduate

◆◆◆

Subject: Fuck you weinstien

Air Force is right to put God in the oath. mikey weinstien is wrong to even still be breething. Air force should save a bomb from dropping on ISIS and drop it on mikey.

(Name withheld)

.

Dear Coward (for using a fake address)

Your use of the language is a tribute to the home schooling to which you apparently didn't pay much attention. There's something called the Constitution of the United States of America you might want to check out, just for laughs. Even the Air Force is trying to figure out a way to resolve this problem, and they intend to fix it without the use of violence, an idea that was promoted in the Ten Commandments. You might want to check them out, too.

Mike Farrell
(MRFF Board of Advisors)

Subject: For "Mikey" the FUCKING LITTLE RAT Shitstain

Weinstein-HAHAHA they finally laughed you out of the house. Nice to see you OUTSIDE the temple pissing and wailing and having no effect any longer. Much like the rest of your inbred cabal, eh? Not doing so well this year? HAHAHA. Your whines are delicious as is your frustration you fucking mutt. NOW you DO have the permission of We The People to FUCK OFF YOU LITTLE RAT BITCH. -NEXT!

.

Dear (Name withheld)

I am writing in response to your email to the Military Religious Freedom Foundation ("MRFF"). I would have addressed this response to you by name, but you were apparently too ashamed of your own words to include it. Please note that I have included mine, as I make it a point to put my name on anything I say.

While I respond to many of the letters MRFF receives, I must admit that the meaning of your email escapes me—we have not been laughed out of any place, nor are we wailing, whining, or frustrated. Further, we have had a very successful year protecting the religious freedom of all soldiers, sailors, airmen, Marines, cadets, and veterans. I am disappointed you are so ignorant of our mission and our progress in pursuing it.

Not only will we not "fuck off" (with or without your permission, which nobody needs), we are not going anywhere. The whines you claim to hear belong to you and your fellow ill-informed "Christians," who care nothing for the constitutional rights of our brave men and women in uniform, as we prepare to fight harder and stronger than ever.

NEXT!!

Blessed be,

Tobanna Barker
MRFF Legal Affairs Coordinator

Subject: business

Dear Mikey

Stop overstepping your bounds and making calls on things that are just not your business. I'm not sure who appointed you judge and jury on matters of God but I can tell you that one day you will stand before that God and have to make account. This is in reference to the historical display that has a flag, appropriate for the display, with the account of a war hero Chaplin. Leave it alone. It truly is non of your business.

Kind Regards,

(Name withheld)
Vietnam Vet

.

(Name withheld), the facts of that display are apparently totally fictitious... thus, it is VERY much our business, (Name withheld)...thx...

Mikey Weinstein

.

Hi (Name withheld),

I suspect it is our business. Maybe you should mind your own. Our business is to support the separation of church and state. In so doing, we protect the right of you and all other members of the military to enjoy the freedom to believe as each of you chooses.

If you'll look at the record, rather than buying the line some zealot pushes on you, you'll find that the organization responsible for the display not only recognized that the story attempting to justify the flag's presence was false, it was moved to take down that part of the display. That left a flag, which was clearly not the flag it had been purported to be, implicitly promoting one particular faith over all others, a violation of our Constitution, our laws and our military regulations.

Contrary to your assertion, it is not "appropriate for the display," which brings to mind a question for you: what if it was a flag representing the Jewish faith, the Muslim faith or some other belief system? Would you have been sending us a message condemning us for calling for its removal? Somehow I doubt it. I suspect someone has gotten you excited by suggesting that your particular ox has been gored. Well, it hasn't. You've been misled.

For the record, we are people of many different faiths and belief systems, so your admonition about our standing one day "before that God and hav(ing) to make account" assumes a great deal. But let me not bother you with the details because you seem to think you've found the answer for everyone.

Be assured that we are perfectly happy for you to embrace the belief of your choice. We are not, however, willing to let you or those responsible for that display, or for that matter the officer in charge at that base, condone the unlawful promotion of one particular belief system over others without being challenged. That's our business.

Best,

Mike Farrell
(MRFF Board of Advisors)

♦♦♦

Subject: unhappy new year to Mickey

You are a disgrace to your country Mickey. You do not Make America Great Again.

You and your liberal minions only hate Jesus Christ and Make America Weak s Again.

You are cancer to the soldiers and aid for abet the muslim and N. korean hordes.

Our President Trump will wipe you mrff and mueller off the face of the earth.

.

Here is a prime example of another coward spouting off under a fake email address. Some of the email addresses and names they use for their email are comical, one could say almost creative, but this one is just fake. As many of these that we get, and we get thousands, they never overshadow the nice ones. Those are always so delightful to receive.

Still, I am shocked at what some people think a president of the United States has the power to do. I guess they skipped one too many civics classes. There is also the borderline illiteracy that one cannot help but note. I guess they skipped English and writing altogether. Then there is being able to create a cogent argument.... Okay, I'll stop!

♦♦♦

The following gets points for creativity but loses a lot for the anti-Semitism.

.

Subject: One Million Dollar Offer to Mr. Weinstein
To: Mr. Michael L. "Mikey" Weinstein, Esq., Executive Director of the Military Religious Freedom Foundation (MRFF):

Our worldwide Christian mission organization is prepared to personally offer you $1,000,000.00 in cash at this present time.

There are 2 nonnegotiable preconditions for your acceptance of this official offer:

(1) You immediately and permanently disband and otherwise terminate the MRFF and forever cease your reign of terror against the followers of Jesus Christ in the U.S. military and at all other locations.
(2) You submit yourself in good faith to a 12 week in-residence course of individualized Christian study and worship to be conducted by our Mens Education Group and which has been especially tailored for your current state of apostatic personal opposition to The Word and The Truth.

Please do not respond via e-mail to the address above as it is not designed for such replies.

We ask you to provide for some serious personal time for private prayer and thought to our bona fide offer.

We will contact you via telephone within the next two to-three weeks to discuss this matter and receive your answer.

thank you, Mr. Weinstein.
In The Name of Our Lord and Savior Jesus Christ

Dear Mission,

I know you said not to respond by email, but since you don't have my phone number I thought it best to approach you this way. Please forgive me if this is considered sinful.

As I am not the Executive Director of the MRFF but only a lowly member of its Board of Advisors, I realize the offer you made to Mikey was not intended for those of us lower on the totem pole. However, given the generosity of your offer to Mikey, I can't help but ask what it would be worth to you if I was interested in entertaining (which, by the way, I do for a living) such an offer.

Here's my thought:
Per nonnegotiable precondition #1, while I don't have the power to "permanently disband and otherwise terminate the MRFF", I can pretty much guarantee to put an end to their "reign of terror against the followers of Jesus Christ in the military and at all other locations."

That's a snap. First of all, they don't rain terror at "other locations". They only direct their attention to the US Military. Second, they really don't "rain terror" anywhere. They just expose hypocrisy, which we all know Jesus wasn't fond of either, and protect the U.S. Constitution. Now, you and I both know the US Constitution wasn't around yet when Jesus was here, but I'm pretty sure he would approve of what it says.

Per nonnegotiable precondition #2, I'm way ahead of you. I already "submit(ted) (my)self in good faith (and a lot of fear) to" way more than twelve weeks, in fact many years of an "in-residence course of individualized Christian study and worship (assuming Catholic counts)." I'll admit it wasn't at the hands of your Mens Education Group, but I can't imagine they're any tougher than Father O'Riley or Father O'Callaghan, and believe you me, those guys were "especially tailored to (deal with my) apo static state of personal opposition to The Word and The Truth." In fact they were determined to use the fear of hell to steer me away from any damned thing that felt good.

So, what do you think? Any chance you might be interested in putting up say a couple of hundred K for the scalp of an MRFF minion that you can hang on your belt?

Let me know. I guess you can't just call me, but Mikey has my number.

Blessings,

Mike Farrell
(MRFF Board of Advisors)

.

Mission Impossible

Your mission Mikey, should you choose to accept it, will be to turn yourself over to be brainwashed in the Evangelical Fundamental Dominionist religion for a term of twelve weeks in lieu of payment in the amount of one million dollars.

As always, should you or any of the MRFF be caught or killed, the Secretary will disavow any knowledge of your actions. This email will self-destruct in five seconds. Good luck, Mikey.

.

Tell them I'll stop answering your e-mails for $250,000.

.

WOWWWWW.

.

They must think it's all about money for you. Cause, ya know, you're Jewish.

.

Wow! I wonder if the option to just partake pre-condition #2 for $999,999.00 is an option?

.

Mikey, This is Unbelievable! This ignorance would be hilarious if it wasn't so frightening. You hang tough my brother! Believe me brother, it makes me sick to my stomach... It is as if they believe they can buy me off as some sort of cheap whore for thirty pieces of silver... Do you understand what I mean? —Mikey

Hey Mikey, Mind if I pretend I'm you for oh say 12 weeks?

...well, this is a brand new approach at least!! ...just can't wait for their promised call...not gonna hold my breath...   :) —Mikey

As you can tell, everyone had fun with this one! I give you a love note to go.

Hey, Mikey -

There are SO many races here that I don't have a dog in, but I am so happy to have this window you provide thru which to peep, to see your good work, in all its pain and passion. I weirdly feel a sense of pride and espirit de corps, vicarious as it were, thru your fierce determinism, patriotism and your thoughtful (thoughtless?) willingness to throw yourself in front of oppression, usually massive in scale, in defense of the little guy.

I am so proud of my association with you and your organization. Surely you already have an awareness but let me reinforce my presumption by saying you positively impact so many more people, like myself for example, than those many whom you so effectively directly advocate.

You, your efforts and basic humanism makes ME a better person and encourages hope and solidarity of a sort, in my existential pursuits of progressive advance my own local sphere of influence.

Hmm. That was a tad sappy, but I'm pretty sure you get it.

Cheers!

Prayer

I CANNOT SAY THAT I have been called upon to talk about or discuss praying much. I always thought of prayers as deeply personal and none of anyone else's business. So, I am finding the introduction to this chapter very difficult.

Today, when people in a position of power give "thoughts and prayers" in response to the horrific deeds and actions of disturbed individuals, I think, well, that is nice. But when that's all they give, instead of enacting new laws to prevent further horrific events, I'm completely disgusted. How dare they! Thoughts and prayers, my ass. Okay, you can tell this situation bothers me a great deal. These people whom we have elected to office to get things done sit and do nothing and hide behind what in this case are belittling words, "thoughts and prayers."

The time has come to move beyond thoughts and prayers and strive towards action and results in order to keep this nation of ours what it is supposed to be; democratic and secular. Prayers such as you are about to read lead us down a very divisive and destructive path.

♦♦♦

Subject: Our prayer for the air force flier

We pray thee Lord Jesus that you protect Major (Name withheld) from the darkness of the grip of the evildoers.

Mickey Weistein and his followers are from Satan. And we pray Thee Lord Jesus to oppose his evil plans to erase Your Word from the Air Force.

Lord Jesus we pray Thee to take his possessions and treasures. Pray Thee take his family. We pray Thee to erase his evil powers from the Dark One over the Air Force.

Lord Jesus we pray you to throw his evil wife and evil children into an early grave for they do not know You as Lord. Consign them to hell eternal.

Lord Jesus bring the just suffering of the Ages to this evil man of Satan. For he is only a man and you are our Lord and Son of Man.

May Mickeys' tears and shouts of sorrow for his losses be endless. May he be destroyed of all happiness and family and friends and future. May he cut himself and bleed out with knives.

May You drive him into the pits of hell with his evil family to burn eternal. May they're never-ending screams be testament to your Holy Sovereinitty.

Haleluyah! We pray this in Your Holy Name.

Jesus Christ the Redeemer.

Jesus Christ Lord and Savior.

Jesus Christ The Word Become Flesh.

(Name withheld)

.

Dear (name withheld)

I am writing in response to your email to Mikey Weinstein. I have had the privilege of responding to many emails received by Mikey - most of which are written by people, such as yourself, who are terribly mistaken regarding the mission of the Military Religious Freedom Foundation (MRFF).

I was excited to respond to your email. I couldn't wait to tell you that the mission of MRFF is to defend and ensure the religious freedom of all soldiers, sailors, airmen, Marines, cadets, and veterans. I thought about how I would enlighten you by explaining that over 96% of MRFF's clients are actually Christians who reached out to MRFF for assistance when they suffered religious discrimination. Frankly, I wanted to give you a detailed education about MRFF, its work, its clients, and its accomplishments.

Then, I sat down to actually write this response and I took the time to read your email again. After a second opportunity to read your hateful words, my only response is this:

How dare you?!

How dare you pretend to be any sort of Christian after praying to Jesus to cause such suffering?!

How dare you wish harm on someone who works selflessly for the rights of others?!

How dare you believe that Jesus or any other deity would take instructions from such an ignorant, narcissistic hypocrite as you?!

Blessed be,

Tobanna Barker
MRFF Legal Affairs Coordinator

.

Dear (name withheld),

Your email is taking my name in vain because I never told you to pray this hateful, vengeful prayer to me. I came into the world to show you the love of the Father and bring you a new covenant and way of life.

"You shall not take the name of the Lord your God in vain, for the Lord will not hold him guiltless who takes his name in vain." Exodus 20:7, Deuteronomy 5:11

"But I say unto you, that every idle word that men shall speak, they shall give account thereof in the day of judgment. For by thy words thou shalt be justified, and by thy words thou shalt be condemned." Matthew 5:36-37

"Be not deceived; God is not mocked: for whatsoever a man soweth, that shall he also reap." Galatians 6:7

"Ye have heard that it hath been said, Thou shalt love thy neighbour, and hate thine enemy. But I say unto you, Love your enemies, bless them that curse you, do good to them that hate you, and pray for them which despitefully use you, and persecute you; That ye may be the children of your Father which is in heaven: for he maketh his sun to rise on the evil and on the good, and sendeth rain on the just and on the unjust. For if ye love them which love you, what reward have ye? do not even the publicans the same? And if ye salute your brethren only, what do ye more than others? do not even the publicans so?" Matthew 5:43-48

"And when his disciples James and John saw this, they said, Lord, wilt thou that we command fire to come down from heaven, and consume them, even as Elias did? But he turned, and rebuked them, and said, Ye know not what manner of spirit ye are of." Luke 9:54-55

Are you following my word or giving me a to-do list against my very own teachings? Are you asking me to kill Mikey like James and John wanted me to rain down fire and kill the Samaritans? You are not aware what an evil spiritand disposition you are of; how much there is of pride, and passion, and personal revenge, covered under this pretense of zeal for me.

"But those things which proceed out of the mouth come forth from the heart; and they defile the man. For out of the heart proceed evil thoughts, murders, adulteries, fornications, thefts, false witness, blasphemies." Matthew 15:18-19

Your email address says "abundantlovofchrist." You do not have my abundant love in your heart. If you did you would pray for your enemies and obey my commandment to love your neighbor as yourself.

You also lack "the fruit of the spirit which is love, joy, peace, longsuffering, gentleness, goodness, faith, Meekness, temperance: against such there is no law." Galatians 5:22-23

I told you "Judge not, and ye shall not be judged: condemn not, and ye shall not be condemned: forgive, and ye shall be forgiven." Luke 6:37

You have judged and condemned Mikey and his family and have the audacity to ask me to kill them for you. An evil spirit abides in you and there is no room in your heart for my Spirit.

"Not everyone that saith unto me, Lord, Lord, shall enter into the kingdom of heaven; but he that doeth the will of my Father which is in heaven. Many will say to me in that day, Lord, Lord, have we not prophesied in thy name? and in thy name have cast out devils? and in thy name done many wonderful works? And then will I profess unto them, I never knew you: depart from me, ye that work iniquity." Matthew 7:21-23

I'll see you at my Judgment Seat. You are not guiltless.

Jesus

♦♦♦

Subject: leave

If you morons don't want Christians praying in America why don't you pack your bags and move to some country you do like and leave us alone ! you stupid liberal, anti Christian, anti American mother fuckers are destroying our country

GET THE FUCK OUT !

.

Hi (Name withheld),

The only morons in this exchange are those making accusations that betray their inability to comprehend the issue at hand. You qualify.

No one here opposes "Christians praying in America." No one here dislikes America. No one here intends on leaving the country. Our work is to defend the country and its citizens from people who want to insist their own particular belief system on everyone else.

The America we support is the America the founders intended and the one

the laws have strengthened, the one that says real Americans believe what they choose to believe and practice it appropriately.

Some of the more imbecilic among the citizenry, however, seem to think their religion is the only belief system that matters and that anyone who holds that the law, like the one that allows for freedom of religious or non-religious belief, should be obeyed as prescribed, can and should be condemned as "stupid liberal, anti Christian, anti American mother fuckers." Again, you qualify.

So, let's add up the score: Moron? You qualify. Imbecile? You qualify. Lunatic who rants on stupidly, grossly mislabeling people he neither knows nor understands? You qualify.

Congratulations!

Mike Farrell
(MRFF Board of Advisors)

◆◆◆

Subject: Pray for Weinstein's wife and daughters

Dear Mr. Michael Weinstein,

It seems that you and your "crucify Jesus as many times as possible" followers at the MFFFR don't like the rape prevention program put on by the Army at the Red Stone Army base in Alabama. Apparently the mere mention of faith in "Jesus" and his healing Grace as being the only reasonable cure for rape is just a little too much for the anti-Christian and anti-American likes of you and your liberal Obummer loving groupies. How dare you try to take Christ out of the Army's anti-rape program you evil leftist. Atheist filth.

We just pray that your wife and daughters get ass raped hard and often and then let us see what you say. Shall we Michael? You will come begging on hands and knees for Jesus to make them whole. But it will be too late You deserve the flames of hell and you will get them. So do your wife and daughters. Do not reply as noone here wants to hear the lies of Satan from your cursed lips.

signed,

.

What a miserable, horrible person this is. This so-called "Walking with the Lord Jesus" makes me want to throw up, seriously.

.

Dear "Bible Believing Americans, Walking With The Lord Jesus"—

I asked Mikey Weinstein to allow me to respond to your email to him and he generously granted my request.

Please note that I placed the name of your "group" in quote marks above. This is sarcasm, as the content of your email makes it clear that you have neither read the Bible, nor follow the teachings of Jesus Christ. Additionally, I suspect that your email is not truly from any group, but is instead the disgusting rant of a single, lonely, and sadly misguided individual. The obviously fake email address was sort of a giveaway.

Regarding the Sexual Harassment/Assault Response & Prevention ("SHARP") Training Program that took place in Redstone, you claim that it is "too much" for MRFF to accept the "mere mention of faith in Jesus...as being the only reasonable cure for rape." As an initial matter, you should know that there is no "cure" for rape—it is an intentional, violent act with an immeasurable impact on the victim and it can never be forgotten or "cured."

That said, you are correct—we have a major problem with teaching service members that the ONLY way to survive and recover from sexual assault is to accept Christ or any other deity or religion. Not only was the presentation an unconstitutional endorsement of Christianity over other religions, or no religion, it demonstrated an utter disregard for the needs of sexual assault victims within the military.

While many victims have relied on Christianity to relieve their suffering, many others found strength from other religions, therapy, pursuing criminal or civil charges, or a variety of other options. Each of these choices is valid and each should be included in a training program designed to both prevent assault and assist victims who have already suffered from such assault.

To teach that accepting Christianity is the only suitable way to recover from assault implies that non-Christian victims are undeserving of such recovery. This is not only false and insulting, it takes advantage of people suffering as the result of a violent act committed upon them to further an agenda of converting our military into a military for Christ, rather than a military devoted to defending the Constitution. While MRFF recognizes and appreciates that Christianity has assisted some victims in their recovery, we refuse to allow any religion to be forced upon all victims as their only option.

You ask, "How dare you try to take Christ out of the Army's anti-rape program?" Well, here is my question: How dare YOU attempt to dictate a victim's recovery process?! Moreover, how dare you even claim to follow Christ or the teachings of the Bible?! Only someone truly vile would pray that anyone be "ass raped" —particularly when the fine women upon whom he wishes such violence have never caused him any harm.

There is nothing Christian about praying for others to suffer extreme harm just so you can feel better about yourself. You are not a Christian—you are a pathetic, narcissistic, waste of space. If you want to honestly say that you believe in the Bible, I suggest you actually read it and use its teachings to be productive instead of spending your life as a useless oxygen thief.

Blessed be,

Tobanna Barker,
MRFF Legal Affairs Coordinator

♦♦♦

Subject: Praying

I am praying that the Light of God would be shown to all of you. I am so thankful for Godly men and women serving in our military and for the testimony they bring. I pray that they remain strong in their faith and that Gods glory will be shown through them.

God Bless,

(Name withheld)

P.S. I should also pray that you aren't intimidated by Christians any longer as well. You are clearly intimidated or you wouldn't be on this campaign against Christians. How do you not understand that what has made America strong for so long is her foundation on Judeo-Christian beliefs? Without God at the center of all we do, this country would never have become what it is today. Unfortunately, people like you are tearing this country down and think that if we take "God" out of everything we do, this country will thrive. It wont and the judgement of God will come down on this country. We Christians should stand up for our faith in WHATEVER industry we are in, military or not.

.

Well, at least the first part of this letter was decent, but his or her true character just could not be held back. Pity, that.

♦♦♦

Subject: Stop hating christians

Please stop this sinful hateful language and behavior toward those who express their religious freedom in this country!

Though I am proud to be a veteran and Christian citizen of this country, I am sickened that you represent out country. I am greatly disturbed at your recent hateful speech toward men and women in uniform who express their beliefs publicly...just as you have done in the media and on your website. Your actions are shameful and quite embarrassing!

By conscience I cannot support your organization.
(Name withheld)

.

I have to tell you here that I stand unwavering in my pride of the work that is being done here at MRFF in the name of the Constitution.

♦♦♦

Subject: Religious Freedom Right

Dear, Sir it is evident to me that you and your Organization has never and will never hold a dying comrade in your arms treating them for their Battle Wounds on the Battlefield. I have and let me tell you there is a God and come judgement day when you stand before him I'm praying you get what's due to you for your opposition to His Word and for helping Our Marines, Army, and airforce personnel be deprived of what they are fighting for. That your just rewards are in the pit of hell. Because when I die I know where I'm going. (Name withheld)

.

Good evening,

My name is Dustin Chalker, former Army Sergeant, Iraq veteran, and combat medic. During my '06-'07 tour in Iraq, I received the Purple Heart for injuries sustained in combat and the Combat Medical Badge for providing care under fire, to include being the only medic on scene at a MASCAL mortar attack for over eighty minutes. I am an atheist, and I serve with MRFF in an advisory capacity alongside many other veterans of Christian, Jewish, Muslim, and other religious backgrounds.

Your resentful and bitter "prayers" are duly noted, and I am certain that any hypothetical god that does exist would be far beyond the arrogant human pettiness that you so blasphemously project onto him. Do you notice how your imaginary god shares all of your own personal opinions about everything? That's because it's a figment of your own imagination. Atheist have too much respect for the concept of an infinitely perfect deity to ever accuse it of actually existing, being guilty of incompetently screwing up its own creation this badly and possessing the vile traits of you ignorant barbarians who ceaselessly endeavor to tell everyone else what god thinks.

In any case, your private views about mythological god(s), heaven, and hell do not concern MRFF. Our organization exists to advocate for the religious freedom of all service members, regardless of their faith (or lack thereof). We believe all service members should be free of religious coercion from superiors in the chain of command. We don't care what anyone believes, until they abuse government power to promote their belief over others. The US government—including the military—does not exist to serve or promote religion but is a shared enterprise that exists to treat all Americans the same.

Regards,

Dustin Chalker, MRFF Atheist Affairs Advisor

♦♦♦

It seems it is not enough for some people to just send horrible letters, they also send pictures, most of which have been cut and pasted from the internet. The following letter was one such email, which is why there is a reference to an image.

.

Subject: I'm sorry I hope this offends you

I'm sorry I hope this offends you, because you certainly offend me. I'm so offended by your lack of understanding how it feels to go into combat and possibly die that a soldier might ask God for divine protection to come home safe.. you offend the crap out of me.. I think I'm going to hire an atty to sue you for emotional damage and pain because you offend me so much...

(Name withheld)

.

Dear Offender—

I am writing in response to your email to the Military Religious Freedom Foundation ("MRFF").

Congratulations – You have managed to offend me. Not because the images you sent show people in prayer. After all, we at MRFF fight tirelessly to protect the religious freedom of service members of all faiths, or no faith at all. Over 96% of our clients are Christians, so prayer is not offensive to us in and of itself.

What offends me is your utter disregard for how these two images put our brave men and women in uniform in danger. Creating the impression that the US military fights for Christianity, rather than for US Citizens and the rights granted by the US Constitution, gives terrorist groups the ammunition they need to claim that the U.S. military is doing nothing more than fighting a crusade against Islam. You may as well personally solicit new terrorists to cause the combat you claim our service members should pray before entering. Perhaps then, the families of our clients should hire attorneys to sue you for causing such deadly combat.

Of course, a Christian soldier, sailor, airman, or Marine would pray before combat—and he/she has every right to do that, as long as said prayer complies with the time, place, and manner requirements of the Establishment Clause of the First Amendment. However, when such prayer wrongfully intimidates their fellow service members to join or becomes an endorsement of Christianity over other religions (or no religion), it not only violates the Constitution they are sworn to defend, it puts their lives in danger.

We at MRFF fight tirelessly to protect the rights of the brave service members who sacrifice so much to protect our rights. I sincerely hope you will think of their welfare in the future instead of intentionally trying to offend a group whose work you clearly do not understand.

Blessed be,
Tobanna Barker,
MRFF Legal Affairs Coordinator

◆◆◆

This article appeared on our web site.

.

"The 310th 'Space' Wing is NOT called the 310th 'Space For My Personal Proselytizing Christian Bible Shrine' Wing for a damn good reason. Major Steve Lewis has created an around-the-clock Christian Bible Shrine on his official USAF workstation desk that has been in prominent static display for YEARS. The pages in his open bible on his USAF desk never change, ever. Thus, it is obviously there as a religious display to promote to others his Christian faith. This sectarian display is a disastrous travesty which completely serves all too well as an absolute textbook violation of Air Force Instruction 1-1, Section 2.12 as well as the No Establishment Clause and No Religious Test Clause of the United States Constitution. MRFF is very pleased that, pursuant to MRFF's specific demand, this bible has expeditiously been removed from Major Lewis' desk pending the the ongoing Commander Directed Investigation which MRFF also demanded. In my nearly 12 minute call with the 310th Wing Commander, Colonel Feltman, yesterday, he promised me that he would be open and fair in all of his dealings on this matter with MRFF and its 33 clients at Peterson AFB and Schriever AFB. We will hold him to his word. So far, MRFF has been impressed with his honesty and responsiveness."

·

Subject: Open Bible On Air Force Major's Desk

Wow, you people REALLY need to find a job that actually matters. An open bible sitting on a desk???? And one that had YELLOW highlighting?? What a danger that must pose?! Unbelievable. Did little people come out and tell you to be a Christian? I PRAY that if you are ever in a position where you might be in real danger, where you might be in danger of losing your life (Again, I pray this does not happen), remember, not to pray for help from God. Just FYI, these are called "Foxhole Christians". Please feel free to pray to Satan, Mohammed, or whomever, but you my friend will be out of luck.

I will pray for your soul.
(Name withheld)

·

Thank you. I believe we have found something that actually matters and there is no need to pray for my soul. So funny you mention it, but I have been in danger; I live in danger from fanatical lunatics who attack my house and put swastikas on the wall next to my front door.

·

Dear (name withheld),

The mission of the United States military is to defend our diverse nation against all enemies—not promote religion. A military member's sworn oath is to "support and defend the Constitution of the United States...and bear true faith and allegiance to the same"—not to a Bible version. Our Constitution 1st Amendment provides for separation of church & state that prohibits our government or its representatives from "respecting" (i.e., favoring, supporting, endorsing, promoting, etc.) any religious establishment (i.e., a religion, church, denomination, sect, cult, etc.). Military service is public, religious beliefs are private. Military members may privately practice the religion (or non-religion) of choice, but they may not lawfully use their service, position or office to force their private religious beliefs on fellow Americans. Military members who disrespect & disregard our Constitution & their sworn oath need to be disciplined & required to take a USA Constitution 101 course as well as be briefed on the legal significance of their sworn oath.

Any person who cannot support the Constitution & honor a sworn oath has the right to seek a career elsewhere.

John Compere (Brigadier General, US Army, Retired)
MRFF Advisory Board Member

.

General,

Let me start my reply with the expression of appreciation for your service to our Country. One should never diminish when someone is willing to put their life on the line for their belief and support of our great nation. It was built on the three most important documents ever written for our country - The Constitution, the Declaration, and the Bill of Rights. Again, thank you.

With that being said, you are completely wrong about the 1st Amendment providing for separation of church and state. NOWHERE in the 1st Amendment or Constitution does it say this.

The metaphor of a "wall of separation" comes from a letter President Thomas Jefferson penned to a group of Baptists in Danbury, Connecticut—a dozen years after the Constitution and Bill of Rights were ratified. The phrase is not mentioned in the Constitution's text or in any of the debates leading to its ratification.

What the Constitution's First Amendment does say is that government shall make no law "respecting an establishment of religion or prohibiting the free exercise thereof." It is well to attend to the actual words of the Constitution. Nowhere is this more important than with the Establishment Clause of the First Amendment: forbidding an official establishment of religion is something quite different from the much looser, imprecise term "separation of church and state." The Constitution only forbids government sponsorship and compulsion of religious exercise by individual citizens. It does not require hermetic "separation"—implying exclusion—of religion and religious persons from public affairs of state.

Having a Bible open on a desk is no more proscelitizing than to say a BBQ cookbook sitting on a kitchen counter requires you to make smoked pork chops. That is a ludicrous and non sensical statement. I say to you, sir, that you need to take the Constitution 101 course that you so profess in your reply. Just saying.

(Name withheld)

.

Dear (name withheld)

You "legal" analysis of our Constitution is deficient & not a correct statement of history or law. It is a misinformed attempt to deny & revise history as well as ignore long established Constitutional law.

"Church and state are and must remain separate."
—President Ronald Reagan
(1984 public speech at Valley Stream, New York)

"We enjoy the separation of church and state, and no sectarian religion has ever been and we pray God, ever will be imposed upon us."
—Christian Evangelist Billy Graham
(1985 sermon at Washington National Cathedral)

"I believe in the separation of church and state, completely."
—Christian Televangelist Rick Warren
(2008 address at Washington National Cathedral)

Constitutional separation of church & state has been publicly acknowledged & accepted by every American President since Jefferson as well as countless Christian leaders with integrity & some knowledge of American constitutional history. Please see the attachments for enlightenment on this subject.

John Compere
Retired Army & Texas lawyer, retired US judge & disabled American veteran (Vietnam)
MRFF Advisory Board Member

♦♦♦

Subject: Just heard about prayer after game

If nobody was forced to pray, than I don't see an issue. Stop knocking on Christianity. I'm a retired Army Colonel, Green Beret, my son is a USAFA grad and my Godson was a West Point football player, so I'm very familiar with your many attacks on prayer. I'm aware that you, and your son are also USAFA grads. I assume that you have never served in combat, or you might have a different view of prayer. There are no atheists in the foxhole, so to speak. Sometimes, SF Chaplains need to be armed, sometimes soldiers need to pray. What is wrong with a football team being thankful for a win, a good game, no one being hurt? After all this country was founded on freedom OF religion, not on freedom FROM religion! Trying to wipe out prayer from the military is terribly misguided - you should be ashamed!

(Name withheld)
COL (Ret) USA

.

COL (Name withheld),

A half century of jurisprudence totally disagrees with your point of discernment between freedom of and freedom from religion. Reality is that you cannot have one without the other. Freedom of religion, or the freedom to choose whichever religion you might desire naturally results in freedom from religion, freedom from one religious view being bolstered with the strength of the governing body. The family of Pat Tillman is a very good place to start debunking your exhaustively falsified rallying cry of there being no atheists in foxholes. If you'd like more examples I'd only ask that you open the door to your mind-deadening echo-chamber and introduce yourself to the world wide web. Try using the popular website "google.com" and search for terms like, "atheists in foxholes". You can call all of these men and women liars and frauds if you'd like, but if that's the level of respect you have for our combat veterans, I have to question your character.

No one is trying to wipe prayer from the military. You can fight that straw man all day long if you'd like. You'll just continue to look silly rolling around in the hay. Read the findings of Lemon v. Kurtzman. Ask yourself why it is that we no longer have faculty led and organized prayer in public schools. Really, please do read the finding now. if you haven't already. I'm sure if I asked you why you think the SCOTUS developed the Lemon Test you'll say something along the lines of "because Satan is waging a holy war and gaining ground!" I ask that you muster what strength you have left and consider the views of another. Let's say a non-Christian. How about a Jewish student, in class at a public school. Let's say that the morning prayer ritual is about to begin and every day that young boy or girl fails the religious test of conformity by refusing to participate. Now we have a totally unnecessary, un-American, separation between in- and out-groups orchestrated by all taxpayers (not just the bible believers). What affect do you think that will have on the way those delightfully prayerful students' view people who aren't like them? Fast forward into the future just a bit. Let's say we have a Muslim soldier, who declines to participate in the mandatory prayer ceremony in formation and is immediately identified by his peers as spiritually deficient. There have been more than enough documented instances of Boykin-esque acts of violence and harassment towards non-Christians in our modern history. Read Mikey's book, No Snowflake in an Avalanche, if you'd like to hear some dozen or so examples. And that's only a fraction of the tip of the ice burg.

It's literally impossible to wipe out prayer. Anyone who claims that as their goal is a fool. Private or voluntary group prayer can be a wonderful thing for those who choose to opt-in. It is possible to stop state-sponsorship of religion. Anytime a service member is given a religious test and must opt-out of participation in a religious ceremony the lemon test has been failed. I hope that has cleared everything up for you, if not keep reading my friend.

Cheers,

Blake A. Page
Military Religious Freedom Foundation
Special Assistant to the President
Director of US Army Affairs

♦♦♦

Subject: may your babies miscarriage

First you destroy the reputation of a American hero like General Boykin.

And then you destroy the career of another American hero like General Grigsby.

For simply inviting General Boykin to address our American hero troops here in Fort Riley Kansas.

How about we do a little destruction on you Mickey?

Oh but thats right we don't have to.

Jesus will take all the care of you jews and your jew seed soon enough. (Matthew 27:25 1 John 5:12 John 3:36)

We pray with testimony that your women kinfolk all miscarry in their abort pregnancies.

And that all your men kin have early heart attack and cancer.

The unquenchable flames await you Mickey. And the MRRF.

(Name withheld)

◆ ◆ ◆

Out of left field, something lovely happens; someone has a sense of humor, like myself. Thank you for the following letter, thank you.

.

Subject: Prayers For You

Hello! I just read the most unbelievable story - or it would be unbelievable if I haven't had an encounter or two with certain types of "Christians" myself. The article included several examples of the mail you receive, and I felt compelled to apologize. I am sure you realize this but not all Christians are so filled with hate and acrimony. Some of us can even spell! Some of us have compassion. Some of us even have a sense of humor (though according to my teenage son that is something I lack). When I read my bible, I find that I am encouraged to go out and smile at people, open doors for them, wait patiently for my turn in line, let someone pass on the street without screaming obscenities, engage in intelligent, respectful discourse with people that do not think exactly like me, and basically be a nice person. My faith in Jesus Christ encourages me to see every other person on this planet as a human being, just like me, with the same hopes, dreams, fears, needs. . . we are all children of God (or whatever other name you wish to use for him or her - hey, I'm flexible). We are all the family of humanity, traveling together, hoping for a little peace in our souls.

And so, as a woman that struggles daily to be a good Christian, I am going to pray for you. I'm not going to pray that you die or even that you eat shit (trust me, I'm pretty sure that's worse than death as I once tripped in a cow patty filled pasture and so I can speak with some authority on this) as so many of my "Christian" counterparts have hoped for. Instead I will pray that you continue on your journey with peace, hope, and a great sense of humor. That you continue as you have, fighting for the personal and religious freedoms of your fellow human beings, with much success. I pray that you will be safe from the hate that some people spew because they seem to have read their New Testament incorrectly. And I pray that, in time, you will find that hate mail comes so rarely that you haven't the material for another book and have only positive messages to post on your website from people that support you.

(Name withheld)

.

Dear (name withheld),

I'd like to thank you for your wonderful letter! It is the rare kind, and I do hope your prayers are answered, so it becomes the predominant filler of MRFF's in-box. Second, I'd like to disagree with your son. I think you gave a great sense of humor—especially that bit about the cow pasture!

Finally, I'd like to thank you for not saying that the others "aren't real Christians." Some try to, you know. It's called the "no true Scotsman fallacy." It's enough that the poison-pen authors consider themselves Christians. And, besides, wouldn't it be judgmental of anyone else to argue otherwise? I hope you'll keep following Mikey Weinstein and MRFF's work. In fact, if you're interested in helping us, we could use another good writer—especially one with such a good sense of humor!

Sincerely,
A long-time MRFF volunteer

GOOD MORNING...
Subject: She'd have to pay me
hey hey hey! On that bill
today. Hello skank whore wif
Kikey Whinestien the Jesus ha
What a crybaby. oh boo hoo
for the jews? Same little fu
who sent THE ONLY Lord t
Cross. Ok she was p
fuck
less
epent fo
children yo
Jesus in th

Hey Bitch:

I see where your chicken
usband doesn't have the bal
list his email address on
MRFF website...no surprise as
(and you) are just a couple
muslim   terrorist   lov
limeballs who are losers in li
e to   et back at tr
n only hope tha
d everyone els
of   shit

husband
od and His
tand before
gment and then go
1. Jesus loves you

struck down
es humanity
don't like
why don't

That Woman, What's Her Name

I WAS RAISED IN a military family and was proud to be an Air Force brat. My family never lived in base housing. The housing on the bases my dad was assigned to either was not available for an officer of his rank or did not exist at all. I was born in Biloxi, Mississippi and was there less than a year before moving to northern California. When I was six, we moved to Athens, Greece. I have wonderful memories of living there and was best friends with the base chaplain's daughter. Chaplin Deming would later marry Mike and me in a Jewish ceremony in the Protestant chapel at the Air Force Academy.

Overseas assignments were only two years in length, but in 1965 my dad was offered a choice to either stay with his family for another tour in Greece, or be transferred to Vietnam. After four years in Greece we finally went back to the States, Southern California to be exact. We lived in a neighborhood filled with girls and two boys who lived on the corner. This was my first introduction to a family of a different religion other than my own. The boys were Jewish, and I was jealous that they got eight days of presents during the holidays and not just one. I was very happy there and had lots of friends, but after just two years, when I was in the middle of seventh grade, we moved to Colorado Springs.

Switching schools in the middle of a school year is not an easy thing to do, especially in junior high. It is hard to be a newcomer at that age. My parents bought a nice house in a good school district. It was walking distance for my little sister to get to her elementary school, walking distance for me to get to my junior high, and a little bit farther but still walking distance for my older sister to get to high school.

Unfortunately, I went into a junior high school where I found it difficult to make friends. It was in geography class that I had the toughest time. Behind me sat a girl who did not like me for whatever reason. I never understood why. She was constantly poking me in the back and doing what today would be described as "talking shit" about me. She was quite effective in making my life miserable.

I am the type of person that when I am upset, I find it difficult to eat. I know some people eat when they are upset and find it comforting. Not me. My mother always referred to me as a gut bucket because at the dinner table I ate everything in sight. She was sure I had hollow legs that I stuffed food into. I was very, very thin and stayed that way no matter how much I ate. It was when I stopped eating and started losing weight I could not afford to lose, that my parents realized something was wrong. They took me to doctors because my stomach constantly hurt and because of the weight loss. It was not until I told them about the girl at school that they put two and two together. One day, the girl told me that I was to meet her on a particular date, after school, at a particular location behind the school.

The morning of the day I was supposed to fight her, I laid in a fetal position at my parents closed bedroom door. They were fighting. From what I could understand, my mom thought I should not be forced to go to school and my dad was insisting that I go. Finally, the door opened in a rush and my dad almost fell over me. He picked me up, got me dressed, and drove me to school.

I made my way into geography class with the greatest of trepidation. When I sat down at my desk, I braced myself for the barrage of taunts that would be tossed my way. For a long time, she did not say anything to me, but then she leaned forward in her chair and whispered to me that she did not think I had the nerve to show up to school today. She then told me that we really did not have to meet after school to fight after all. It was at that red-hot moment that my blood reached a boiling point. It took absolutely everything I had to stay seated and not launch myself over her desk and beat the shit out of her. I often think about it and wonder what would have happened if I actually threw myself at her.

It was also at that moment that I realized that after all of that torture and turmoil this girl put into my life, I would never be one to take any more of it. She brought out the fighter in me and ever since then I have stood up for myself and have become quite the strong individual. It was weeks later, after that fateful day of the fight that never happened, that I was with my dad in Kmart. We had gone out to do an errand, and I was walking beside my dad holding his hand. We were in a wide aisle walking toward the front of the store when around the corner came that girl. I have never remembered her name. My hand got entirely clammy and slick with sweat so much so that my dad looked down at me to see what was wrong. I whispered to him, "That's her, that's the girl," as we continued to walk toward her. I felt the anger in my dad and thought he was going to say something, but when we walked by each other, she said hi to me and I said hi back. What has stayed with me even to this day was that she was alone and wore a camo-type boys jacket during a time when the girls I was friends with did not wear clothes like that and certainly did not go out after dark by themselves to a store. I felt sorry for her, very profoundly sorry.

I often think of the amount of time, efforts, and energies it takes to be hateful, to hold grudges, or to just simply hate. I am not that type of person. I am a positive person and usually see the glass as half full. What would it be like inside the body of a person who would bully someone and constantly be angry at something or someone, so much so that you feel the need and desire to act on it? The time it has taken an individual to do so much hating is such a waste and a travesty of epic proportions.

The protagonist in *American History X* at the end of the movie says, "Hate is baggage. Life's too short to be pissed off all the time. It's just not worth it." Followed by a quote from Abraham Lincoln: "We are not enemies, but friends. We must not be enemies. Though passion may have strained, it must not break our bond of affection. The mystic chords of memory...will swell when again touched, as surely they will be, by the better angels of our nature."

Lincoln said the above quote to reconcile with the states that had seceded from the union. In his first inaugural address, he denounced secession as anarchy, and explained it had to be balanced by constitutional restraints in the American system of republicanism.

I believe that the time we have on this earth is a very precious resource and I try to not waste too much of it. Therefore, I will not waste yours with too many letters in this chapter. The letters presented here are ugly, needless, and completely useless, and were written by bullies. I also do not need to bash you in the face with all of the shit these letters bring forth. A few of these letters are all that you will need to understand what I now deal with, so in this case, less is more. Should you want more, then please read my first book, *To the far-right Christian Hater, You Can Be a Good Speller or a Hater But You Can't Be Both*. It is chocked full of nasty letters to me.

◆◆◆

Subject: Bible on desk

Hey Bitch:

I see where your chicken shit husband doesn't have the balls to list his email address on the MRFF website...no surprise as he (and you) are just a couple of muslim terrorist loving slimeballs who are losers in life and have to get back at true Americans! One can only hope that the both of you and everyone else in your piece of shit organization will be struck down with the worst diseases humanity can offer! And if you don't like what I just said then why don't you suck my cock, cunt? I live in Virginia and I'll be more than happy to discuss this with your faggot hubby in person...but we both know he's a coward and would never show up! Don't forget to show up for your part time job in the evenings...walking the streets as a 2 bit whore!

.

Stupid idiot. My husband's contact information is everywhere on the website. Why is it no one else has any trouble contacting Mikey, you idiot!

.

(Name withheld),
Aren't you just the bravest little hero?

Takes a big man to berate and insult the family of someone you disagree with instead of taking them on directly. The love of Jesus really shines through his followers such as yourself. I hope your foxhole on the front lines of Fort Couch is well secured and stocked with all the pop tarts and mountain dew you need to get through the tempest night. Push on, though, and maybe you'll get that carpal tunnel purple heart with a valor device. Post that citation all over your fb page, "For injuries sustained while executing a mission of sexual harassment, keeping with the highest traditions of the keyboard warrior... while choking on his own spittle and cross eyed with stupidity fueled rage..."

You might disagree with what we do, but we would never stoop to the slime pit of amoral scum you seem to enjoy splashing about in.

Blake A Page

Military Religious Freedom Foundation
Special Assistant to the President
Director of US Army Affairs

♦♦♦

Mrs. Weinstein,

I really can't believe you are wasting your life hating people and trying to erase religious freedom. It is such a waste of one of Gods greatest gift..a meaningful life and you are a waste of space in America. It takes so much energy to hate and will make you look old and ugly. You should move to a Muslim country where they treat women like disposable dish rags since you seem to be so taken with their religion. I have never been in church where the preacher says you should go and kill all people who don't believe like we do, which is what Muslims do. Why would you as a thinking woman support that? Why would a free woman ever want that evil to get a foot hold in America? Good always triumphs evil so I full faith your evil organization will never win! As a wife of a retired Air Force Officer, when you mess with a military man you better be aware their wife will have his back because if they get a hold of you will praying for the good Lord to help you! Sincerely,

(Name withheld)

♦♦♦

Subject: HMMMMMMMMM.............................?

SO, NOW, YOUR EVIL WIFE DIE YET? HMMMM......................? SHE PUNISHED FOR YOUR SIN? HMMMMMMMMMM............................?

♦♦♦

Subject: Mystified

Bonnie:

After reading the 'objectives' of the mrff I am completely mystified at what I read. The mrff obviously has no Christians or Hebrews that truly are devoted to the GOD of Abraham, Issac and Jacob. We love America and Israel with an intensity that HE has created us for. Israel is the 'apple of HIS eye' and America is here to be the greatest of allies.

I have no intention of trying to persuade you of anything, just daring you to find out what Christianity really is (you will be amazed!). I have left the letters mrff in lower case purposely to bring the letters to the level of your misguided attempts of destroy the one true Allie of Israel and yes, I understand that you are Jewish by birth.

(Name withheld)

·

Hello (Name withheld),

Bonnie is quite busy dealing with issues important to her, so has asked me to respond to your message on her behalf.

I'm sorry the "objectives" of the MRFF are difficult for you to understand. Many, I'm happy to say, don't have the problem you apparently do. But when I read your message, including your judgment of some of the people associated with our work, it became clearer to me why you find it so difficult to follow and understand what it is we do. Whoever the "WE" that you arrogate to yourself the right to speak for might be, he, she or it has a rather monocular view of the world, of religion and of God. That being so, it's no wonder our 'objectives' are mystifying to you.

We, for starters, have a very different view of why America is here. The idea that our country was created to be the "greatest of allies" to a nation that wasn't even in existence until 172 years later would be confusing to some, you must admit. Given the quite extraordinary flight of fancy that powers your vision, I'm happy to say on Bonnie's behalf that we're delighted to know you "have no intention of trying to persuade (her) of anything." She, being a rational person, would, I think, find it more than a bit difficult to join you in your amazing journey. It would be interesting to know just what it is that prompts your apparent belief that the MRFF is attempting to destroy anything, much less someone named Allie of Israel. I can personally assure you that Allie of Israel, whoever she is, has nothing to fear from the MRFF.

Best,

Mike Farrell
(MRFF Board of Advisors)

(Name withheld), you send an email yesterday to my wife, Bonnie. I happen to be "completely mystified" as to what YOU are completely mystified about, brother? We currently represent thousands of active-duty United States marines, sailors, soldiers, airman, and veterans, and about 96% of them are practicing Protestants and Roman Catholics. We have nearly 300 paid and volunteer staff here at the foundation, and well over 80% of them are practicing Christians, stop—half my own family are Christian. So what again is your point please, sport?

Mikey Weinstein
Founder and president of the Military Religious Freedom Foundation.

◆◆◆

Subject: Why?

Please ask your retarded husband why he wants, and feels the need to be such an obvious asshole. Why does he not grow some juevos and publicly tell all of us why he has such a rat up his ass about religion, especially Christian? Even if he hates religion what harm does it do to allow others their faith. Your husband is a straight line agitator and for no good reason accept I guess his twisted perceptions of what is important. At least religion helps some people to deal with life in a positive way but for the life of me the only thing I see your husband doing is stroking his ego with no real positive effect on anything except maybe his hateful psyche. What a waste of human tissue.

(Name withheld)

·

Dear (name withheld),

Bonnie and Mikey have both read your email and shared it with me, asking if I would offer a response. One of the ways that I assist is with email correspondence such as this, a task that I normally enjoy a great deal.

This time, though, I've got to challenge you on a personal level—

Why in the world would you send such a nasty note to a very nice lady about her husband? Based on your email address it seems you are married (as am I). So for you to make such a vile personal attack through a spouse is—and I say this gently as I can—completely gutless and totally lacking in "juevos."

That said, the general content of your note, being long on unpleasant attitude and short on specifics, makes it difficult to craft a response...but I will try my best.

I can assure you that Mikey does not "hate religion", nor does he have "twisted perceptions" about it. He does not do what he does to "stroke his ego", nor because he has a "hateful psyche." Finally, and perhaps most importantly (at least to Mikey)—to my knowledge he does not have, nor has he ever had, a "rat up his ass."

What he DOES possess is an honorable, steadfast and courageous commitment to stand opposed to hateful people such as yourself, sometimes at great personal risk, in order to lead an organization that is dedicated to ensuring that all members of the United States Armed Forces fully receive the Constitutional guarantees of religious freedom to which they and all Americans are entitled by virtue of the Establishment Clause of the First Amendment. The fact that such a logical and reasonable goal would cause someone like you to lose his mind is, in my opinion, ample evidence that there is a need for a watchdog organization such as MRFF.

Mike Challman
Christian, AF Veteran, MRFF Supporter

·

Dear (name withheld),

Please ask your retarded... No. I take that back. It would be beneath me to lower myself to your level. For that matter, I intend to use proper spelling (it's "huevos," not "juevos"), grammar, punctuation, and sentence structure, as well. Oh, and no profanity.

Mikey Weinstein asked me to respond, a couple days ago. Sorry I couldn't get to this, sooner, but I was busy doing other things to protect our American citizenry from misguided missiles of Christian defense, like yourself. The fact is, nearly 40,000 individuals have come to Mikey for help, because their *military chains of command were attacking them, and 96% were being attacked for being Christians! Wait. Let me clarify that: They were being attacked for not being Christian enough.*

So, (name withheld), what do you think is Christian enough? Do you think you're Christian enough? Well, what if your boss said you weren't, and that you had to go to his church, believe in his version of God, and follow his particular religious rituals, or you'd get the most dangerous assignments? What if your refusal meant going to prison for disobeying a military order? Would that be acceptable?

Such behavior is illegal according to the Constitution, the Bill of Rights, and a couple centuries of case law, as well. Every military member must take an oath to "support and defend the Constitution"—not the nation, not the politicians, not the land—"against all enemies, foreign and domestic." That Constitution is the absolute foundation of our nation, our land, and the laws our politicians, who also take that oath, write—or should write. Those who, within our military (as that is MRFF's focus), use their rank and power to force their religion on others or mistreat others for not being what they consider the right religion, are breaking their oath, breaking the law, and working in breach of the rights of their underlings. This has to stop.

You can be part of the problem or part of the solution. The choice is yours.

Sincerely,

An American veteran, proud patriot, and staunch MRFF supporter

·

Dear (name withheld),

I'm tempted to assume (name withheld) is neither as angry nor as ignorant as you are and address this message to her. The temptation arises from the fact that you were classless enough to send your pitiful and obnoxious message to Mikey's wife. But I won't stoop to your level and insult Susan. I'll send this to you in the hope that a little information will seep into your brain and enlighten you at least a small amount.

Unlike you, apparently, Mikey believes everyone has the right to her or his own belief system. He founded the MRFF because that right was being attacked by zealots who wanted to impose their belief on those in the military who had no recourse because the wrongdoers were officers and others in positions senior to them.

Like Mikey, we at the MRFF feel that everyone should have the right to believe as she or he chooses. We oppose the use of one's position to push a religious faith on those in inferior positions. We oppose it because it is wrong, because it is illegal and because it is unfair, especially in a hierarchical relationship like that of the military.

I hope that is clear and helps you understand a little more about the reality of the situation into which you have inserted yourself in such a boorish manner. You see, it doesn't matter to the MRFF if the proselytizing is done by a Muslim, a Buddhist, an atheist or a Christian. It is wrong in any instance. However, when this is done by a fundamentalist Christian, as is the case in our military, people like you leap to the assumption that Mikey and the MRFF are anti-Christian and fire off brutish assaults filled with wrong-headed opinions and lots of foul language.

You assume a great deal, Paul, on the basis of no meaningful information at all, and you embarrass yourself and your wife in the process. Your pig-headed assumptions are entirely incorrect and, if you have any pride or sense of personal honor, I suggest you send a message of apology immediately.

Everyone makes mistakes, Paul, and you've made one big time. Fortunately, Mikey is a big man and strong enough to withstand this kind of stupid assault. But your kind of nonsense is not easy on Bonnie, who unfortunately has to deal with boorish assaults like yours too often. So, let's see what kind of man you are.

With hope,

A proud MRFF supporter

·

Dear (names withheld),

Bonnie appreciates your letter but is very busy dealing with issues concerning MRFF and thousands of complaints we have received from our young men and women in the Armed Forces who have been subjected to command centered and coercive Christian proselytizing.

She has asked me to follow up on your note.

First, Mr. Weinstein is not retarded. He is an honor graduate of the United States Air Force Academy, an Air Force veteran, a lawyer and a White House Council during Ronald Reagun's presidency. Secondly, he has founded the Military Religious Freedom Foundation to help guarantee religious freedom to each and every member of the armed forces.

We of the MRFF have no bias against Christianity but only against those who attempt to use Christianity to advance their personal agendas to the detriment of others.

It is our goal to keep government religion neutral and fair and balanced for members of all faiths.

Although your letter was insulting and the work of a very disturbed person we make it a point to fairly answer each communication, fair or biased.

Rick Baker
Capt. USAF (Ret), MRFF Volunteer

♦♦♦

Mrs. Weinstein.

Unless you and your husband repent for attacking God (Jesus) and His children you will stand before Jesus in the judgment and then go straight to hell. Jesus loves you and bore the punishment we all deserve for our sins by His death on the cross. John 3:18 He who believes in Him (Jesus) is not judged, he who does not believe has been judged already because he has not believed in the name of the only begotten So of God. Everybody who's in hell or ends up there is because they choose to go there. The choice is yours. Don't continue to be stupid fools. God's words and not mine.

(Name withheld)

.

And you know this how?

◆◆◆

Bonnie,

Why are you such a hateful person?   What happened in your life to make you so angry?   Why such disdain for God?   I hope you can be healed on day.

(Name withheld)

·

(Name withheld) What is the matter with you? Speaking of hateful, look in a mirror. What in your life has made you so incredibly superior that you have the right to make judgments about people and condemn someone you don't know? Have you met Bonnie? Have you spoken with her? What gives you the right to assume she has "disdain for God"? And, by the way, who made you God's protector? Does the same authority give you healing powers? If you have a question or concern having to do with the work of the MRFF I'll be happy to help you deal with it. But grow up and stand up. Act like a person with a legitimate issue, if you have one, and get back to me. I'll personally see that you have an appropriate response.

Mike Farrell, MRFF Board of Directors

◆◆◆

Subject: She'd have to pay me

hey hey hey! On that billboard today. Hello skank whore wife of Kikey Whinestien the Jesus hater. What a crybaby. oh boo hoo hoo for the jews? Same little fuckers who sent THE ONLY Lord to the Cross. Ok she was pretty hot for a she-jew. I'd fuck her. But only if she paid me 1st to do her. start with anal. No checks just cash. Or you're kikey head on a platter.

·

Dear (name withheld),

As a former Air Force officer and rescue pilot, I have had occasion to meet some pretty low class people, including enemies of the United States. You are on the bottom tier of all that I have met.

We at MRFF do not use personal insults against adversaries but rather try to gain their trust and support through logic and truth.

You have already destroyed your case with banal and insulting rhetoric so I will not attempt to change your mind about MRFF but will only say that you probably would not understand our goals anyway.

Bonnie Weinstein is a beautiful and educated woman of class and substance. She would not accept your advances in any case and is so far above your gutter mentality as to obviate any contact.

I believe you mentioning Christ is the most egregious blasphemy possible. I would be careful about using sacred names if I were you.

Please extend my heartfelt sorrow to your family for having to even be around you.

And as for paying you, all you can expect is the standard thirty pieces of silver normally paid to the Judas's of the world.

Rick Baker
Capt. USAF (Ret)
MRFF Volunteer

♦ ♦ ♦

Subject: feckless cunts are Mikey's bitches

Samantha Bee calls Ivanka a feckless cunt cause Ivanka can't get her dad to ease up on the criminal spics coming into our country?

You want feckless cunts Samantha? Look at Mikey Weinstein's daughters and wife.

There the real thing.

They can't stop Mikey from attacking innocent followers of Jesus Christ in the armed services.

Fair is fair and feckless cunts do exist. But not Ivanka.

Its Weinsteins little brood of feckless cunts.

(Name withheld)

.

(Name withheld)

If you are going to send hate mail, it would be good if you knew how to write good, rudimentary English. Perhaps another year of school would be helpful.

Peace,

Herb

.

Dear (Name withheld)—odd how your "name" sounds like a "Bronx Cheer," a fitting prelude to your comment which approximates continuous flatulence): Your insults and cowardly attacks on Mikey & his family are exactly par for the course from the type of lizard-brained, scum-sucking, bottom-feeders who only rise to the atmosphere to expel their foul comments and then slide back beneath the slime under which they hide that you so exactly personify. Yeah, Samantha Bee was wrong to call Ivanka what she did; especially so since had she wished to be descriptive rather than insulting, she'd have called her a privileged brat of a gilded-age criminal oligarch, promoter of Capitalist exploitation, Zionist supremacy, and the violation of human values in the pursuit of obscene wealth.

And, "innocent followers of Jesus Christ"??? Where have you been hiding? Those "innocents" are prosecuting illegal wars and covert murders around the globe under color of "national defense." Were there such a thing as a "god" as you seem to believe exists, they'd all disappear in a flash of sulfurous vapor! The crimes committed in the name of the "Prince of Peace" demonstrate you are either an utter ignoramus, a dupe, or a tool. So, while you may call Mikey's family names, the only thing I can see, while reading your e-mail, is a fart exiting a soiled anus.

Fuck you very much!

Marshalldoc.

.

(Name withheld)

You are a disgusting, mindless, soulless coward. Hiding your sickness behind a fake address doesn't make it any less perverted, it only proves you don't have the guts required to expose your twisted mind to the light of day. Being a pain-filled wretch has to be personally excruciating, but there are people and places than can help one who is so pathetically weak he can't control his tormented brain. But lashing out anonymously proves only that you're on a path to the Hell you so fear. I pity you.

Mike Farrell,
(MRFF Board of Advisors)

.

Mikey, Guess the moron hasn't realized that Ivanka converted to Judaism...

A MRFF ally

♦♦♦

Subject: Trump and you wife

Yo Mickey. Your a goddamn disgrace to America.
I hope you get fucked by the greatness of Trump even harder than my posse
and me will be fucking your wife tonight.
Consensual.
She begged us.
We'll send you the sex tape.
jews can't satisfy Christian women. Any better than they can serve as loyal
soldiers.

.

Hi (name withheld)

You disgust me, just as I'm sure you disgust anyone who comes within smelling distance of you. (Name withheld) is the perfect name for one who stinks as terribly as you do. That's a slightly twisted historical allusion which I don't expect you to get, but the twisted part might cause a faint echo of recognition back in the reptilian recesses of what passes for a mind around you and your posse. May the 'greatness of Trump' elevate you to his level of understanding. I'm assuming the fake address you use is self-identifying: the five represents your IQ, the star your inability to think of another number, and the 326 your waist line. Tell your posse I send the bird.

Mike Farrell,
(MRFF Board of Advisors)

.

I just love reading responses from all my champions.

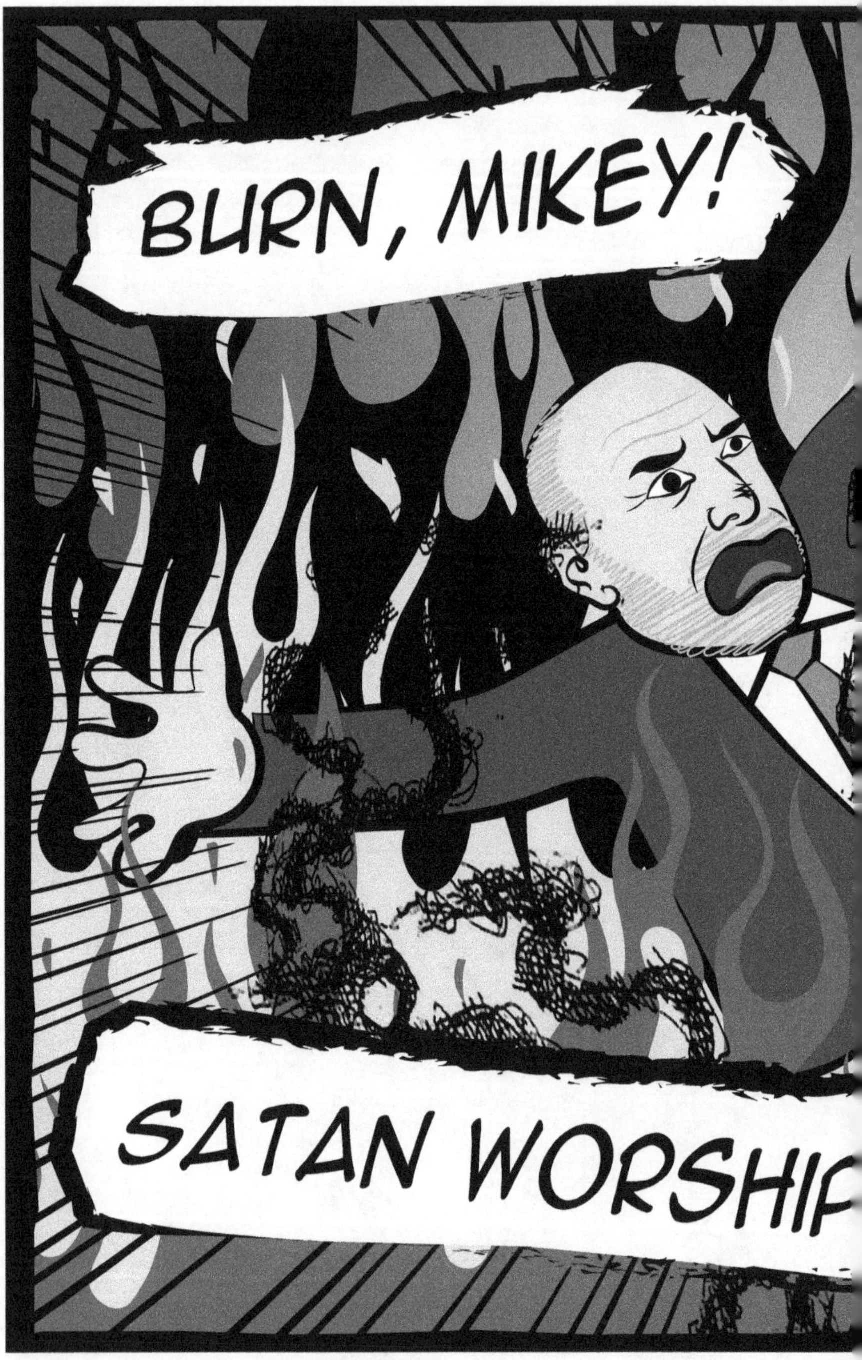
BURN, MIKEY!
SATAN WORSHI

Burn, Burn, and More Burning

OH, HOLY DAMN SHIT...WHAT THE FUCK?

Sometimes there are no real words, but a little cussing goes a long way!

♦♦♦

Subject: dream of mikey

I dream of mikey whineystien the perpetually offended little jewboy who wanted to be a real man.

Take him down Jesus!

I dream of him burning in hell forever with his buddies bin Laden and Saddam. May mikey scream in eternal agony as his flesh is consumed aflame.

Let your howls be drowned out only by the screams of your wife bonny, your children and, friends as they roast forever with you.

Hooah! Payback is a bitch mikey.

Have a blessed day and always remember that 'arbeit macht frei".

(Name withheld)

.

Vulgar fighting words, as my husband would call them, need no verbal response. That the quote "arbeit macht frei," "Work Will Set You Free," words that were placed above the gates at Auschwitz, are quoted here only prove the depths to which this person will stoop.

.

Subject: UnChristian

Mickey Wienstein,

You are un-american and unChristian and unhuman. Un-fit to live. May our Lord and Savior damn you and your sour family to the depths of hell to burn for all eternety. Your MRRF is just full of fake Christians, athiest commies and women and men queers. Too bad none of you served in uniform. We hope the Lord's critters poop and pee all over your unmarked grave. We plan to dance on it every Christmas and Easter.

(Name withheld)

Dear (name withheld),

You really just wished that some critters "poop and pee" on our graves? I think you should go ask permission from your mommy and daddy before playing with their computer next time kiddo.

—Blake

.

Hi Mikey.

Doubtless I'd be ECSTATIC not to be this kind of "Christian"—and it's "too bad" this typically ignorant moron is so illiterate that it can't even read the bios to see most of the MRFF staff and clients have not only "served in uniform" but many have served in combat. As for "un-american" (sic), what's un-American in my book is a snarling, sniveling, putrid little cowardly cur who makes threats from behind phony Es that they (mistakenly) think are hiding them. And yes, as always, you may publish this—under my own real name. (Unlike this slimy, yellow-bellied, candy-ass!)

Semper Fidelis,

Jim
F. J. Taylor
USMC (Ret.)

♦ ♦ ♦

Subject: Whinestein Burn in Hell

You, Michael Whinestein are a Jesus hating faggot who is communist and a athiest and a husein obama kissing leftist jew bastard islam loving kike feminist lawyer. You will burn for eternity in hell for your many crimes against Jesus Christ and our national armed forces. You have ruined our military by forcing Jesus out and keeping arabs blasphemers abortions and queers in. Can you picture this final destination for you Michael? Can you feel it? Can you smell the fire and fear? Can you sense the absense of all hope?

We can. And can't wait you to be aflame in torment. For anguish all eternity. Amen and Hallelujah! Hell is real and awaits you Mickey. As its never waited so much for anyone ever before.

Sooner than you think for our Saviors is an awesome Savior. And you are just little bald jew with a big mouth. Like your mouth on fire in the snapshot of your soon future below.

(Name withheld)

.

Dear (name withheld),

I'm sure you can sense an absence of hope. Just as surely as you can sense your absence of education. Abortions can't serve in the military in the same way that dances, surgeries, or tooth extractions. Actions of any variety are ineligible for service, largely due to their lack of being human. As for the rest, I hope you burn for your crimes against the English language! And by burn, I mean burn the midnight oil in deep and much needed study.

Cheers,

Blake A. Page

Subject: You are going to hell

Dear Satanists,

Since you hate God and Jesus Christ, you are will burn in the lake of fire and brimstone beginning in 3015 for eternity. On the first sliver of the new moon in March-April is your judgment day before Jesus Christ. You will be judged by Jesus Christ on every thought, word spoken and written, and every action performed since the age of accountability. Read and reap losers for you have less than 3 years to live. If you are an American and live in the USA, you will die within probably less than a year and that includes all of your family, friends, and relatives. Welcome to the Book of Revelation coming alive in September of 2015 on the 14th.

(Name withheld)

Jesus in 2015 to 2017. Are you prepared to meet your maker this year?

.

Mikey—

Hey, I admit (being somewhat slow of thought), I'm confused. Are you in trouble starting (in order):

(a)   3015? Or is it ...

(b)   "the first sliver of the new moon in March-April"? (of 3015? Or of 2015?) Which, by the way, the first sliver is either just before or just after the new moon, but now I'm just being nerdy! And since the New Moon is only a snapshot, not an extended period of time, it's either 20 March at 0936 Zulu, or 18 April at 1856 Zulu. If it's 2015, that is. (If it's 3015, then dude, I'm movin' in with you, because you are the SAFEST GUY ON THE PLANET for the next 100 years!) Or, is it...

(c)   Just when was the "age of accountability"? Was that just after the Renaissance? Or was it when the big meteor hit and wiped out most of the dinosaurs? (Now THAT's "accountability"!) I think there's an ark in there somewhere....

(d)   Or is it "less than 3 years," which actually could give hope to get you into 2018? That's better than 2015, but it does beg the question: What happened to the New Moon of March (or April)? What happened to 3015?!

(e)   Or is it…"Ooops! We're back to "probably less than a year"! As prognosticators go, this guy's right up there with Jeanne Dixon and Nostradamus!

(f)   And then…out of NOWHERE…ZING!!! It's 14 Sept 2015!!! Sure as Hell!! (Umm…so to speak!)

I'm glad we go that settled, "once and for all".

(Name withheld)

OMG! I was wrong! It's "Postscript Time" (even if he doesn't use "P.S."!) It's "Jesus in 2015 to 2017."

P.S.—(And this time, it's ME using the P.S.) I actually think you should send one of those cutem free internet "Thank you's" or "Valentines" to Ms Senese… she was actually NICE!!

P.P.S.—I'd still vote for "eating shit" over "death" pretty much any day. Especially if it was an accident, like hers. But hey, that's just me!

A MRFF ally

.

Dear Sinner,

I see that you have taken it upon yourself to judge, despite the admonition which Jesus made against it: "Judge not, lest you be judged." You also make predictions worthy of false prophets, witchcraft, and sorcery. Whether you came up with these on your own or have chosen to follow a false prophet, preaching as though he speaks for God and Jesus, it is incumbent on you to choose whether to continue this sinful behavior or to follow in Jesus' footsteps, beg God's mercy, and really read your bible. In the meanwhile, I will continue to support the organization that protects our military members from others in the military who spew threats like yours, trying to force them to change their beliefs. Each to his own. Let each military member choose for herself or himself who and what she or he cares to believe in and let no one force his or her beliefs on anyone else. That freedom of belief is embedded in our Constitution, and that is what MRFF protects.

Sincerely,

One who knows, having served in our military and faced the force of evangelical threats

♦♦♦

Subject: jew from hell

Hello Mickey. Your jew right? Of course the nose the curly hair and LOVE that $$ right? 30 pieces of silver to give up the Lord. Gimme Gimme Gimme. You can stop pretending to be a "civil rights activist" now you conniving jew lawyer. And just fess up to the truths of being a Christ hating jewboy from the deeps of hell.

Leave the servicemen who guard our Christian faith alone. You little fuck. What do we do to jew like you? And think bout your fellow jews who baked in the ovens for mouthing off once too often. Don't your kind ever learn? So typical of a jew to wine Winerstien. Just like you do all the time.

We who love Jesus Christ and America are sick of hearing you wine. Your done jew. The new ovens are ready for you.
And your wife and kids. And all the little satin worshipers of Mffr.
Your kin burned in the ovens mickey didn't they?
Have to ask your self why? why why why?
Here is why.

Spare the whip to the jew and hear the wining. Hear them try to attack Jesus and Christians and worship the $$. But bake a jew in the ovens and love the silence. No jews know peace. No mickey know quiet. Best part is that after we bake you in ovens you will still bake for all time in hell. You loose and Jesus Christ wins jewboy.
Feel the burn yet mickey? OUCH huh?

(Name withheld)

Hey (name withheld),

You stupid, right? You a knuckle-dragger, right? A coward who hides behind a fake address; back in the not-so-old days you hid behind the robe and the hood, right?

Oh, we know you, pal. We recognize you by the pot belly, the slobber and the bad breath. You're the gutless ones who call themselves Christians and burn the big crosses to show what men you are.

Howl in the night, slobbo, spill your hate before it devours you, you poor frightened mouse.

Mike Farrell
(MRFF Board of Advisors)

Dear Mikey and Bonnie.

Every time you get one of these ignorant emails, you need to remember that you are loved and appreciated by so many people. I'm one of those people. I've never had any interest in being in military service, but that's not even the point. You are defending our constitution. Please, keep doing what you're doing, and never, never, never let these ignorant people keep you from the mission you have chosen.

With deep respect and love for you and your family,

Your friend,

A MRFF ally

♦♦♦

Subject: you Cant fight God

Mr. Whinestien and all of the MRRF evilersMy wife and I have 2 sons in the service and we read the story of you in The Blazes on the about how you want to declare war on all the Christian chaplins. For hating the gays for there disgusting non biblical corruptions. Get this. if your a faggit you belong in hell. If your a faggit lover then the same. The bible makes it clear. Oh you seem to be fine with your jew-kin and raghead chaplains tho. You and the MRRF only attack chaplins of Christ. Well we have a good message from the Lord Jesus Christ for you Mr. Whinestien.

FUCK YUO! BURN IN HELL JEW FAGGIT!

Same for your whores wife and hellbait children of wickedness. Same for you demon followers at the MRRF. May the Son of God curse them all to have their eyes pecked out by demons in hell. May you be cursed to suffer there never ending screams of righteous pain.

Mr. jew read the bible. There is only ONE way to salvation. And only 1 true religion and one savior here to give it as a free gift. His blood shed makes us pure. There is only 1 county which is the most pure and precious to Jesus and that is the USA.

Our soldiers are soldiers for Christ. No separation of Jesus and state in the constitutions. We dont need no queers or jewboys and sand niggers to bring down are once proud red white and blue.

The Christian chaplin is right you are todays king harrod. But actually no. You are the antichrist for all to see. You fool noone anymore jew demon. You will soon be tossed to the Lake of Fire to burn for all eternity. Youll have company with all your fag jew and camel jockee buddies.

We plan on enjoying your howls all the way in heaven. Stars and bars forever! For the Glory of Christ!

BURN Mickey and demon family for time immemorial

(Name withheld)

.

Dear Stars and Bars,

I understand that in the New Testament Jesus offers salvation as a free gift. According to the New Testament, Jesus did that by dying for mankind, by allowing the spilling of his blood. I understand that in the New Testament Jesus gave his blood by dying for mankind so that mankind gets the free gifts of salvation and purity. I do not get what you are saying about " His blood shed makes us pure." Are you saying is that we human beings can be pure if some of us choose to kill for Christ? Where in the New Testament has Jesus actually killed others by shedding their blood to make us pure? What do you mean by "you Cant fight God?"

Please explain what you said "His blood shed makes us pure?

A MRFF ally

◆◆◆

Subject: Your Destiny

After reading about your paganistic activities, I only wish that I were at the pearly gates when you take your last breath, and I hear the Lord say " Depart from me your sinful scumbag, and forever enjoy the fires of hell". Your eternal fate is sealed.

.

Dear Mr. (withheld)—

I am writing in response to your email to Mikey Weinstein. I am not sure what "paganistic activities" you believe damn him to "forever enjoy the fires of hell," but I somehow doubt you are not accusing him of participating in an earth-centered religion and preparing for the upcoming Sabbat of Mabon. Instead, I suspect you use the term "paganistic" in the derogatory sense sometimes used by so-called "Christians" to refer to anyone who isn't Christian.

I will not explain the history of the various pagan religions or why your use of the term is so insulting, nor will I attempt to educate you about the fact that the Constitution protects the religious beliefs of ALL people—both Christians and non-Christians. Understanding such things requires a respect for others that you clearly do not have. I will only point out that you would damn a man to hell because, in your mind, his actions do not conform to what you believe is required to avoid such a fate. It is incredibly arrogant to assume that because YOU dislike something, it is inherently wrong.

You seem to believe that YOUR opinion somehow determines another person's destiny. I must admit, it has been a while since I picked up my Bible, but I'm fairly certain that the term "scumbag" doesn't appear anywhere in it. You, sir, are no Christian. Any true Christian would know that it is not his place to declare punishment—particularly without knowing all of the facts. For example, over 96% of MRFF clients are Christians who reached out to MRFF as a result of religious discrimination and persecution. Additionally, MRFF has been nominated for the Nobel Peace Prize numerous times. These hardly seem like the actions of someone destined for an eternity in hell. What have you done lately besides write fatalistic emails?

Unlike you, I will not venture to predict what your fate holds, but perhaps you will be the one who is surprised when you reach those pearly gates and the Lord says to you, "That's NOT what I taught!"

Blessed be,

Tobanna Barker
MRFF Legal Affairs Coordinator

♦♦♦

Subject: snap crackle and pop

Hey Kikey jew Mikey. Yo! You are a dirty filthy faggot leftist athiest communnist lying clever Christ-killing raghead-loving socialist tool of-Satan kike scumbag. Drained the blood out of any Christian children lately for your matzah snacks? We pray the Lord for the ruin of your diseased children and wife. And all who are at the MFFR and all who give you santuary. You are jew enemy Number 1.

You think Obummer can save you from the White house? Niether you or him have favor with Christ Jesus. Our savior know you both not. (Matthew 7:23) And you deserve no mercy from Jesus for how you attack our soldiers. Even the girl negro fighter pilot. And all those spirit-filled chaplins who you turn you evildoer jew hate upon, For your jew $$. and you jew ego. Stiff necked jew! (proverbs 29:1). Be destroyed!

You are what worse than Isis and al quayda and tailban. Jesus is done with you now. Praise The Lord! The Son will have you burn in hell eternal. But first He will have you watch as your wife and children burn before you. You and all darkness are helpless before Jesus.

There skin will snap crackle and pop under hells clensing flame of righteous and grace and veangence. you will hear it you will see it you will smell it before you to are sent there mikey. Heat wave coming for you! How will your family smell on fire? Oh hallelujah! you will howl in sorrow for youre burning kin and clan Snap crackle and pop. snap crackle and pop. Just like that matzahs you eat jewboy.

(Name withheld)

.

His ignorance is astounding and seems to fuel his hate. His stupidity is evident even while his use of hyphens is not. I would lay odds that this person could not define a single chosen word/combination of words. A Jew/Atheist and a Communist/Socialist are quite opposing, are they not? It just numbs my mind when I realize that all of the vile, hate-filled fanatics feel that they know exactly what Jesus wants, and they feel completely free to speak on Jesus' behalf.

.

Oy vey. I wish they would learn the proper spelling of the word "atheist." If you can spell "scumbag" correctly, why can't you spell "atheist?" Sometimes I wonder what is whirling around in the heads of these creeps when they aren't writing hate letters. I mean, it must be a burden to carry around all this hate inside all the time. I can't help thinking that this is the kind of person who one day picks up a rifle and shoots 26 kindergarten children thinking he is sending them to Jesus.

(Name withheld)

.

The spelling in this hate letter is so bad, it should come with a glossary. Here's one that might help your readers:

Obummer = When President Obama trips going to the podium

Tailban = Banning girls from the bar on the military base

Al quayda = Al's Dada-ist bar on the Quay in Paris

clensing = What Uncle Clen did when the cops caught him

chaplins = Military pastors who think they are funny

santuary = An estuary that has been sanitized

A MRFF supporter

.

Dear "info"—

I am writing in response to your email to Mikey Weinstein. First, let me say that it is truly inspiring that someone as clearly ignorant as you has learned to use a computer. We at MRFF receive a number of uninformed, profane, and poorly written emails, but yours really deserves some sort of "Moron of the Year" award. Sixth-graders have forged notes to get out of gym class that are more intelligent than your email—at least these notes are based in reality and they sign a real name, even if it's not their own. Not only are you incapable of forming a complete sentence and clueless regarding the true mission of MRFF (which represents thousands of Christian soldiers, sailors, airmen, Marines, cadets, and veterans, as well as service members of other faiths or no faith at all), you plainly do not understand the principles of your own professed Christian faith. Last I checked, Jesus never felt pleasure at the thought of people burning alive—you're thinking of psychopaths, not Jesus or true Christians.

On that note, in light of the unadulterated glee you seem to receive by threatening such vile acts against Mikey, his family, and the rest of us at MRFF, I sincerely suggest that you make an appointment with a therapist as soon as possible. I trust there is a doctor somewhere who will delight in treating the merry-go-round of crazy and stupidity you have to offer.

Consequently, I trust that the only thing going "snap, crackle, pop" is your tiny brain as you attempt to understand the multi-syllable words I have written. Good luck with that. Do you smell smoke?

Blessed be,

Tobanna Barker
MRFF Legal Affairs Coordinator

♦♦♦

Subject: When you MFFR finally pass away off God's earth

We will be in heavan at the right hand our Lord and Savior Jesus The Christ.

And watching you and your little brood of Christ haters fry in hell for your crimes against Jesus.

It will be fun for us the faithful. FUN!

The fun will be watching Mikie scream and squirm to stop the fires all over on his angry little jew bod. FUN!

it hurts huh Mikie? Maybe it'll stop some year? Nope.

Hey good luck on that Mikie.

Plus the fun of watching him watch his burning wife bonny. Howling with their kids and grandkids and great grandkids all burning together.

A Wienstein family fire affair! FUN!

And all them other MFFR people will burn together. Flaming eternal with there mouths screaming for the Devine justice to stop.

Oh andn it never will jewboy.

'Stop! Stop the burning! I can't take the pain! Help! Help! You are our only Savior Lord Jesus. Forgive us!" FUN! FUN! FUN!

But too late little Mikie and the MFFR. You had your chances to bow your knees and confess Jesus as your onliest King.

too many chances.

Maybe you should'nt have taken the Air Force prayers to Christ Jesus away from the players at the football games?

Opps maybe your thinking you like a do over? Too late too late too late.

ya think little Mikie?i

Hey hows the whether down there wth Satin!

What? No begles and lox for you down there? NO FUN FOR MIKIE AND FAMILY! NO FUN FOR MFFR PEOPLE! hot hot hot hot hot!!

(Name withheld)

·

Dear (name withheld),

Mikey would have replied to you himself, but he was busy and sent me this in case I was motivated to do so before he flushed. Understand, what follows are my thoughts alone. They do not represent Mikey or the MRFF.

First, your illiterate and dyslexic reference to the MRFF as MFFR (repeatedly!!), your misspelling of Bonnie Weinstein's name, and a plethora of other assorted ignorant misspellings and syntax errors identify you as sufficiently ill-educated, illiterate, and 'challenged' as to be included in the next edition of Bonnie's book To the Far-Right Christian Hater...You Can Be a Good Speller or a Hater, But You Can't Be Both. *That's not something in which you should take pride...just sayin'. All I can say is that you would be the prime illustration of the meme "All I need to know about Christians I learned on April 19, 1995" [look it up] had I not had a lifetime's experience with authentic believer's in Jesus' message.*

I'm curious about how you expect people to want anything to do with a religion [such as you represent it] that revels in the thought of eternal torment for those who disagree with it? I understand that your mythology demands eternal damnation for those who transgress...it's the "FUN! FUN! FUN!" part that seems so entirely un-Christian, not to mention perverted. You're obviously obsessed & overjoyed at the prospect of watching not only those with whom you disagree, but their innocent and unborn descendants as well, suffering torment for crimes they didn't have anything to do with [presuming your twisted theology has any relevance to reality]. It is evident that you clearly suffer from a sado-masochistic sexual disorder. Did you ejaculate while writing your screed?

Having been, during my youth, rather aggressively proselytized by my childhood companions and their parents, it was—then—my conception that the religion Jesus preached was one of kindness, compassion, and very importantly, forgiveness…remember that "forgive them Father, for they know not what they do" thing [Luke 23:34]? Based on what I've learned over time about what Jesus' adherents believe I suspect you're not one of them. Please get moral and psycho-sexual help, you're badly in need of both.

Marshalldoc.

.

Dear (name withheld),

I would rather spend eternity in flames for the crime of living a life of true empathy and devotion to the wellbeing of others than spend one week among the pathetic, morally bankrupt, cesspool of evil that is your ilk. You salivate at the wildly detailed fantasies of human suffering you've concocted, and all the while think you're taking the moral high ground. That's laughable, not laudable. I pity you, because I understand that you must carry an enormous amount of pain in your heart to genuinely feel glee at the thought of other's pain.

Get well soon,

Blake A. Page
Military Religious Freedom Foundation
Special Assistant to the President
Director of US Army Affairs

♦♦♦

Subject: Anti Christ Revealed!

Mr. Weinstein you are now NAMED by our church. Lo behold the anti Christ. Or of the word and whole flesh of the anti Christ. You are such a evil leader of dark forces. Head ring leader. But you are at last exposed!

You will suffer eternity in hell for driving Jesus Christ out of the armies of USA. And under the orders of your cohort black moslim president from africa husien obama. But a new day is dawning in America where your rebel kind will be cast into the Lake of Fire. So closest we can smell it.

No rest for day or night. And the smoke from your burn flesh will rise high up in to the heavenns. (Revelations 14:11)

Your of jew kind so you know all about that burning flesh. Oh it stinks and yours won't never stop burning. You pridefully defy Jesus and He will make you pay the pride price.

We proclaim Christ Jesus as Lord of the Military in America. With the new President The Lamb will cleanse earth of your Weinstein seed filth.

Soon with new President you and you ugly wife and disease spawn and rat followers will be thrown by The Son of Man to burn forever and ever and ever.

And ever and ever and ever and forever. As it is written so shall it be. The flames await you're flesh Mr. Weinstein. Prepare to burn.

(Name withheld)

.

Dear Sir,

As if the email address is legit, you left off your name so the assumption is that you are a man. Your email to Mikey is interesting as I know him and can assure you the last thing he wants to do is drive any religious preference from the military. I should know as I just retired as a Command Chaplain for the United States Army. Now I could argue your points—ad infinitum; however, I sense that would be useless.

Since the Rapture has not occurred yet, unless you and I have been "forgotten" (I am a student of Eschatology) then the basic requirement for "the revelation" has not been met. I can tell as well that Mikey has not suffered a mortal wound to his head, nor have the two witnesses come forth. As a final statement, Mikey has impact; globally, with seven (7) Nobel Peace Prize nominations. As busy as he is I am sure that his objective does not include being the leader of the world.

Respectfully,

(Name withheld)

Subject: You will BURN in hell

The only reason you and your MFFR don't want a war hero like Gen Boykin to speak at fort Riley is because your a FUCKING JEW COCKSUCKER CHRIST KILLER WITH A NAPOLEON COMPLEX!!

I HOPE YOU WIFE AND CHILDREN AND GRANDCHILDREN DIE SCREECHING BEFORE YOUR EYES BY THE WRATH OF THE ONLY TRUE LORD REDEEMER AND SAVIOR PROVIDED TO MANKIND.

WHICH IS JESUS THE CHRIST! JESUS WILL NOT LET YOU FURTHER HARM HIS FOLLOWERS AND HE WILL HAVE YOU BURN IN HELL FOREVER!!!

Mickey have a nice eternity burning with your wife and kids and grandkids. Say hi to obama and hillary.

(Name withheld)

.

Hi (name withheld),

I hope this is not a fake address. Most of the cowards that send slime like this use a fake address, so if this gets to you it will be a surprise. Having said that, let me say that it surprises me not a whit that someone with the lack of decency you demonstrate would be attacking us for opposing having our honored military offer a government-sponsored speaking opportunity to a homophobic, Islamophobic Christian-supremacist bigot. He's had his invitation revoked, as I assume you know, but I'm sure you can find someplace to hear his drivel if you're capable of sneaking out from under your rock.

Mike Farrell
(MRFF Board of Advisors)

Subject: Jesus will send you to hell

Mr. Wienstien

What does the communist organization MFFR have against the love of Jesus in the military? You think you won that court case yesterday about that poor Marine lady who wasn't allowed to show her simple and pure love for Jesus? You think Jesus won't make you and those liberal communist judges pay for such blaspheme?

Jesus is the only life truth and way for the military. For the whole world.

Read His Word.

There is no doubt.

Jesus will send you directly to hell for what you have done to stop the spread of his innocent and saving grace. For what you are still doing.

You and your fellow MFFR villains will pay for this unholy defiance.

But none will pay more than you Mr. Wienstien. For you are the blackest and evilest soul on earth.

My husband and I know we are not supposed to say but we will enjoy watching you be consumed forever in flames.

Enjoy your little court case "victory" while you can.

The only true victory is in Christ.

Think on that sir while you are on fire for eternity.

(Name withheld)

·

Mr. (name withheld)—if this is a real name and email—which is doubtful:
Your email to Mr. Weinstein was somewhat ill informed and harsh without reason. You see Mikey only engaged due to a complaint from a person involved and the Surgeon was way out of place. You see I served almost thirty-three

years with the last seventeen as a Chaplain in the United States Air Force and The United States Army. Having spent numerous visits and an occasional tour into our military hospitals and I can assure you that this Surgeon was very wrong. My question to you is simply this, would you be as offended if a Muslim Doctor came out and prayed with the family? Or how about a Wiccan, or Buddhist, the list could be endless? Would you feel that Mikey should "burn" if the role were reversed and it was a Jewish Doctor offering a prayer? You see as a Chaplain I learned very quickly that we have myriads of beliefs and non-beliefs in the military and so I took to heart the directive to either perform or provide services. This Surgeon was to provide a service (surgery) and if he had a strong Christian belief nothing in the world would prevent him from praying before providing said "service." However, he crossed the line - without the affected members permission—and demanded that all pray. Even as a Chaplain I could not demand everyone to pray even when I became a Colonel. So, the Surgeon was not innocent! He was guilty of pressing his beliefs on someone who neither wanted the prayer or asked for it. Please peruse your facts next time you go into a fray, as you may come out looking a whole lot less foolish. As you showed your conclusion leaving a hanging adjective—eternal (sic) what? I hope this email reaches you; but, you and the thousands of cowards never let us address you personally.

Sincerely,

Quentin D Collins, US Army Chaplain (Colonel-Retired)
MRFF National Advisory Member

.

(Name withheld)

It is quite obvious you do not understand the mission of Mikey Weinstein, he is not anti-religion, he stands for the constitution that does not allow religious overtone in the military. there are too many upper ranking in the military who demand those under them observe whatever religion they themselves observe, that- is against military code and the constitution. I'd rec commend you take a better look at what he does and thank him for protecting the rights of all religions as well as those with no religious affiliation. remember- your religion is the blueprint for life you have chosen it is for you to follow it is not for anyone to uses to judge any other. that is arrogance and very far from the teachings of any bible except for the old testament where death to the blasphemers was accepted. Mikey is not your enemy he works for everyone...

A proud MRFF supporter

◆◆◆

Subject: you will burn forever in hell

I hate you Mike Weinstien and I hate your stupid organization of Jesus haters. When you pass away when decreed by Jesus and we pray the Son takes you soon to judgment. It will be a holiday in heaven when Jesus sentences you to burn in the Lake of Fire. The cheering from the Host and angles will be defeaning and glorious to behold. Hallelujah. I promise you this. You satanic demon. After you are buried I will find your grave and deficate all over it. And I will use strongest apoxy glue to attach bibles to your headstone. Just like you won't let bibles in Japan for the troops. Your grave will have bible on it forever. As you burn in hell I hate you and your silly little MRRF minions.

—from a retired policeman and Sunday School teacher who loves Jesus and the Bible. And our servicemen and our Flag

.

I am sure that I can speak for everyone who works with and volunteers for the foundation, that being a MRFF minion is a badge worn proudly and with honor.

Subject: Mikey weinstein is the traitor

You are a traitor to Jesus Christ you jew dirt. And you are the traitor to America. We know who you are and the evil you have done.

Our new president knows too. He knows that our military needs to be led by Jesus. Your fight against Jesus is over now.

The old nigger in chief is gone thank Christ. He was a raghead commie monkey moslim who has a transvestite chimp as a wife. He loved you jew monkey. But he all gone now.

Can't wait for mikey to die and then burn forever. The pain of the flame is your eternity jew killer. jew **traitor.**

Maybe you can get a raghead moslim to fuck your white traitor wife? She wants a big raghead dick for a change. OINK Oy VAY!

Traitorism runs in the Whinestein family. A fine family of traitors to Christ and America. And you know what President Trump does to traitors mikey?

You about to find out. You're cell in guantanamo is waiting. bread and water hard labor. Then gallows. Then fires of hell. Halleluyah!

HALLELUYAH

(Name withheld)

.

Dear (name withheld),

If the filthy pig who wrote this didn't use a cowardly fake address, I hope he can read better English than he can write.

You, sir, are a cheap, repulsive repudiation of Christianity. Your addled brain spews vile, soul-defiling garbage in the name of Jesus, a fact so grotesquely ironic that only a diseased spirit could claim responsibility for it. Of course, hiding behind your robe and hood you haven't the courage to take responsibility for anything. But in the dark of night, when you tremble in fear for having so demeaned the name of the one you claim to represent, know this: the worm that is eating away at what's left of your mind is laughing as it fattens itself, little knowing it will soon die of the poison that fuels you.

Mike Farrell,
MRFF Board of Advisors

◆◆◆

Subject: weinstein is leading you all to the eternal flames

Do you fine folks at the MFRR even know that when you die you will not be going to heaven?
You will going to your father in Hell. The devil.
You will be set on fire to roast for your evil in opposing the Son of God for our military men.
And you will have satan's right hand man to thank for your burning alive forever.
Michael Weinstein.
Mikey your fearless leader is of satan by satan and for satan.
And he is a jew as we can all see so well. (John 8:44)
Mikey is satan's little helper.
Condemn him for his demonic evil before Jesus will make you pay for not doing so.
(a service member's wife who knows what she is talking about)

.

Hi (Name withheld)

You may actually be a service member's wife, there's no way to know about that, but you sure as hell don't know what you're talking about.

The sickness that permeates your "knowledge," your apparent belief system, is alarming because it is what promotes this ugly assault on people you don't know yet feel free to condemn. I urge you to talk to your service member husband and see if you can't find some psychological help through him or his medical connections.

Just to be as clear as possible in the face of your perverse views and accusations, none of us is going to the hell you envision, a place the idea of which obviously torments you. Nor are any of us "opposing the Son of God for our military men," as you claim to believe. We support those in the military

245

and, in particular, support their right to believe as they choose rather than having them left to suffer while misguided hyper-Christian zealots like you insist their personal, twisted and in your case wacky beliefs on them.

Mikey takes a lot of heat from bigots like you for being "a jew," as you put it. But you know, so was Jesus. And he took a lot of crap too. I see no reason to condemn Mikey; instead I applaud him for his steadfast dedication to supporting the constitutional rights of every woman and man in the service of their country.

You might think about being a fraction of the American citizen he is. If you were you'd find a lot of ways to be of value to your husband and your country rather than being a pathetic bigot spewing hatred in the name of God.

Mike Farrell,
MRFF Board of Advisors

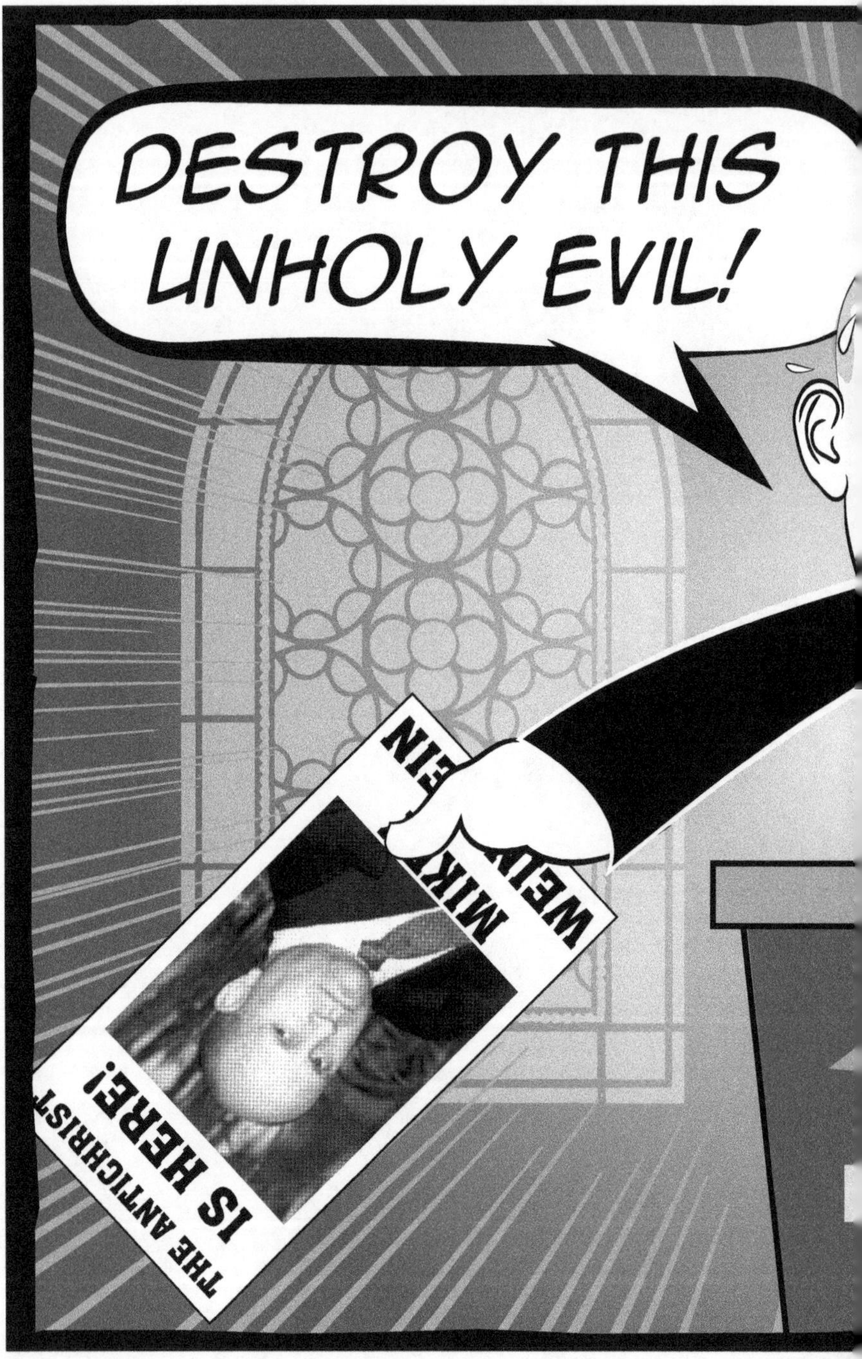
DESTROY THIS UNHOLY EVIL!
THE ANTICHRIST IS HERE!

Anti-Christ

MY HUSBAND AND I have been called many names. They call me a lot of cuss names; however, some very creative ones have been hurled at Mikey. He has been called a Jew lawyer, a soulless jew, a pussy ass Jew boy, Mr. jewgooder, a jew coward, a stiff neck jew, jewfuck, jew asshole, jew boy, goddamn jew, a thievery jew, a jew trouble maker, a stinkin jew, a little jew, a whimpering jew, a conniving jew, a leftist jew bastard, a jew liar, and a pissy jew. Besides the Jew name calling, which I guess should be expected from this level of lowlife, they move on to calling Mikey a worthless piece of garbage, a bully, a disgusting little prick, a dip shit, a fucking moron, shit for brains, a pussy, a worm line (what the hell does that mean?), little Mikey boy, a stupid liberal, a Jesus-hating faggot, and a communist atheist.

However, in this chapter they concentrate mostly on Satan, coming up with the names of Satan's Lawyer, a disciple of Satan, a tool of Satan, a devoted senior servant of Satan, the soul of Satan, the devil incarnate, a false profit of darkness, an unrepentant sinner, Christ killer, the Anti-Christ, a commie Christ hating satan lover, the great eviler of our age, and my personal favorite, the field general of the godless armies of Satan. I like to be called by my given name, which is Bonnie, or more formally, Mrs. Weinstein, especially from people whom I have never met. My mom calls me Bonnie-mue. I like that. It is without doubt cowardly, to say the least, that people hide behind a keyboard and toss out mean spirited, ugly names to my husband. If they had a chance to have a reasonable, sensible discourse with him, I think they would come away with a different opinion of him. However, I have a feeling that is asking way, way too much of these emailers because I mentioned the words reasonable and sensible.

What on earth was I thinking?

I like to call him sweet heart, or honey, and I know he likes that. It's when I call him Michael that he knows for sure I am upset with him.

◆ ◆ ◆

Subject: Is Mikey aware he is walking dead?

Hi,

I've just seen this latest stupidity of Mikey's over the Bible on the desk and have to think he must be a disciple of Satan and eager to destroy the truth of Jesus and His Second Coming!

When Mikey's ancestor's successfully slaughtered Jesus as an offering to Satan they saw GOD tear open the veil of the temple showing that Jesus's death ended the law yet now 2,000 years later the Mikey's of this world still prefer to follow Satan to their doom and refuse the simple offer of eternal life Jesus made to all who would accept it by simply believing He is the Son of God.

I do wish you Jews would burn your Torahs and get good NKJV Study Bibles and learn the truth of Jesus and see how simple is the way to eternal life with Him on a renewed Earth.

Good luck for when Jesus returns to destroy all who lie: 1 Corinthians 6:9

(Name withheld)

.

I think someone has seen a few too many zombie movies and TV shows!

.

Sadly, (Name withheld),

You appear to reside in the broken pieces of a fractured self. As a woman of faith, while I was reading such a diatribe of garbage in your email, it left me cold, suspended in an empty vortex. This type of vortex brings nothing good to the earth .

An evolved soul recognizes the value of "others." Our friend, Mikey Weinstein, is a man of perseverance, diligence, dedication of the highest level, and deeply authentic. . .

Sadly, what a loss for you by remaining just a broken piece of a human being. . .you could be so much more, like the vase below. . .

Be well,

Jude

♦♦♦

Subject: Behold the Anti-Christ

As a true Christian mother of 5 and wife of a career active duty spirit-filled Marine I'd just like to tell you to FUCK OFF. The only words you deserve. The Corps teaches the love of Christ to all and runs on it and fights with it. Our country's enemies (like YOU and your MRFF) fear the USMC because the Corps is of Christ and has Christ in it. You take Christ out of the Corps and you cripple it. Do that and America falls and its YOUR fault Weinstein. Your last name its jewish right? This all makes sense because we all know who killed Jesus. Don't try to blame the Romans either. I pity you. I even more pity your poor wife and children and grandchildren to have to live with a Christ hater like you. A Christ killer. Ruthless and brutal. Guess you can't help it. Its in your blood.

.

Dear (Name withheld),

If the only words we deserve are "FUCK OFF" you've surely gone above and beyond the call of duty with your love letter to us. I often hear from "spirit filled" believers. Interestingly, the one characteristic that I've seen which distinguishes these "spirit filled" folks from other believers is that they in no way reflect the unconditional love of others taught in their book of magic stories. Usually they're hateful little pricks that express themselves by aligning with the Christian love that Hitler showed the Jews and that the KKK showed to non-whites. I'm sure when you learned about the horrors of the holocaust in school you never would have dreamed that one day you'd be sympathetic to their racist disgusting ideology, and yet here we are. Funny how things work out.

You've said that the Corps is a Christian organization (albeit in more words, but the message was received). Please tell me more about this. Are there Marine Corps policies in place at your husband's installation which have led you to believe that your religion has conquered a branch of our military? I'm very eager to learn more about the sources which support your claim.

I do wish you luck in reconciling your depraved self righteous indignation with the messages of love you seem to have ignored in the bible. Perhaps the next time you applaud a lynching, and throw slurs towards a person simply for having a Jewish name you'll at least have the confidence to openly admit that you, Brenda, share the same bigoted principles as the most vilified scum of the past several centuries, the Nazis and other white Christian supremacist groups.

Cheers (and go fuck yourself),

Blake A. Page

♦♦♦

Subject: Hope you Choke to death on You Own Vomit

We learned all about you at bible study tonight on post satan Mickey. You are now revealed for all the world of loving Christians to see. Evil doer of jew blood ancestory. Educated by Uncle Sam and turns on the Christian hands who fed him. Eat vomit and choke till you croak on it. You anti Christ.

.

That is what a Bible study is for, is it not, to discuss how much you hate someone and say anti-Semitic things about that person?

♦♦♦

Subject: Re: Our Church Feels Bad for your Kids

Mr. Wienstein,

As Youth Pastor at our town's largest church of spirit-filled followers of our Lord and Savior Jesus Christ and the father of 5 children myself I find myself pitting your poor children.

From many media sources it seems that you have 2 or 3 sons and 2 daughters. You even have grandchildren. We have some their pictures up in our Young Family Prayer Center. We pray on them each day to finally see their evil father for what he truly is.

Do these poor creatures have any idea that their father and leader of the family is a devoted senior servant of Satan? How can they not see you evil as the world does?

Do your poor children know how evil you are? How invested in the dark Father of Lies you are? Millions around the world do know. More clever dangerous and evil than atom bombs.

Do they have any idea how badly you have injured our American army by taking Christ Jesus away from their lives? You won't even let the Marines have a God Bless sign on base now?

Do your sons and daughters understand that their father will burn in flames for all time after he breathes his last breath? You will be a hallelujah bon fire of revenge for the Son of God.

Your children better get the blinders out of their eyes and see you for what millions in this world already do.

The Number One Prophet for Satans' plans for doom and chaos. Michael Wienstein is The apple Satan's evil eye.

(Name withheld)

.

That is really creepy…they have our kids pictures up on the wall to pray on? I suggest they pray for their own family's religious education and leave mine out of their small minded and negative belief system.

.

At first, I chuckled at the wording of this letter. Then I read it for content and my words left me. In fact, I've had to walk away from the computer several times and delete a couple of 'over the top' responses. Here is hoping this attempt succeeds. I understand the letter writer wants you (MRFF in general and The Weinsteins in particular) to know they are praying for you. In a vague way that sounds harmless enough until the writer tells you they have pictures of your grandkids up on a wall where they are the focus of much prayer.

I've been reading on your website for a while now and the idea of children being exposed to the amount of vitriol you face every day makes my blood run cold. Who takes innocents and uses them this way? And why would they think this is in any way OK? Shall we find pictures of all their loved ones and do the same thing? I can guarantee the cries of WITCH would be so loud the internets would not be needed to hear them.

I get MRFF works hard to maintain the constitution against attacks by Christian supremacists. I guess exposing the hypocrisy is a side benefit. All I do know is none of you are paid enough to do this job (snark intended as I know many of you volunteer—grins).

A MRFF ally

.

Couldn't be more proud to have you as my dad. I would love to go into their church and rip my picture off the wall in the middle of their class.

Curtis Weinstein

.

Well, you've been known quite publicly as the field general of the godless armies of Satan for quite a while, and I think I can speak on behalf of your kids to say that we're still quite happy to stick by you.

.

So funny to see this crap, from these people. I've met almost all of your family and they are AWESOME! I can't believe they say this stuff without actually meeting anyone.

.

Isn't it comforting to know that youth pastors not only do not know the Constitution, they don't know how to spell either!

.

Mikey: I am speechless after reading this! Are these people for real? (He can't spell either). I never knew we had people like this living in the US! I don't know how you stand it!

.

Dear Youth Pastor,

Wow. Talk about hypocrisy. You mention being invested in the "Father of Dark Lies"—well you are promulgating the biggest lie in the world and to children no less! What kind of low life are you, taking advantage of impressionable children and filling them with the lie of an omnipresent and omniscient being? Shame on you. You are exactly the kind of person you think Mikey Weinstein to be. Give people a code of conduct—but don't spread falsehood.

Signed, Supporter of truth and realism

♦♦♦

Subject: Research Report on You

Mr. Weinstein, greetings.

My bible study Womens Group was asked by our Pastor to prepare a oral report on you and your anti-Christian MRRF and we did a lot of research. No surprise to find out that you are a communist and an atheist and that you are a soulless jew. That last thing always seems to go with the first two doesn't it. Also found out that you have been attacking innocent Christians for years now in the armed services. Now like that poor Marine Col. on Hawaii. All because your precious children supposedly got mistreated at the air force academy? You and your wife have raised a bunch of wimps. She's a soulless jew too and a cripple. satan brought you two hate birds together and taught to breed more hate birds. satan made your wife a cripple and you a High leader of darkness. Can't you see?

Come to find out that all that happened to your brood of kids is that some good folks at air force academy tried to respectful expose them to the love of the Gospel and to The Word of Christ. To save them from eternal damnation for rejecting Jesus Christ as you have done. Like father like children. Stupid is as stupid does. You and your children and wife are so ungrateful to those who Walk in The Word. And for showing such Christian grace and love their "jewish lawyer' father goes postal forever on innocent Christians in the uniform services. You are a waste and a fool. America was built on Christian values and is a Christian nation with a Christian purpose to fulfill. You can't fight Jesus Mr. Weinstein so give it up. We will give our report on you tomorrow evening at our church.

The Spirit of the Living Christ will be with us all as we do it. We will sing the Israel national anthem and the American national anthem too as we always do.

We will pray that you be given a final chance to come to the Lord before satan rewards you for your disservice to America. Your dishonor to the services. You make Jesus just weep. If anyone ever deserved to burn in the lake of fire it is you Mr. Weinstein. Hell was made with commie soulless jews like you in mind. You are very Lost and so shameful.

Do not reply to this e-mail as your demonic attempts to attack us will not be allowed to received by the Children of The Lord.

.

Wait, they did a lot of research and they came up with all of that crap? What pray tell kind of research is done to find out if you are soulless or not? Did they fact check anything? Sorry, stupid question. How did they jump to the false and ridiculous conclusion; that I am a cripple simply because I have MS? Oh, sorry. I am throwing out reasonable questions to an unreasonable statements and a really stupid letter.

My bad.

.

Dear Children of the Lord,

Urgent! Please let me know immediately how to reach your pastor!

He needs to be warned that there is someone in his congregation who is insane. This is a person or persons whose drunken ramblings (I assume drunken because they include such poor spelling and mangled syntax - of course it could be drugs) make little sense but manage nonetheless to constitute libelous and scandalous insults to Jesus Christ and Christian values. This person (or these people) is (are) so unhinged that unless he, she or they are immediately separated from the Church Chochkee it will lose all credibility in the community of the Spirit of the Living Christ.

I know this may sound like an overly dramatic plea, but please know your congregation is in serious danger of being tainted by the obvious sickness of this person who claims to be a woman in your church's Women's Group. Of course it's hard to know If anything she or he says is verifiable since it's clear she/he/they has or have been struck by the curse of the Tower of Babel and everyone with whom she, he or it comes in contact is in danger of being exposed as part of a cult of fanatics because of the ravings of the poor demented soul in your midst.

I hope the pastor of the Church Chochkee is capable of doing the necessary exorcism to rid she, he or it of the demons that are clearly possessing him, her or them.

I'm happy to be of assistance in the event he needs any help, because this may be the worst case of demonic possession I've ever seen. Normally demons manifest as powerful and intelligent, if nefarious, beings. This one is trying to trick us by appearing to be unutterably stupid.

Thanks.

Mike Farrell
(MRFF Board of Advisors)

◆◆◆

Subject: Fuck The MRRF

Our local Christian radio station call in show was all about you and your little band of Christ hating bastards today. You have a problem with the Army fighting for our Lord and country Wienstien? You and your little clone followers of satan can just get the fuck out of our USA! Scram you blasphemers!

I hope the Isis captures you and skins you alive for your family to see. For the world to see. Then watch you beg our marines and soldiers who walk in Christ to save your pussy ass jewboy. But it will be too late for you as you will burn in hell. Still not to late for America to drop to its knees and confess Christ over all else. To include your constitution and bill of declaration independence rights. Where do you think that all came from anyway? From Jesus thats where. Your a doomed and stupid fool. A false prophete of darkness

Dear Ignoramus,

I think the only thing clear in your message is... no, I'm wrong. There's nothing clear in your message. You listen to a "Christian radio station" that doesn't, apparently, know what it's talking about. You don't know anything about us except what some bigot told you, and you're stupid enough to repeat it while insecure enough to hide behind a fake address. You give voice to some ugly threatening fantasies aimed at us and do so while pretending to believe in Christ and Christ's teaching. You show your ignorance of the country you pretend to be defending by calling one of its founding documents a "bill of declaration independence rights. And you are an anti-Semite. Other than that, I guess I can be charitable enough to thank you for providing more evidence of the accuracy of Bonnie's book. In case you missed it, it's called, "You can be a good speller or a hater, but you can't be both."

Mike Farrell
(MRFF Board of Advisors)

·

After sending a letter like this out to supporters and friends we often receive little tidbits of comments and support back. Now, it all depends on your level of sarcasm and sense of humor here, but you've got to love some of the comments even though they may be a little rough around the edges...

I'm betting he masturbates to "Oh Come, All Ye Faithful" while hurting himself, because he "knows it's wrong..."

"A corpse torch forever burning in the Lake of Fire." I like that...sounds like some brutal lyrics to a sweet death metal song!

And one I particularly enjoyed: "I believe there's something in the New Testament somewhere that specifically mentions Jesus ordaining the bill of declaration independence rights. I think maybe it's in Luke, but I'm not sure. So, clearly, he's got you there."

I had no idea that Jesus authored the US Constitution. I must have missed that lecture in law school... Stay strong.

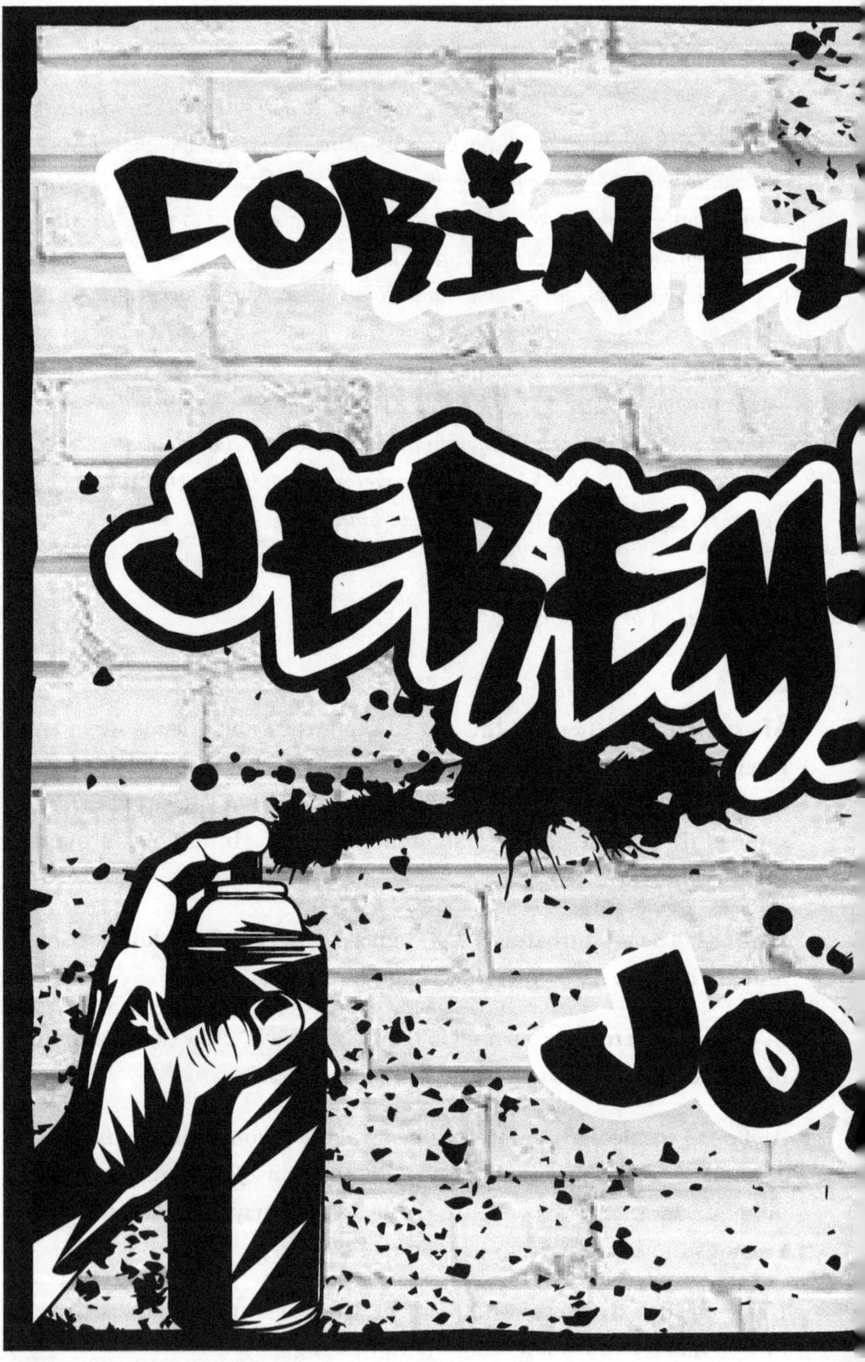

ANS 10:17

AH 29:11

N 3:22

RANDOM BIBLE VERSES

INTERESTINGLY ENOUGH, THERE ARE thousands of different distinct denominations of Christianity, and what separates them is that each of them has an entirely different opinion on what the scriptural texts say. I didn't know there were thousands, not by any stretch of the imagination.

I wonder how many of these Jesus-loving people have ever sat down and read the Bible cover to cover. I think, in actuality, very few. I would put money on it. I think they rely on preachers at their Sunday sermon to give them tidbits of biblical information, then cherry-pick Bible verses to use here and there when they think it's appropriate.

So, here we have a chapter filled with the love of, and devotion to, quoting scripture—and not in a good way. Having read enough of it over the course of thirteen-plus years, I have found a pattern. The long and short of it is simply this: scripture is used to justify hate toward other religious faiths, people of color, homosexuality, and anything else they decide to dislike. This, then, is all wrapped together to blame whomever they choose for any supposed infraction they feel qualifies as wrong according to their personal belief system. Rarely, if ever, have I heard someone quote scripture to bless someone or for a happy occasion.

♦♦♦

Subject: A verse

A verse for Mikey "For we are to God the aroma of Christ among those who are being saved and those who are perishing. To the one WE ARE THE SMELL OF DEATH; to the other, the fragrance of life." 2 Corinthians 1:18 J There you go weinstein. Have a nice Easter week. The man without the Spirit does not accept the things that come from the Spirit of God, for they are foolishness to him, and he cannot understand them, because they are spiritually discerned. 1 Corinthians 2:14

(Name withheld)

.

Dear (Name withheld)

Being Jewish, Easter has no meaning for me. But I hope you have a nice one.

Mikey Weinstein

.

Dear (name withheld),

This does confuse me, I have to say. People like you, who apparently believe in a Jew and feel they were saved by a Jew yet delight in indulging in such crass antisemitism, cause me to wonder if they understand the meaning of hypocrisy. That ever trouble you?

Mike Farrell
(MRFF Board of Advisors)

♦♦♦

Subject: Last Birthday

For a guy who says he's a lawyer you know nothing about how American law is derived from the New Testament and the miracle of Jesus Christ. You and your stiff-necked cohorts seem to get off on constantly trying to destroy the peace and love of Jesus in our armies. (Acts Chap 7) You are but flesh and blood and will whither as the grass. But the King of Kings reigns supreme forever.

Lord Jesus shed his precious blood to guarantee your place with Him in Eternity. Accept His free gift and disciple others to do the same. Or play the fool and reject His love and be consigned to satan and his flames in hell forever. A little net research shows it's to be your birthday soon Mickey? Inching ever closer to your special place burning in hell. Apostate Weinstein My unit and me will pray to Him and His Son that it will be your last birthday. (Psalm 109) And so your efforts to cleanse the military of Christ's power will perish with you.

(Name withheld)

·

I just want to know, how many of you raised an eyebrow when you read the first line of this letter? Megachurches teach that this is a Christian nation and revisionist history authorities spout this horrible misinformation and people eat it up. So, there you go...American law was derived from the New Testament and Jesus.

·

Dear (name withheld),

Like most religious misfits you seek to replace Jesus in the judgement department. Jesus is qualified to handle this stuff on his own without the help of those such as yourself.

American law was extracted from English common law and has nothing to do with the Bible or any other religious document. The United States Constitution contains not one word about religion or Gods.

You would do well not to attempt to commingle religious and secular life.

Please hold and respect your religious beliefs while respecting the beliefs and non-beliefs of others.

Rick Baker
Capt. USAF (MedRet), MRFF Volunteer.

♦♦♦

Subject: What's Wrong with Spreading the Love of Jesus Christ

What's wrong with spreading the love of Jesus Christ. Our country is in a downward spiral and it's because we've turned are back on God. Psalms 9 verse 17- The wicked shall be turned into hell, and all the nations that forget God.

(Name withheld)

·

Well, there is absolutely NOTHING wrong with spreading that "love"... But you must realize that America is NOT a Christian country... We are a secular country... Therefore, in order to "spread" that love it must be done in a time, place and manner that complies with our US Constitution, it's construing federal and state caselaw and, in the case of the military, in accordance with all department of defense directives, instructions and regulations... Can you understand that please...?

Thank you for your consideration,

Mikey Weinstein...
Founder and president, Military Religious Freedom Foundation

·

Dear (name withheld),

I am writing in response to your email to the Military Religious Freedom Foundation ("MRFF"). Contrary to your ludicrous assertion, the separation of church and state is not "a lie from the pit of hell." It is a right granted by the Constitution of the United States. I understand from your email that you don't like this fact, but that's just too bad for you. I don't like Mondays, but that doesn't stop one from coming around every week. MRFF fights tirelessly to protect this right for all of our brave men and women in uniform. Perhaps you can find something about helping those in need in that book you claim to have read.

Blessed be,

Tobanna Barker
MRFF Legal Affairs Coordinator

Subject: Happy Last fathers Day

Hello Mr. Mikey Weinstein. I'm the mother of 4 God fearing children of the Lord Jesus Christ. Do your kids and the Lord's whole green earth a favor today and choke to death on a chicken bone. You're a servant of Satan and deserve the flames which will surely await you. 2 Peter 2:4 1 Thessalonians 2:15

(Name withheld)

.

She has four children; that's sad. Children are a blank page, and as parents we write on that page whatever we choose. I think that raising children is the greatest of responsibilities one could ever hope to take on and should be done with great care and unconditional love, not fear and hoping someone chokes on a chicken bone.

♦♦♦

Subject: Help Build the Wall??

Dear Mr. Weinstein,

I call all Christians to start tearing down the wall of separation and to bury you underneath it, metaphorically speaking of course! Christians will start rising up and defying the governments rulings of separation of church and state no matter what is the cost to us!

Jesus was a revolutionary and an activist and we will follow His example of overturning the status quo and pushing back the powers of darkness!

May Jesus receive all the glory!!

"Righteousness exalts a nation, but sin is a disgrace to any people." Proverbs 14:34

(Name withheld)

♦♦♦

Subject: Devil

Mr. Michael Weinstein. You, sir, are the devil incarnate.
Get thee behind me, Satan. Matthew 16:23

(Name withheld)

.

Some of the most stupid and hate-filled proclamations are all easily justified with scripture...how very convenient.

.

Dear (name withheld),

It amazes me that so many of you faux-Christian Bible-spouters manage to employ certain passages of the good book for your own purposes without any comprehension of its overall message and do so while completely ignoring its other timely admonitions, such as "Judge not, lest ye be judged." Next time you kneel, if you do, to pray, if you do, I'd suggest you consider asking for forgiveness. Remember what pride goeth before...

Mike Farrell
(MRFF Board of Advisors)

.

My goodness it is wonderful theater. Bravo to Mike Farrell. Shakespeare could not have said it better! Someday, I'm going to write a scathing, hateful email to Mikey just to get an email from Mike Farrell. #Swoon

A MRFF Friend and supporter

.

Mikey, when religious haters email you their excrement-filled hate, you should just respond with the following passage taken from Jesus' Sermon on the Mount:

Matthew 5: 10-12 verse 11: Blessed are ye, when men shall revile you, and persecute you, and shall say all manner of evil against you falsely, for my sake.

Then just say "thanks for simultaneously ensuring my salvation and your damnation" according to your own beliefs.

A MRFF Supporter

♦♦♦

Subject: universal response to haters

Mikey, when religious haters email you their excrement filled hate, you should just respond with the following passage taken from Jesus' Sermon on the Mount:

Matthew 5: 10-12 verse 11: Blessed are ye, when men shall revile you, and persecute you, and shall say all manner of evil against you falsely, for my sake.

Then just say "thanks for simultaneously ensuring my salvation and your damnation" according to your own beliefs.

A MRFF Spporter

.

Can I have an amen here?

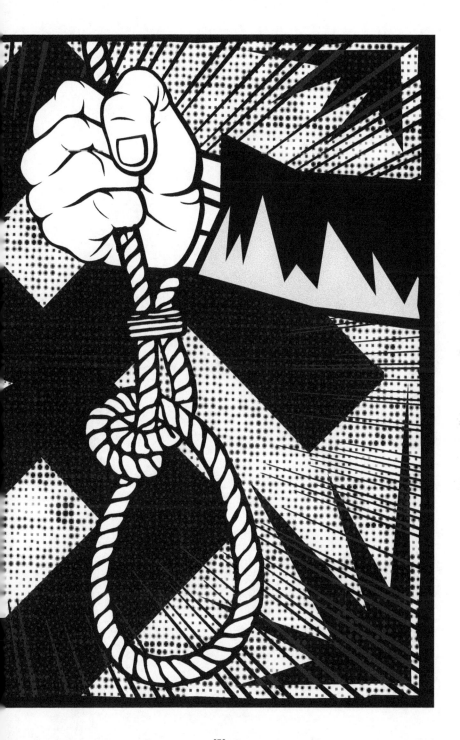

THREATS

WE TAKE ALL THREATS seriously, with security being our number one priority! That is a sad statement but necessary in the environment in which we now live. We have become targets. I can say with absolute certainty that most people do not live with the kind of intense security that we have had to develop around ourselves and our home. People may choose to have strong security, but does the average person need guns, protection dogs, cameras, personal hand to hand combat training, and bodyguards? I am pretty sure that's a no. Unfortunately, since the beginning of the foundation, that has become our new normal and I hate it.

We get many grotesque and threatening phone calls, and you are about to read a small sampling of the threats that come in daily via snail mail and email. Our windows have been shot out of our house, while I was home... twice! Swastikas and crosses have been spray painted on our home, innocent animals have been beheaded and disemboweled and left on our front porch. Our car tires have been slashed, and feces and beer bottles have been thrown at the house.

I was not home when the house was attacked and spray painted. I was in DC visiting friends and family. I came home to find my mother, who is in her eighties, on the front porch using chemicals to try and remove the swastikas and crosses from the house. She had hoped to have this done before I came home. Even though we live just outside the city, the then mayor of Albuquerque sent a graffiti team over to remove the mess from the front wall of our home.

The worst of the threats are immediately reported to law enforcement. We have had the local police at our house more times than I care to count. Our lawyers also write directly to those who threaten us. My husband and I are fighters and I love that about us.

◆◆◆

Subject: So sorry for you!

So sad for you Mikey!
We are many, We are legion, We are Anonymous

(Name withheld)

.

Of course you are anonymous, you coward!

◆◆◆

Subject: RE: News Article Today

Little man? Comical. Sort of like CNN and MSNBC, heh?
Those are your Holy Books, right? Pure BS just like your propaganda.
Gonna shut you down soon, 'ol boy. No one, I repeat no one likes a damn
RAT! We shoot all RATS in these parts.
FYI: I don't miss nor do I flinch.

(Name withheld)

◆◆◆

Subject: May God Have Mercy

May God have mercy on your soul for your unbelief. Don't ever threaten
me. You won't like the outcome.

(Name withheld)

.

*I am not quite sure what you're talking about? I do not believe that I have
ever threatened you? I'm afraid that I do not even seem to remotely remember
who you are?? Having said that, what do you mean "that I won't like the
outcome"? Kind of seems like you're threatening me, doesn't it?*

Mikey Weinstein

.

I mean exactly what I mean. You know exactly what I mean and I do not fear you Mikey.

(Name withheld)

.

Again, quite on the contrary, I actually do not know what you mean. Not in the slightest. Actually, I do not even know who you are? But we do get a lot of threats and are, thus, very used to it and so we will just add you to the list, little fellow.

Mikey Weinstein

.

I am honored that you regard me as a threat to your tyranny but you should really fear the wrath of God, not me.

(Name withheld)

.

I do not fear threats from either entity. I also offer you no honor whatsoever.

Mikey Weinstein

.

With threats of this nature we always do a lot of research to find out anything we can. We have an excellent research department. We also report activities like this to our local law enforcement and security. The information we unearthed on this individual from his twitter account was not surprising. His tweets involve a plethora of extremist right-wing thought, racism, and violence. Below are just a few of his tweets:

.

Why do young black men who are the minority commit well over 90% of violent crimes and make people like myself have to shoot them in defense You will suck on the barrel ad my .357.

I will bust your teeth out.

Are you surprised by his tweets? I sure am not but find it par for the course.

◆◆◆

Subject: intolerance

you have reached a new low for groups like yours. truly intolerant and bigoted. thank God you are in such a minority in our military and elsewhere.

fully expect to be attacked and welcome it

(Name withheld)

Dear (name withheld),

Really? We take these threats seriously, so you better be prepared to see the FBI knocking on your door!

Pastor Joan
MRFF Advisory Board Member

welcome it. please do as you threaten

(Name withheld)

Dear (name withheld),

It's not a threat...it's a fact.

Joan Slish

then I expect them at my door. you folks are so predictable. I do not get intimidated by the likes of folks like you. you are an embarrassment to what made this country great.

(Name withheld)

Dear (name withheld),

Ditto. You're not the first of your kind to contact us nor will you be the last.

Joan Slish

.

(Name withheld),

You've made several assumptions here that I'd contest, but frankly when someone writes us with threats of violence I prefer to just forward those threats on to our security folks. We are each prepared to be attacked, and to defend ourselves as needed.

Blake A. Page
Military Religious Freedom Foundation
Special Assistant to the President
Director of US Army Affairs

♦ ♦ ♦

Subject: Your recent negative, nasty comments concerning an Air Force general who spoke about GOD in public

Each person in your organization should be summarily shot or hanged for you suggestion the general should be court marshaled. You are obviously a bunch of far left extreme liberal democrats. You should be ashamed of yourselves.

(Name withheld)

.

Did you just read what he wrote? Each of us will be hanged or shot? What kind of sick fucks are these people?

.

Oh my dear (name withheld),

As one of the people associated with the MRFF whom you have suggested should be shot or hanged, let me offer a few thoughts. This offer, of course, assumes you're capable of understanding some rather complex facts, and I realize that may be a stretch.

Aside from being loose-lipped and a lousy speller, you are acting on assumptions based on false information. That information may have been passed to you by people with their own agenda or you may have heard some partial information and leapt to a hasty and false conclusion. You are clearly capable of the latter, as your assumption about our political affiliation demonstrates.

As far as shame is concerned, you've got a lot to answer for.

So here's the deal. If you just wanted to shoot your mouth off because you've had another bad day, we can just consider it done and forget it. If, on the other hand, you have a serious complaint about something that you'd like to pass along, make sure your spell-check is working and send it to me. I'll be happy to provide a response that will, I'm sure, make you angry as hell because it proves your assumptions wrong and you'll have to find something else to get mad about and someone else to threaten.

OK?

I'm standing by. (I've been thinking about your email address. Is there a Starsky in your life?)

Mike Farrell
(MRFF Board of Advisors)

♦♦♦

Subject: Hey jewboy freak

stay the fuck out of transfuckers in the Army

we don't need no faggots or jews neither

and no haji arabs

you got eyes in back of your head?

to go with the horns in front?

(Name withheld)

More than anything else, these people are racist against Jews first and then the other groups follow.

IIey stupid,

Your message betrays your IQ, which explains a lot. However, threats are still against the law, even for those who can claim mental incapacity.

I apologize for using words you probably can't comprehend, but those of us at the MRFF aren't comfortable with stooping the the level of some of our correspondents.

I hope you can find someone to read this to you. It's important that you understand that we take threats as seriously as we abhor cowards, bigots and those of your ilk.

Mike Farrell
(MRFF Board of Advisors)

♦♦♦

Subject: YOUR ON!

You want a fight you have one!!!! Back the fuck off.

(Name withheld)

Mikey Weinstein wrote:

Or what, sport?

Just see how many veterans,Veteran bikers,VFW,D.A.V. members come visit your office. Bitch!!!!!

(Name withheld)

...thx for the heads up...... passed this on to our own security and law enforcement.....our security team and our local police/FBI will be ready.... and our lawyers will be in touch.....

Mikey

.

Good because we mean no violent acts what so ever just a nice peaceful protest,and may God Bless you.

(Name withheld)

◆ ◆ ◆

Subject: Mikey

Mikey Mikey Mickey

Obviously, you have not read your comment pages lately .... I have the feeling someone is tracking you and yours. Be careful out there

(Name withheld)

.

(Name withheld)

....thx for the heads up....just turned your name over to our security folks for law enforcement coordination......plz tell us more as to why you have that "feeling" and, further, why we ought to "Be careful out there."......we're all ears, sport.... Mikey

.

hi Mikey.

Your types of organizations like to "stir the pot" then walk away claiming innocence. What you haven't yet realized is this "division" is festering and growing. At some point in time, you will realize that. Also at that point in time, you will re analyze, but I am afraid it will be to late. Cheers.

.

Your threats and threatening innuendos are well understood and will be further reported to our security in coordination with law-enforcement.

Mikey

.

Mikey, Is she stupid or what? She comes back at you with another veiled threat. Joan

.

I know....stupid is the correct answer here

Mikey

♦ ♦ ♦

Subject: Can You Grow Them Hebe?
You better be able to grow eyes in the back of your head jewboy.

Lovers of Christ will not be taking anymore of your menacing in the military.

Christ's message of salvation will conquer your kike attacks as Christ was victorious over the Pharisees.

(Name withheld)

.

You cowardly pissant. You wouldn't know what a "Lover of Christ" was if she or he washed your feet. You and your friends who pervert Christianity make me sick.

I assume the "eyes in the back of the head" remark is an unintended confession that you don't have the cojones to meet face to face.

I look forward to hearing from you.

Mike Farrell
(MRFF Board of Advisors)

♦ ♦ ♦

Subject: Sick

Sick fucko. We will crush you and hang you out to decompose.

(Name witheld)

.

(Name withheld),

What exactly do you intend to do? When you say you want to crush us, are you saying you have an active intent to cause us harm in order to change how we live our lives? You must be a big fan of Daesh's methodology. Hanging the bodies of an enemy out to decompose is straight out of their playbook. It's refreshing though that you openly confess that you are an aspiring terrorist and were kind enough to give us your name. If you don't take a few moments to clarify that you have no actual intent to commit an act of violence, I'm sure the FBI will have lots of interesting questions for you in the near future.

Blake A. Page
Military Religious Freedom Foundation
Special Assistant to the President
Director of US Army Affairs

♦ ♦ ♦

Subject: Mikey

I've had enough of your stupid shit.
Stop your bullshit , or pay the consequences.

(Name withheld)

.

hello, (name withheld)....your specific death threat, cowardly expressed below to our Development Director, is being taken very seriously and has been referred to MRFF Security, MRFF Legal Counsel and law enforcement for immediate review and appropriate action.....

Mikey Weinstein
Founder and President, MRFF

♦♦♦

Subject: Please

PLEASE, do every real US citizen (ie true patriots) a huge favor & point a loaded 1911 at your temple and pull the trigger.

If you're too chicken-shit to complete the task, I volunteer to assist.

This isn't a threat, I'm merely offering you an opportunity to move the humane race forward.

FUCK YOU !!!

(Name withheld)

.

Recognizing reason, or reasonable arguments based on the axioms of formal logic requires a certain level of intelligence. The symbols symbol-mapping process can't occur in an ill-equipped mind. I could explain to you in using those clear, simple, and elegant processes, that offering to point a gun at another human being and end their life is tantamount to a threat. Or I could invest a month of my time explaining to my dog how WiFi works. I hope the analogy isn't lost on you, but I've amused myself at least.

Thanks for all your hard work and dedication to being an asshat.

Blake A Page
Military Religious Freedom Foundation
Special Assistant to the President
Director of US Army Affairs

♦♦♦

Subject: Fake ass military bitch

I demand the Weinstein weenie be taken out and "fragged"! He no longer serves a purpose in this world to the living or the human gene pool! That goes for his followers too! They had no business on an Air Force base to begin with as they are antireligion terrorists and zealots looking to get their heads blown off anyway!

WHEN ARE ALL MEMBERS OF THE MILITARY RELIGIOUS FREEDOM FOUNDATION GOING TO BE ELECTROCUTED FOR DENYING A 1st AMENDMENT RIGHT TO AN AIR FORCE MAJOR FOR DARING TO SUGGEST HE BE "AGGRESSIVELY PUNISHED" FOR HAVING AN OPEN BIBLE ON HIS DESK AT PETERSON AIR FORCE BASE IN COLORADO SPRINGS, CO? THESE PEOPLE ARE FOAMING, MAD-DOG INSANE.

I THINK THROWING THEM ALIVE INTO AN INDUSTRIAL WOOD CHOPPER WOULD ALSO BE FAIR & JUST RECOMPENSE FOR THEIR OUTRAGEOUS CRIME.

(Name withheld)

·

simply answer yes to no....are you threatening me/MRFF?.....your answer is important.....need your address please.....your threats are being sent to our MRFF security to coord. with law enforcement.....standing by for your answers...

·

You were in the military that's fucking hilarious!!! Navy bitch huh!? Hahaha omg you could swab my dick tonight after I'm done beating your ass!!! Bitch!!! Punk ass pussy lipped baked headed jewish shit turd! Don't even watch stupid television but I'll beat your ass and we can put it on pay per view but no one would give a shit about me beating your pussy ass up! Now a live faggot feed on the Internet of my beating your ass all day that might be worth enjoying!!

HAHAHAHAHAHA your no threat...your weak Mikey soo weak it's awesome! You have to admit my disgusting hatred fuels your love for another mans Dick !! You gotta have this hatred in your pathetic bald headed punk ass to continue!!!! Now type me back some more juicy comments I love imagining you reading my stuff and gripping your boyfriends ass !!!! U pussy!!!!!

(Name withheld)

.

just to clarify for our MRFF security and law enforcement we will coordinate with and to whom we will now send this e-mail of yours; you ARE threatening violence against me and/or MRFF here, correct?

♦♦♦

Subject: There are Good Jews and Bad Jews

Hey there Mickey. The good jews are dead. See ya. Be good now.

(Name withheld)

.

(Name withheld),

if that's your name. I assume the 666 is your description. We deal with fools all the time, most of them not self-described. Thanks for saving us the trouble.

Mike Farrell
(MRFF Board of Advisors)

♦♦♦

Subject: Dickbag

What's up dickbag. Sorry you took to many cocks up the ass during your time in the Air Force maybe next time you should join a real branch. I see your whole family for the last 3 generations have served between the Air Force and the Navy what kind of fags are y'all? Well go back to sucking your bags of dicks you silly cock boy and keep your head down never know when someone's coming for you bitch.

(Name withheld)

.

Hi (name withheld),

Your pathetic message to Mikey is a sad reminder of how many incredibly stupid and terrified people there are out there.

We've heard from your type before, the kind of sad little dweebs who are so threatened about their own lack of manhood they beat their breasts and declare their homophobia in the most juvenile terms possible. You bring to mind Shakespeare's admonition about protesting too much.

We've dealt with your kind before, pal, and sadly will probably have to again. But in the off-chance you meant the threat about "someone's coming for you," do me a favor, will you? Stop and see me first.

Mike Farrell
(MRFF Board of Advisors)

♦♦♦

Subject: I see your whole family for the last 3 generations have served between the Air Force and the Navy

what kind of fags are y'all?

(Name withheld)

.

(Name witheld),

Do you mean fags such as the Navy Hospital Corpsmen assigned to Marine Corps infantry platoons; or do you mean the Navy SEAL fags who took out Osama bin-Laden; or maybe you mean the Air Force PJ fags who make HALO jumps from 20,000 feet; or could it be the fag pilots who fly the infantry grunt's good friend, the A-10 Wart Hog?

I'm confused about exactly which fags you mean.

The American military dragon is quite large and it has very sharp teeth. There is nothing to do but respect and admire the men and women who make up those teeth. But here's the thing: Teeth make up about 15 percent of the dragon. The other 85 percent, presumably, are fags.

You know, the fags who feed everybody; the fags who make sure everyone gets paid; the fags who process leave papers so you can go home and hug Mom; the fags who make sure the tanks and Bradleys and Black Hawks and Hueys all work properly. Without the fags, the dragon's teeth surely would rot and fall out.

So many fags, so little time.

A MRFF supporter

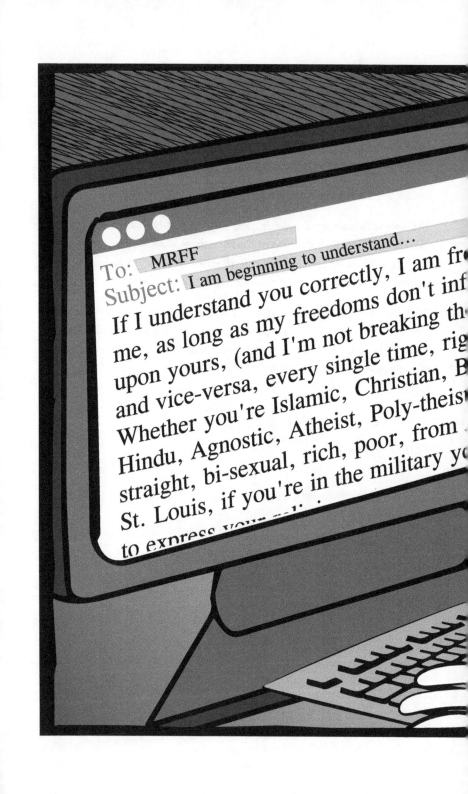

A light comes on

EVERY NOW AND THEN we experience small and wonderful miracles.

Miracle number one: They write under a real email address with their full name and contact information.

Miracle number two: For the most part, they are reasonable and rational and can spell correctly.

Miracle number three: The attackers have actually read the responses our foundation writers sent to them.

Miracle number four: They have actually thought about what was written back to them and ponder the idea that they may have been wrong or have jumped to an incorrect conclusion.

Miracle number five: They apologize.

This is why we write. This is why we take the time to respond to every email that comes in—because once in a great while miracles do happen.

◆◆◆

Dear Michael Weinstein;

I am writing this e-mail to you, asking that you truly carry out the mission that your home page proclaims. Please stop using it as a cover-up to just outright attack Christianity. I accept the fact that you Proclaim to be an atheist, but if your organization operates truly by the words of the First Amendment, then you will stop attacking people who are Christians. I have friends who are Buddhist, Hindu, Muslim, agnostic, and atheist, and I don't attack any tenant or belief system that they have, although I am a Christian. If all your organization is doing is making certain that no religion is forced down the throat of others, who disagree or practice another religion, or choose to embrace no religion, then I completely understand. But, if you are you are using your organization, as a cloak of deceit, to single out and attack Christianity, then you should be so ashamed of yourself, that you will immediately change your policies and practices. Thanks for your attention to my concerns, tho I'm fairly certain you won't take time to respond.

Sincerely

(Name withheld)

·

(Name withheld)......thx for reaching out....plZ call me in 15 mins....

Mikey Weinstein

·

Good afternoon Mikey,

Thanks for your prompt reply. I will do my best to give you a call tomorrow. I've got two different tasks to complete today.

Sincerely,

(Name withheld)

Dear (Name withheld),

I see that you have or may have had a conversation with Mikey. If so, this response is superfluous and I'm sorry to bother you. If the conversation has not yet happened, though, let me try to clarify things a bit in the hope that your confusion about who and what the MRFF is can be resolved.

A lot is said and written about the MRFF. In certain circles it is almost always biased and ill-intended, I'm sorry to say, so it's good of you to want to hear our side of the story.

Many people are confused by the First Amendment, the concept of freedom of religion and the separation of church and state. That's certainly fair. But it's important, when one doesn't understand something, to try to fairly and objectively search out information that can help clear up the confusion. In too many cases, some find it easier to leap to conclusions and make judgments. In a number of cases they go to sources whose information is not unbiased and it strengthens their worst assumptions.

I'm glad, that being the case, that you wrote us and tried, at least, to get our side.

So. We are not using our declared mission as a coverup or excuse to attack Christianity. Over 95% of those associated with the MRFF are themselves Christians. They are not, however, the kind of Christians who insist that their views, their belief about Jesus and their particular doctrine are the one and only true Christianity and that all others are false. They are devoted Christians who not only understand that others can have different views, perhaps different faith beliefs or even no faith belief at all, and still deserve to be respected as human beings who happen to believe differently.

Though there are probably a fair number of MRFF supporters who are atheists, they do not recruit or proselytize, as that is not what the MRFF is about. It is, as advertised, about believing the business of belief or non-belief is a private matter and no one in a position of authority over others in our military should be, whether intentionally or carelessly, promoting one belief system over another.

If you've spoken to Mikey you may already have had the question answered to your satisfaction, but in my opinion he is not an atheist but a man of very deep belief.

Our purpose is not to attack people who are Christians, atheists, scientologists, Jews or people of any belief or non-belief. I wouldn't support the organization if that were true. We certainly do object to the more vicious attacks on us or on others by religious totalitarians who rage and condemn and sometimes, I can tell you, the exchanges can become very ugly. But from my perspective the things said from this side are critical of the invective and dishonesty we are faced with rather than the individual's belief. In our view, he or she is welcome to believe whatever she/he chooses. But in the US military they are not free to impose it on others.

From the way you describe yourself, you appear to be an open person who is comfortable with his belief system and not threatened by people who see things differently. I couldn't be happier to hear that.

We feel the same way.

I hope you've had a chance to speak with Mikey. I think that will be a great experience for you.

And if you have any questions or concerns about anything I've said or not said that leaves you unsure, please feel free to write again.

Best,

Mike Farrell

.

Good afternoon Mr. Farrell,

Thanks so much for your timely and accurate response to my original e-mail to Mikey Weinstein. (After reviewing it, my apologies, for its slight abrasive tone) :-) I did speak w/Mikey at length this afternoon, and was greatly relieved, that some of my original assumptions about the Military Religious Freedom Organization, are indeed incorrect, and pretty much opposite of what your organization is about. I greatly enjoyed our conversational exchange, and realized that both of us have had instilled in us, the long standing desire to take up for those who are subjected to bullying techniques, whether it be physical, verbal, sexual harassment, etc. ad infinitum. My father raised me to always take up for those, who are the victims of bullying. I retired honorably from the U.S. Army, as a Staff Sergeant, had good bosses, not so great bosses, and mediocre bosses, but whether I was a team leader, squad leader, or platoon sergeant, I always sought to treat each of those individuals subordinate to me, w/respect, fairness, and the willingness to go to bat for them, if they were in the right, every single time. I would like to offer a heartfelt thanks, for what I now believe to be the heart of your organization, and that is to represent each person, each organization, equally, and to the letter of the law, and within the entire premise of our great First Amendment. I believe in closing, that I am free to be me, as long as my freedoms don't infringe upon yours, (and I'm not breaking the law) and vice-versa, every single time. Whether you're Islamic, Christian, Buddhist, Hindu, Agnostic, Atheist, Poly-theist,etc, gay, straight, bi-sexual, rich, poor, from Kabul, or St. Louis, if you're in the military, and are at the right place, at the right time, with the right uniform, ready to do your job, I commend you, and would always fight for your right to party. (Oh wait, that's Twisted Sister. LOL) Seriously, we as a nation, need to concentrate on these things that bring us to together in unity, and applaud our differences, which is a portion of why our nation was founded. Remember: It's always okay, to agree to disagree. But, in the case of the this fine organization that stands up for those who sometimes don't think that they have a voice, or anyone to represent, and/or rescue them, I applaud you, and your continuing efforts.

Sincerely,

(Name withheld)

P.S. Thanks so much B.J. Honeycutt, for being a humble human being, willing to give freely of yourself and abilities, for what I've very recently come to believe, is an incredible humanitarian organization. And I guess my only claim to fame, is I was priviledged to play the piano and sing for Wayne Newton on his USO tour on Yongsan Army Base, in Seoul, Korea. It remains to be seen if he thought it an entertaining performance. Ha

Pss. As I told Mikey, I am highly interested in serving in a volunteer capacity w/you guys, and possible if needed a recompensed position in the future. Have a great remainder of the week.

.

Dear Ms. (Name withheld),

Thank you for this thoughtful and quite moving response.
Your acknowledgement is deeply appreciated.

I'm pleased to know that you are not among the troubling cohort I described. And I do hope you now understand that we have no antipathy toward either the Bible or Christianity. In fact, over 95% of those associated with the MRFF are themselves Christians. Some of them, I believe it's fair to say, probably struggle daily as well.

My best to you.

Mike Farrell
(MRFF Board of Advisors)

♦ ♦ ♦

Subject: Freedom of Religion

To Whomever,

What is your point of getting so upset at Major General Craig Olsen's comments regarding his Christian faith? I truly want to know. As a Christian, we must profess Jesus Christ as our Lord and Savior. If we deny Christ before men, He will deny us before The Father. After all, wasn't America founded upon Christian principals? Jesus tells us that the end times will reveal an increased hatred for followers of Christ and you're evidence of the truth Jesus spoke about. So, who do you represent? A court martial, really?? Perhaps you should give Jesus a place in your life and let him reside in your heart. If you do, your life will change dramatically and you will actually support those like Craig Olsen.

(Name withheld)

.

Dear Mr. (Name withheld):

I am writing in response to your email to the Military Religious Freedom Foundation ("MRFF"). You ask some very good questions and I hope to adequately address your concerns.

First, you ask, "What is your point of getting so upset at Major General Craig Olsen's comments regarding his Christian faith?" This question is more complex than it appears and, consequently, my response will include a detailed explanation of the Establishment Clause and how it applies in this situation. However, the simplest answer is this: The facts surrounding Maj. Gen. Olsen's speech amount to a violation of the Establishment Clause and the wrongful endorsement of any particular religion over others can have very real consequences for those under Maj. Gen. Olsen's command. While all service members have the right to freely practice and express their religious beliefs, the Constitution requires that such expression be made in the appropriate time, place and manner. One of the ways MRFF protects the religious freedom of service members is by ensuring that military leaders adhere to these Constitutional mandates.

Now for the complex part: The Establishment Clause prohibits the establishment of any particular religion. This prohibition has been held to include actions or policies by state actors if (1) the purpose is not secular; (2) the principal/primary effect either advances or inhibits religion; or (3) it fosters an excessive entanglement with religion. Lemon v. Kurtzman, 403 U.S. 602 (1971). In this case, several facts are relevant to the issue of how Maj. Gen. Olson's remarks amounted to a violation of the Establishment Clause, rather than a permissible expression of religious beliefs. Maj. Gen. Olson is the Program Executive Officer for C31 and Networks at Hanscom Air Force Base in Massachusetts. He is also the highest-ranking officer there, leading 2,200 subordinate Air Force personnel. In his speech, he admitted that he has neither the ability nor the training to perform his job:

"He put me in charge of failing programs worth billions of dollars. I have no ability to do that – NO TRAINING TO DO THAT – God did all of that.
"He sent me to Iraq to negotiate foreign military sales; deals through an Arabic interpreter. I have no ability to do that – I WAS NOT TRAINED TO DO THAT – God did all of that."

"I also went in as a very self-sufficient person. I thought if you work hard you'll do fine and that was working great in high school. Did not work very well at the Air Force Academy. That's where I realized I had a very limited intellectual ability.

"I still carry in this pocket my transcript from the Air Force Academy – as Exhibit A in the court of law – that you're not a gifted intellect; you have no real academic skills."

In addition to admitting that he is not qualified for his own job, Maj. Gen. Olson requested that the audience pray for Defense Department leaders and for troops preparing to re-deploy. While this request might be a perfectly acceptable expression of religion under some circumstances, he specifically stated that Defense Department leaders "need to humbly depend on Christ" and requested prayers for the troops so they can "bear through that by depending on Christ." Moreover, he made these statements in his official capacity as a military leader while wearing his uniform, thus giving the impression that his statements clearly endorsing Christianity over other religious beliefs were made on behalf of the Air Force. This situation does not involve a service member merely expressing his own personal religious beliefs in support of God, which might have little or no impact on those under his command.

It should also be noted that Maj. Gen. Olson was speaking at a National Day of Prayer Task Force event. The mission of the National Day of Prayer Task Force is to mobilize the Christian Community "to intercede for America and its leadership in the seven centers of power: government, military, media, business, education, church, and family." Therefore, he was speaking in his official capacity for a group whose sole purpose is to inject its own Christian beliefs into all areas of government, in direct violation of the Establishment Clause. Consequently, Maj. Gen. Olson's speech (1) had no secular purpose; (2) had the primary effect of advancing Christianity, while inhibiting the practice of any other religion; and (3) created an excessive entanglement with religion.

Maj. Gen. not only violated the Establishment Clause, he also violated USAF Instruction 1-1, Sec. 2.12: "Leaders at all levels...must ensure their words and actions cannot reasonably be construed to be officially endorsing or disapproving of, or extending preferential treatment for any faith, belief, *or absence of belief." Pursuant to the Uniform Code of Military Justice, the violation of a lawful regulation "shall be punished as a court martial may direct" (emphasis added).*

MRFF understands the belief of many Christians that they must profess Jesus Christ as their Lord and Savior. MRFF does not oppose anyone's right to declare devotion to any deity, nor does it expect or require that Christian service members deny Christ before others. It simply works to ensure the profession of Christ as personal savior – or any other expression of religious belief – is made in a permissible time, place, and manner pursuant to the mandates of the Constitution and military regulations.

In response to your second question, this country is not founded upon Christian principles. While the Founding Fathers may have been devoted Christians, they clearly established a government based on democratic principles, rather than religious principles. It is possible that these men may relied on their religious moral standards in determining the rights and restrictions included in the Constitution, but even if that is true, it does not change the fact that they declined to establish a Christian nation.

You state that, according to Jesus, "the end times will reveal an increased hatred for followers of Christ" and that MRFF is "evidence of the truth Jesus spoke about." I hope my above explanations of the Establishment Clause and MRFF's mission have already made it clear that MRFF does not hate followers of Christ. As previously stated, the majority of service members it represents are Christians and MRFF does everything it can to correct wrongs they have suffered as a result of their religion, just as it does for its clients of all other faiths or no faith at all. Similarly, I hope that I have already clarified who it is that MRFF represents – it represents all men and women in uniform who suffer wrongful religious discrimination or persecution.

I hope I have addressed all of your questions and concerns regarding the work of MRFF and the facts surrounding Maj. Gen. Olson's recent speech. If I have missed anything or if you have any additional questions, I would be happy to address them.

Blessed be,

Tobanna Barker
MRFF Volunteer

Tobanna,

I truly appreciate your thorough explanation to my questions. I also appreciate that you did this in a very tactful manner. Although I don't agree with you 100%, I do have a better understanding of your stance. Yes, our founders certainly established a country based on democratic principles, but it was through Godly inspiration that our constitution was born. Not all founding fathers even believed in God, but even those did understand the significance of Godly morals as is well documented. I don't expect another reply, because we obviously disagree here.

I do thank you for reading my email and your reply.

Thank You

♦♦♦

Subject: Operation Christmas Child

To whom it may concern,

You should be ashamed of yourselves, but I know you wont be. You put a stop to people helping other people all because YOU have a problem with religion. Last I checked people in the military are adults and can make their own decisions on weather or not they want to participate in things like this. Why do you feel that your existence is necessary? If someone does not want to participate in religion, they will not do it, but because of your beliefs you keep those that WANT to participate in religious humanitarianism from doing so. The only losers in this situation are the poor children of distant countries that would have received the gift from these generous people.

Hang your head in shame, you took gifts out of the hands of children...

GOD BLESS!

(Name withheld)

Hi (Name withheld)

Mikey Weinstein asked me last week if I'd like to reply to you, but I have been slow in doing so. Still, I want to toss in my two cents because it's clear to me that you have reached a wrong conclusion about the objection raised by the MRFF, re: Dover AFB. As for who I am—I'm an active Christian, a USAF Academy graduate ('85), and a veteran Air Force officer.

So no, I certainly don't have a "problem with religion". For that matter, MRFF is not an anti-religion group. Rather, we are pro-Constitution and we advocate on behalf of military members when they request our help. Specifically, we are dedicated to ensuring that all members of the United States Armed Forces fully receive the Constitutional guarantees of religious freedom to which they and all Americans are entitled by virtue of the Establishment Clause of the First Amendment.

With regard to the Air Force specifically, that means expecting all military leaders to honor their obligations as spelled out in AFI 1-1, which says the following --- "Leaders at all levels must balance constitutional protections for their own free exercise of religion, including individual expressions of religious beliefs, and the constitutional prohibition against governmental establishment of religion. They must ensure their words and actions cannot reasonably be construed to be officially endorsing or disapproving of, or extending preferential treatment for any faith, belief, or absence of belief."

Our sole objection at Dover AFB was the manner in which a clearly sectarian religious effort was promoted. The commander deserves great credit for acting swiftly and decisively to correct the misstep, although he is being unfairly vilified by conservative media outlets for doing the right thing.

What should have happened at Dover was for a program of this sort to be advertised via appropriate means, notably the chaplaincy. And as far as I know, no one at Dover AFB has been prohibited from participating in Franklin Graham's evangelistic efforts, so I'm unclear as to how it is that we "took gifts out of the hands of orphans".

Hope this perspective helps.

Peace,

Mike Challman
Christian, USAF veteran, MRFF supporter

Mike,

I appreciate the explaination, the story I read did not explain these aspect, and I apologize for my conclusion. Thank you for all you do.

(Name withheld)

·

Thanks for the reply. The reporting on stories like this one is invariably driven by lots of agendas. In the case of anything involving Christians, the knee jerk reaction from the conservative sphere is to cry 'persecution'!

I appreciate your willingness to consider the other side of the story.

Peace,

Mike

♦♦♦

Subject: I want to give you a piece of my mind

Dear Mister Weinstein

I am a retired US Army Sergeant of twenty five years service in the National Guard and Regular Army. I want you to know at the very outset that I am not writing to you because I admire or respect you (the "dear" is formality only). I want you to know that I consider the MRFF to be just a hate group and nothing else. You are not about freedom at all and I consider you nothing more then a bully and a coward who wants to push a selfish agenda. I cannot believe that they let someone like you in the military.

Listen mister we are one nation UNDER GOD. You wanted to punish a poor cadet at a service academy because he had a Bible verse written on a board outside his room that didn't hurt a thing. You wanted an officer court martialled because he had a Bible on his desk and another because he mentioned in a speech that he believed in God. I cannot believe that ANYONE takes you seriously. The only time that I have every liked Bill O'Reilly was when he called you a jerk and turned off your mic. You even objected to having Bibles at a MIA display. If I had been one of those commanders you had sent a threatning letter to I would just have told you to stick it! I have read books by so many Vietnam POWs who spent years in hell and talked about how only their faith in God kept them sane and saw them thru. When Admiral Jeremiah Denton was released from captivity at Clark Air Base he said "God bless America".

A Soldier swears to defend his country and his God. I love to write to World War II veterans as a hobby and so many of them told me that faith in God got them through the war. Joe Louis said that we would win because we were on God's side. General Washington prayed at Valley Forge and Lincoln regularly sought God's guidance and help during the Civil War. Gee would you have filed complaints against them? I was a chaplains assistant in Operation Desert Storm and let me tell you something moron there are no such things as athiests in foxholes. Of course you wouldn't know because you've never been to war.

I have read the letters you have written threatning people and so often you use overblown words like "disgraceful" and "disgusting" to describe people you want-to hurt. I want you to know that you are one of the most despicable, disgraceful people I have ever read about. I cannot believe that they let someone like you wear a uniform. Bullies are basically cowards at heart because they attack people who don't fight back and someone should have told you off a long time ago. I await your reply if you have the guts COWARD

SGT US Army (Retired) and someone who loves the Lord and proudly serves him

·

SGT (Name withheld),

This is in response to your classless personal attack on the Military Religious Freedom Foundation (MRFF) Founder & President, a former USAF officer, military veteran & patriotic American you do not even know.

Your diatribe proudly proclaims your private religious beliefs. Apparently, you believe you have the right to determine, enjoy & practice your own religious beliefs. Obviously, you do not realize the MRFF represents over 52,000

military members, veterans & civilians (96% of whom are Christians) who have requested-their right to determine, enjoy & practice their own religious beliefs be respected & protected. All want freedom from imposition of someone else's version of religion, especially superiors, in the military work place so they can perform their military duties without unwanted interference. Surely you would not hypocritical deny the same right you demand for yourself to others serving our Country.

Your declaration "A Soldier swears to defend his country and his God" is wrong & indicates you do not know or remember the military mission & sworn military service oath. The military mission is to defend our country against its enemies - not promote a religion. The sworn military service oath is "to support and defend the Constitution of the United States...and bear true faith and allegiance to the same" - not to any deity or religion. The Constitution lawfully prohibits our government or its representatives (which includes the military) from promoting a religion. Simply stated, military members have the right to privately practice their own religious beliefs, but not publicly on other military members.

It has been my experience that a man who resorts to hateful name-calling does so because he cannot address a subject matter with intelligence & integrity. Your malicious message reflects only on yourself and not on the MRFF or its leader.

1st Commander-in-Chief GEORGE WASHINGTON publicly acknowledged military freedom of belief when he wrote the military chaplaincy "has a tendency to introduce religious disputes into the Army, which above all things should be avoided, and in many instances would compel men to a mode of worship which they do not profess."

40th Commander-in-Chief RONALD REAGAN affirmed this fundamental liberty in a public speech "We establish no religion in this country, we command no worship, we mandate no belief, nor will we ever."

Most Sincerely,

Brigadier General John Compere, US Army (Retired)
Disabled American Veteran (Vietnam)
Military Religious Freedom Foundation Advisory Board Member

Dear SGT (Name withheld),

Thanks for your service to our nation—your devotion and sense of duty are clear and admirable. I've volunteered to respond to your note to Mikey for several reasons: because I, too, have served more than 25 years (AF) and I have experience and perspective on these issues that may prove helpful.

If you don't mind, I'd like to excerpt from your letter and respond to specific comments.

"You are not about freedom at all and I consider you nothing more then a bully and a coward who wants to push a selfish agenda."

The MRFF's agenda is simple: to allow all who choose to serve our nation in the military to do so honorably without bias concerning their religious beliefs or lack thereof. The oath these soldiers take is to the Constitution of the United States. And, while some may choose to add the phrase "So help me god," at the end of their oath, those last four words are not mandatory and there is no clear indication that the "god" to which they are requesting help is the Christian god of one of several available textual translations and compilations, Allah of the Koran, the Jewish god of the Torah, or Odin of Viking legend. It could even be the spirit of the rocks, springs, and trees of the forest as some active duty pagans believe.

"I cannot believe that they let someone like you in the military."

Who are you to judge? Mikey's family is, in my view a paragon of service. Several generations of graduates from our service academies and a combined decades of honorable service by his family speak otherwise. I deeply admire Mikey, his service, and that of his family.

"Listen mister we are one nation UNDER GOD."

Who's god? Heck, if it was that clear, would we have Catholic, Protestant, Jewish, and Muslim chaplains in the military? We have chaplains who are Lutherans that disagree with others who are Evangelical Baptists. In my mind, everyone has a different, individually developed notion of what god is or isn't or what role spirituality plays in their lives. You're welcome to do *the same, but you are not welcome to define "GOD" for those around you or to require all serving in the military to define their religious beliefs as you or anyone else do. That's the first amendment of our Constitution.*

"You wanted to punish a poor cadet at a service academy because he had a Bible verse written on a board outside his room that didn't hurt a thing. You wanted an officer court martialled [sic] because he had a Bible on his desk and another because he mentioned in a speech that he believed in God."

The area outside of a cadet's room isn't private. It's public and government owned/controlled. It's shared by superiors and subordinates and is part of the cadet work environment. Unofficial statements written based upon personal opinion or beliefs on those boards are not appropriate. The statements he/she writes on that board are not unlike writing graffiti in a public place on a military base. Any soldier would be rightfully punished for putting a partisan political message or private corporate endorsement on a work-area message board for subordinates to read. The same is true of religious statements. Ask yourself this... 'How would I feel if I was assigned to work FOR someone of different beliefs and everyday when I walked to their office, I had to read, "Religion is the opiate of the masses," or "Allahu Akbar!". If a religious (or atheist) statement is important to a cadet or officer, then they can put that in their personal space INSIDE their room or private residence--that's their right.

As for the officer with the bible on his or her desk, the same rule holds true. If he or she closes their door for a moment of private reflection, then it's absolutely appropriate for them to have a bible as reference. Their bookshelf might contain any religious text or even Mein Kampf. BUT, if a subordinate reports in to the office, then religious and sectarian texts must be put aside to do business. An officer can't have a bible open, facing the subordinate, for example, with highlighted text—which was the case in which the MRFF was engaged.

"I cannot believe that ANYONE takes you seriously."

The fact that the MRFF has tens of thousands of clients throughout the military that depend on the MRFF's strength to fight discrimination in the military workplace--including hundreds of cadets at our service academies-- argues the opposite.

"The only time that I have every liked Bill O'Reilly was when he called you a jerk and turned off your mic."

Being called a jerk by a serial sexual harrasser is no insult.

"You even objected to having Bibles at a MIA display. If I had been one of those commanders you had sent a threatning letter to I would just have told you to stick it! I have read books by so many Vietnam POWs who spent years in hell and talked about how only their faith in God kept them sane and saw them thru. When Admiral Jeremiah Denton was released from captivity at Clark Air Base he said "God bless America"."

While we all admit that many (even most) POWs found solace and strength in their religious beliefs during captivity, one cannot assume that every one did, not that all POWs were Christian or even religious. The MRFF defends the rights of these brave men to state their personal beliefs, but not to proclaim that religious belief was a necessary or sufficient condition for survival.

"A Soldier swears to defend his country and his God."

Wrong. A soldier swears of affirms to support and defend the Constitution of the United States. There can be no religious test for public service or office. Again, if you feel that you are defending your god when you defend the US, then that's your right. I don't. That's my right, too, and my service should be judged on its merits, not the god or belief system I choose to represent in my mind.

"I love to write to World War II veterans as a hobby and so many of them told me that faith in God got them through the war. Joe Louis said that we would win because we were on God's side. General Washington prayed at Valley Forge and Lincoln regularly sought God's guidance and help during the Civil War. Gee would you have filed complaints against them?"

If they required me to believe in their god to serve or judged me as inferior for not believing as they do, then you're damn right that I would. BTW, the legendary painting of Washington kneeling in prayer at Valley Forge is nothing more than legend, unsubstantiated by any documentation. You can choose to believe he did not not. I can't prove he did or didn't. But, there's no evidence the painting represents any verifiable act.

"I was a chaplains assistant in Operation Desert Storm and let me tell you something moron there are no such things as athiests in foxholes. Of course you wouldn't know because you've never been to war."

I have have, and I am. I know MANY others that have been to war and are atheists. That doesn't mean they weren't afraid. It just means that they didn't believe that any myth or legend was responsible for their fate or salvation.

I won't respond to your other ad hominem attacks, other than to say that it is you, with your poorly spelled attacks that is acting the bully today--accusing others of cowardice.

Good Day, Sir

An Air Force Veteran of 30+ years of active duty and 9/11 survivor (Pentagon attack) survivor

.

Mr. (Name withheld),

I am a recipient of the Combat Medical Badge and a former atheist in a foxhole. I served in Iraq as a medic for route clearance and about 20% of our unit consisted of non-religious atheists. This is roughly average for the military as a whole. Your statement that there are "no atheists in foxholes" is false, offensive, and easily disproven. Anyone who actually served in the military would be well aware of our presence, so I have serious doubts that you were ever in the military at all, much less in combat. You are either a liar or a self-absorbed prick oblivious to the people around you. Which is it?

The United States Constitution is the document that replaced the Articles of Confederation, establishing the government of the United States. You swore to uphold and defend it, so you may want to understand what's in it. When you are done reading it, please inform us all where in the Constitution it establishes a nation "under God"? You won't find any such language to support your claim.

Instead, you will find that our government was established on the authority of "We the People". There is not a single reference to divine authority or establishing a Christian nation. You'll find that the only time religion is *mentioned is to limit religious influence over the People's government. For instance, "no religious test shall ever be required as a qualification to any office or public trust under the United States." - Article VI, Section 3. Do you understand what that means? The framers were specifically sending a message to people like you that there is no place in our shared government for religious bigotry. The United States government has no business concerning itself with people's religious beliefs.*

We the People are a diverse group who make up a pluralistic society that is most certainly NOT "under God". That disgusting un-American perversion was added to the pledge during the Cold War era by theocratic traitors in Congress. You are mindlessly parroting the un-American slogan of traitors, not a foundational principle of our Republic.

MRFF Atheist Affairs Advisor,
Dustin Chalker

.

Thank you very much for your service and I am proud to count you as a fellow veteran. Now please take me off your list and don't send me any more emails. My box has been flooded today and enough is enough

(Name withheld)

.

.........roger wilco.........you will get no more e-mails from me after this acknowledgment......I'd still like an apology from YOU, for the TOTAL crap you said about me from the get-go...but I doubt you have the integrity and character and class to so apologize?!.....there was NO need to come out at me and mine right at the start by throwing hand grenades of defamation.......

.

Mister Weinstein

I'm very sorry for what I said. I have been under a lot of stress and have had a lot sickness in my family and I didn't mean to blow my top. I was reading some of the things your staff wrote in response and it made me sit down and think which I should have done in the first place. I was angry when you had those Bibles removed from those MIA displays and wanted "God" taken out of the Air Force oath. But I've been doing some research on you and your organization and you HAVE done good work like fighting prejudice and commanders FORCING religion on their soldiers which is wrong.

I went back to college after I retired from the military and got a history degree and I studied in one class about how religion played an important part in our nation being founded. The colonists under British rule were sick of the stuffy traditions of the English church and they wanted to be religious in their own way. They began to realize they wanted freedom period don't you see? In the Declaration it is said people are endowed by "Their creator".

God got me though Desert Storm and I had a terrible health crisis in the military in 2006 I spent a month in the hospital and I almost died. They had to perform seven surgeries on my leg and I almost lost it. I'm 90% disabled and live with pain every single day. I will never have a day without pain for the rest of my life My faith in God got me through and it still does. I'm a proud member of my church and I love to visit veterans hospitals and pray with them especially WWII veterans. I DO believe to my dying day that we are one nation under God and God got me though a wonderful military career and I couldn't have done it without him. I want to tell you a story about a special letter I got from a famous flyer who was on the Jimmy Doolittle mission. He told me that he and the others made it through because "we were all mortals but there was one IMMORTAL watching over us" beautiful.

I'm very ashamed of the horrible things I wrote to you in that hurtful hateful email and I wish I could take them back. Could you please delete that letter from your inbox? One of your staffers in his reply accidentally mentioned my name. We have a right to disagree with other's opinions but I should have respected yours and not been so "disagreeable". I watched that interview you did with O'Reilly and I agree that he is an idiot and a bully.

I had two things I wanted to ask. Mike Farrell was one of the people who wrote me, is he that one that was on MASH? That was one of my all time favorite shows. The other thing is do you disagree with Nativity scenes on military bases that are not in front of chapels.

Happy New Year and God bless

.

Dear(Name withheld),

I appreciate your apology to Mikey and I respect the courage it took to make it. We all have moments of thoughtlessness we regret, but too many times we fail to do the right thing and make amends. Your having done so says a lot about you, and I know I speak for Mikey as well when I say it means a great deal to all of us.

It's good of you, too, to expand on your thinking a bit by way of explanation. Your doing so helps me better understand what motivated your response, beyond the awful stress and pain you describe.

If I may say so, per your mention of history studies, while it's clear many of the founders of our nation were believers, that's certainly not true of all. Read a bit of Tom Paine, for example. And, as regards those who were believers, many were Deists, not Christians. As you suggest, some dissented from the strictures "of the English church and wanted to be religious in their own way." But further, some wanted to be free of all the trappings of religion so as to exercise their imaginations and develop their beliefs, outside the bounds of what was then, as it is now, thought of as 'religion.'

For some, it was at a minimum confusing to see that many of those who were 'believers' could somehow justify owning human beings as slaves, could casually dismember families and engage in what today, when thought about at all, is painfully recognized as unconscionable cruelty.

And of course there was the "problem" of the indigenous people, those who were already here when our earliest settlers arrived. Those folks, quickly categorized as 'savages,' actually had – still have – their own carefully and thoughtfully developed belief system. But it was not one respected – even recognized – by the invading newcomers.

So you see, there were many belief systems extant in our New World during the years leading up to the formation of our country. And the great thing about America is that, for all their faults, those drafting the foundational documents of the country understood the necessity of recognizing that the government of this new nation should not be in the business of telling people what they must believe.

This quite revolutionary idea was fore-runner to the recognition that it is a fundamental human right of each individual to determine for her or himself what to believe about the meaning of life, its purpose, its reason for being and in which kind of construct, if any, to place it.

You express a deep belief in God, "the creator," which some of us share and all respect. But some who believe in and pray to such an entity fail to recognize that Allah and Yaweh and The Great Father, Mother Nature, the Force and other such characterizations are arguably one and the same. Therein lies the basis for much strife and pain.

Many others, of course, feel no need for such a relationship at all, and that is their right as well. One of them might be inclined to ask, per your mention of a correspondent who took part in the Jimmy Doolittle mission, if his belief that an "IMMORTAL" was watching over them meant that his God not only approved of but championed the destruction of so many human lives.

Per your question about nativity scenes on military bases that are not on chapel grounds, I hope you'll take advantage of Mikey's invitation to call him, as he can provide a much more thoughtful explanation than I. For me, it's simple. On chapel grounds a nativity scene is appropriate, as would be an artifact of their belief on the grounds of a base synagogue or mosque. But off the chapel grounds, such a display suggests a government endorsement of one religion over others and is neither legal nor appropriate.

Per "M*A*S*H," I'm glad you liked our show. I did too.

Thanks again for your thoughtful apology.

I wish you an end to your pain and a happy, healthy and loving New Year.

Best,

(MRFF Board of Advisors)
Mike Farrell

It is a wonderful gift for all when just one person broadens his horizons past the constrictions of his own religion.

Epilogue

AND WITH THIS, THE epilogue, the end of the book is here for most of you. Most of you will want to close the book and call this the end. There is, however, one more email and its responses which I purposely have not included in the main body of the book. Remember I had said that I usually skim and read a paragraph or two before filing? This email came to my inbox along with the following warning from my husband to everyone he sent it out to.

****PLEASE STOP and READ this specific warning before deciding to make the personal decision to proceed to review the 3 hate mails from the same apparent source below: The trio of hate mail sent to MRFF below is EXTREMELY SHOCKING and HIDEOUS .....I have never done this before, but I AM going to do it this time....I am warning you, please, PLEASE do NOT review unless you are prepared for the worst...I send it because you need to be aware of the ASTONISHING degree of inhumanity with which our enemies will go to in order to try to intimidate and try to stop our MRFF civil rights activism

So naturally, I did not read it. I never opened the email. At the time, I did not think anything more about it, nor did I ever mention it to anyone. What I did do was a simple click on the keyboard and filed it under "book two" and with a swoosh it was filed.

Once I started compiling the letters and writing for this, my second book, I came across this file again and realized I had a very serious decision to make. Do I read the file? Do I need to read it and decide if it should go in this book, or do I just not include it and never even read the file. I did not ask Mikey or talk to anyone about this decision; I felt it was my decision to make and I needed to do it alone as this was affecting me personally. Well, please trust me when I say that I did not make this decision lightly and I am not sure I made the right one. As you can tell, since you are reading this, my decision was to open the file.

And now it haunts me.

This single email has caused me too many wakeful nights tossing and turning or outright walking and pacing back and forth, unable to wash the thoughts away. Some nights, I would go out to the living room and sit in a chair along with a generous two fingers of bourbon….I hate bourbon…and just stare out at the horizon while the hours ticked away.

To make matters worse, the picture that came with the last email popped up on the screen and I saw it. I am not a hardened criminal investigator, or a person in the various crime fields that would see images like this, so I was shocked and horrified. I shut my eyes quickly and looked away, but the image was seared into my brain.

As an average person I have goals, wishes and dreams, wonderful children, grandchildren, and friends. I am also not an average person, far from it. I have hideous trash that comes into my email every day and the filth filters into our daily lives as a matter of course; it has come with the territory.

And it has come at a cost.

Boy, do I long for those average days again. I would love to be in the same boat all of my friends are in—retired, secure, mortgage paid off, relaxed, unencumbered—and have "do what I wanna do" kind of days. But that is not the case. That fateful decision those many years ago now to stand up for our own children and for the tens of thousands who cannot, to give voice where a voice is needed, has had a steep price to pay. I remember telling a friend that we have been nominated for the Nobel Peace Prize, then for the fifth time. She asked me how it felt. I told her that it was not a feeling as much as it is a complete and total emersion of sacrifice. The extent to which our lives have been affected by the path we chose has been profound. So, if we were to go back in time, would I take the same path? If I did not know the future, yes, I would. But, if I had a crystal ball and saw the future, I would have to say that I would not. I tell you that knowing how incredibly selfish it is of me because the foundation has helped thousands of people. If the foundation were not in existence, all of those who came to us would have no recourse. But, I am only human and apparently very selfish.

Of course, when we formed the foundation, we thought it would not take long before this entire situation was resolved. After all, look at the case law, and the Constitution that stands with us. And now, "I'm ten years burning down the road" (yes, I am a Bruce Springsteen fan) and we have worked for 64,000 clients, all of whom are grateful, I know. My husband has found his calling, and I, for better or worse, stand by my man.

I have turned in this manuscript with a note to my publisher that he may choose to include the following email or not, with or without the picture. I only asked that my comments stay.

WARNING

Extreme warning and shocking

◆◆◆

Subject: Hungary: Migrants should go back 'where they came from'; threatens mass arrests

Hungary: Migrants should go back 'where they came from'; threatens mass arrests.

Mikey Whinerstein must be sent immediately to ISIS so that they may bake him in a sodomite oven.

.

Subject: Elton John urges Ukraine to accept gays

Elton John urges Ukraine to accept gays.
Mikey Whinerstein and Elton John pump each other in the Anus.

.

Subject: Drone shot down at Inhofe fundraiser

Your worthless ass will be set to ISIS so as to bake jew bread.

To bad that drone wasn't fudgepacker Mikey Whinerstein.

.

Subject: Whinerstiner pumped a little too hard. Falala

◆◆◆

The image attached to this email is not displayed in this book due to its extremely violent and shocking nature. The image can be found on the MRFF's website. This is the link to the landing page: mrff.org/wcbb.

The publisher

◆◆◆

My dear brother, Mikey, what I have seen and read is intolerable. The individuals responsible must be, as a matter of law and justice, criminally prosecuted. If the

individuals responsible are prosecuted and determined to be guilty they should be incarcerated for their outrageous, willful domestic terrorist threat. Not to do so empowers these violent offenders to continue with their campaign of terror. I love you.

·

Subject: I am reporting you to the FBI

It is unfortunate that you have chosen to issue threats of bodily harm to a citizen of the U.S. I am not quite sure on what basis you think such behavior is legal, but the Federal prosecutor will most certainly be successful in bringing you to justice.

SAMUEL W FAIRCHILD

·

Good!!! Those emails were the worst I have seen. The worst of humanity. I hope this coward is truly brought to justice.

·

Subject: For Mr. Kenton Barlow, Muncie, Indiana

Dear Mr. Barlow,

Before I refer this matter to the FBI, I thought it might be helpful to you if I share the language and explanation around the federal law that you are breaking in your repeatedly-sent threatening and hate-filled emails to Mr. Michael Weinstein. The law in this matter is clear:

18 U.S.C. § 875(c) states: "Whoever transmits in interstate or foreign commerce any communication containing any threat to kidnap any person or any threat to injure the person of another, shall be fined under this title or imprisoned not more than five years, or both."

From the wording of § 875(c) it is clear that the legislator did not require the element of 'intent.' Thus, it is irrelevant if the accused claims he/she did not have the intent to produce any injury on the victim; the mere act of sending the e-mail with threatening messages typifies the criminal conduct.

The holding in United States v. DeAndino, 958 F.2d 146 (US Ct. App. 6th

Cir. 1992) confirms this statement. In DeAndino, the court held: "A criminal statute such as 18 U.S.C.S. § 875(c) does not contain a specific mens rea element. However, such a statute is not presumed to create a strict liability offense, because mere omission from the statute of any mention of intent will not be construed as eliminating that element from the crime denounced." In other words, 'federal stalking,' as this crime is also known, is not a strict liability crime but it does require prosecutors to prove that the accused committed the offense. Thus, the 'wording' of the e-mails and the e-mails themselves are critical evidence in these cases. Threats of injury must be found in the e-mails sent by the accused. As the Court held in DeAndino, the words in the [e-mail] message must fully, directly, and expressly set the elements of the statutory offense. For instance, in Tuason, the wording of one of his e-mails said: "Mulatto kids are ugly freaks that should be destroyed. . . The blackie should be castrated. I want people in public malls, photo shoots, TV studios, radio, concerts, arenas, restaurants, NBC TV, Bravo TV, parties, sidewalks, etc. to stare and stab dead any blackie with a white girl like "SS". . . If not, I "HK" WILL BOMB THE PLACE." These words are a clear example of threatening words of injury under the federal statute.

Many other US circuit courts have followed this interpretation in DeAndino. For instance, the First, Second, Fourth, and Fifth circuit courts have followed this interpretation of 18 U.S.C. § 875(c) as not requiring specific mens rea (mental state of intent).

DeAndino held that this crime requires three specific elements: (i) there must be a transmission in interstate commerce; (ii) there must be a communication containing the threat; (iii) and the threat must be a threat to injure the person of another.

Therefore, according to 18 U.S.C. § 875(c) sending e-mails with words threatening injury is a federal crime and can be easily proven by showing that it was sent to a person in other state, showing the e-mail, and the wording the e-mail contains. Thus, individuals prompt to explosive reactions should be cautions when wording their e-mail messages. A simple 'mistake' in wording e-mails threatening its recipient with an injury, even if not intended, may typify a federal crime with a harsh imprisonment sentence.

There is a high likelihood that the Seventh Circuit, where the offending emails were sent from, would reach the same conclusion as the First, Second Fourth *and Fifth circuit courts. There is an equally high likelihood that the Tenth Circuit, where the offending emails were received, would do so as well.*

One way to avoid my referral of this matter to the FBI and most-certain Federal prosecution is first for you to send to Mr. Weinstein a hard-copy letter apologizing to Mr. Weinstein and his family for the hate-filled email correspondence from you. It can be mailed to me at The Tadpole Group, PO Box 2, Brookside, NJ 07926, and I will forward it to Mr. Weinstein. Secondly, you will need to post the fact that you sent a letter of apology to Mr. Weinstein on your Twitter account - I will be following your Twitter account to ensure that you comply with this step. And thirdly, you must not post on Twitter or any other internet-based account any further threatening or hate-filled messages, nor "take-back" your public apology.

If you will agree to do these three things, I will suspend my intended referral to the Federal prosecutor, in this case Josh Minkler, who serves as the US Attorney for the Southern District of Indiana. Please affirm this by return email within the next 48 hours. Please be clear— if I do not hear from you by then, I will continue with my referral.

On a personal note—you are 52 years old. While I am about nine years older than you, I cannot imagine that you do not know better. I suggest you move quickly on this. Spending a significant portion of the rest of your life in jail because you cannot seem to manage your emotions seems to be a very poor outcome for this matter.

Samuel W. Fairchild

.

Mr. Fairchild,

I never had any intention of harming anyone just went a little overboard. I don't have any Intention of going to California either. Mikey Weinstein throws jabs at everyone else so I threw one back. I will write a short letter and send it to you if that will help.

Sincerely,

Kenton B. Barlow

Mr. Barlow — My conditions are clear in my earlier email. It appears that you are quite wiling to comply so please:

1. Send me a letter of apology address to Mr. Weinstein and his family—a sincere one, please—and mail it to me so I can forward to Mr. Weinstein.

2. Use your Twitter account to certify that you have sent such a letter of apology.

3. Refrain from contacting Mr. Weinstein again or publicly attacking him in any way.

I do not expect you to agree with Mr. Weinstein's positions on a range of matters, nor do I expect you to change any of your views. I only expect you to act lawfully, and you have not.

Thank you for your response. I will wait for your return email confirming that you will do all three things, then I will expect action on your part on the first two conditions. I will monitor both your Twitter account and other internet fora that you use to ensure your compliance.

And, I apologize for getting your age wrong in my previous email - I think I said you are 52, and in fact I think you are 47.

Thank you. Samuel W. Fairchild

⸱

Well, after almost an hour of trying to figure out how to compose some lucid and hopefully life and freedom affirming personal response to this kind of off the rails emailed hatred and vile imagery, especially considering that the unique MRFF and the entire family of the honorable Mikey Weinstein have devoted their lives to defending the most basic of Constitutional principles, I still can only come up with this: When any one citizen of a democracy walks in wisdom and principle (especially with an unadulterated love of the US Constitution,) there are bound to be fellow humans of lesser moral clarity who will do their pointless best to tear you down. Nevertheless, for the sake of humanity's ongoing efforts to be better in all of its complexity, stay the course as long as you can because you benefit so many millions more people than you might count among your immediate ranks. Your reward is oddly reflected through a glass darkly, a mirror darkened by the unhinged hatred that knows no bounds and incurs no personal risks. If ignorance persists then your wisdom is the only light that can lead the way for humanity's further greatness, denying the ignorant of their hold upon history's advancements.

Thomas Cardellno.

.

I took the following comment from one of many supporting emails that were sent in from those who also chose to open the email. It says simply and honestly:

"We are fighting barbarians—barbarians who have email."

CPSIA information can be obtained
at www.ICGtesting.com
Printed in the USA
JSHW020732171119
2409JS00007B/2

9 781644 280485